Western Psychology

WESTERN

Edited by GARDNER MURPHY
and LOIS B. MURPHY

Basic Books, Inc., Publishers

PSYCHOLOGY

From the Greeks to William James

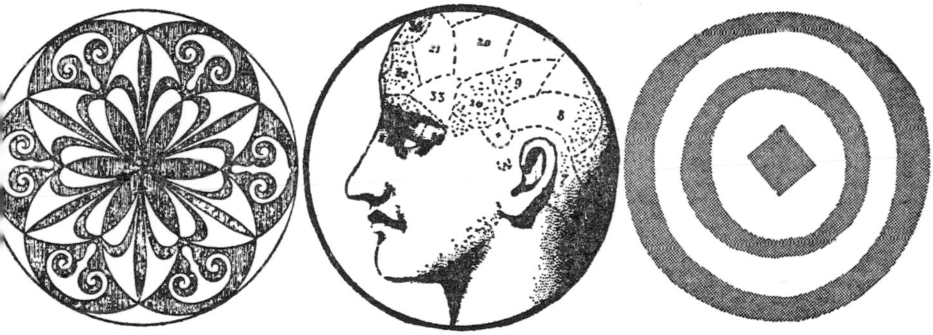

NEW YORK LONDON

Library of Congress Catalog Card Number: 72–78454
Manufactured in the United States of America

Editors' Introduction

Man's perennial desire to understand himself has been intensified through the general growth of science since the time of Galileo. This was partly because of the increasing insistency of questions about evolution and the relation of man to his animal ancestry; partly by virtue of the development of experimental research skills which treat man as a natural object; partly a reflection of the new clinical evaluations of human difficulties; and partly an expression of the increasing awareness of the nature of culture and personality. We are seeking to make available to the Western reader representative selections from the seminal thinkers about human nature, its origin and development, introducing and interpreting several dozen new insightful contributions scattered through the history of psychology, and creating as much integration as possible. But we are allowing disparate authors to speak in their own idioms. In the first volume of this series, *Asian Psychology,* we dealt specifically with the psychology of India, China, and Japan, which for most of us has been poorly articulated with the psychology of the West. The present volume is concerned with the great procession of Western thought from the pre-Socratics through the Greek classical period, through the Roman and patristic eras, through the Renaissance and the Age of the Enlightenment, up to and including the first great formulations of an evolutionary psychology. We believe that William James is an appropriate exponent of the last great phase in this development.

But there have been launched in the Western world several hugely important ways of looking at psychology which cannot be included within the present volume; they remain for independent treatment. These are: (1) developmental and psychoanalytic psychologies; (2) the Soviet psychological system stemming from Sechenov and Pavlov; (3) altered ego states (or states of consciousness). We hope to work on these groups of problems later.

What we offer here—with grateful recognition of the assistance of Professor Richard P. McKeon of the University of Chicago in reference to the Greco-Roman period and the psychology of Islam—is a psychology known to students of philosophy and of psychological systems. Each section offers an attempt at integrated treatment of psychologies in their relation to the various great eras in Western history but written with a consistent effort at psychological coherence. We can offer only *psychology*. The *philosophy* of the West would be much too much for us. We deal, for example, relatively little with epistemology, the science of understanding, on which there is profound philosophical material that we cannot properly include. We cannot do justice to the philosophy of ethics, and of esthetics, and the philosophy of the social order. We are writing as psychologists, not as philosophers in the more extended sense of the term; and although philosophy frequently batters down the doors of any isolationist psychology and insists upon raising its answerable or unanswerable questions, we shall have to maintain some sort of consistency in the conception of psychology as a growing science concerned with the mind.

Let us then simply restate our purpose: To give, parallel to our *Asian Psychology,* a view of the major psychological contributions from the Greeks through to the evolutionary period, and terminating with William James, allowing the authors for the most part to speak for themselves, but offering enough interpretative material to give an overall view of where psychology has been and where it stood at the end of the nineteenth century.

As already noted in the introduction to *Asian Psychology,* there are two quite different senses in which the term "psychology" can be understood in any such effort as the present one: (1) We may have in mind direct illustrations of psychological principles as they appear in folklore, drama, fiction, biography, and other types of literature, in which human behavior and experience are directly portrayed in some rich and explicit fashion. Or (2) we may have in mind the effort to make *systematic sense* out of these observations, as when Aristotle or Shakespeare pause in the midst of descriptions of human action and reflect upon the causes or the forms or the meaning of the conduct represented. In the *Poetics* and the *Rhetoric,* Aristotle gives us not only examples of the way in which human beings respond to one another but basic conceptions as to the reasons why. Shakespeare, in the midst of a theme of love or death, has his actors reflect on what it all means.

The distinction between these two kinds of "psychology" is, of course, not absolute, but to make some sort of distinction is absolutely essential to our purpose. We cannot include all of history merely because it is "rich in psychology." We cannot, for example, include all of Thucydides' incredibly vivid account of the Peloponnesian War, nor even try to use such reflections as he may offer us as to the conditions of human life in which such things as a Peloponnesian War could occur. We can at times use the dramatist and the biographer in this way. We can use Shakespeare when he tells us that "all the world's a stage" because he is reflecting upon the form and meaning of human development from the cradle to the grave. But we cannot make it a principle of selection of our materials to try to introduce every supernally vivid and brilliant account of human thought or action.

We shall attempt to clarify this distinction concretely, as we determine ground rules for the inclusion or exclusion of materials. Blaise Pascal comes to mind as an illustration of a psychologically rich and philosophically penetrating analyst of his own experience. When we try, however, to consider Pascal from this point of view, we cannot honestly differentiate a sense in which Pascal is a psychologist, as contrasted, let us say, with Benjamin Franklin or Abraham Lincoln, who also are, in a sense, profound psychologists. In preparing this volume we have limited ourselves to what, in the Western tradition, has been called "psychology."

Contents

Western Psychology

Prologue / WESTERN CONCEPTIONS OF THE MIND FROM THE GREEKS TO THE NINETEENTH CENTURY

From ceramics and music to religious rites and family customs, cultural history has been expanding its domain in recent centuries. Our era has been discovering the cultural history of the sciences. When this is better known, the roots and the branches of science at each phase will be more visible, along with the forces which nourished them, including both earlier concepts and new forms of inquiry.

No one, even the general historian of science, can write this story today. For with regard to earlier phases of science, not enough historical material is at hand. And with regard to the last century or so of science, the facts are too rich, the interbranching too intimate and complex to permit perspective. But in recognition of thc impossibility of doing this today we now suggest a simplified version of such an attempt at what will assuredly sometime be available, as perspective becomes possible, as the methods of historiography become more refined, and as the instruments for such dissection become more subtle.

What we shall attempt will be a brief definition of various cultural phases of Western European history, presupposing study of the chart on page 13 and indicating at each half-millennium point in history since 500 B.C. some simple and tangible aspect of the history of Western Europe broken down in terms of (1) economic organization, (2) political structure, (3) military skill, (4) religious attitude and organization, (5) scientific imagination and achievement, (6) philosophical spirit, and (7) psychological assumptions and trends. This chart is obviously not for historians, who would inevitably be very unhappy with the oversimplification, the cliché-like character of the phrases chosen to depict a vast movement through a vast period of time. It would be obvious at a glance, for example, that our characterization of 500 B.C. as representing an economic order based on agriculture and commerce is unduly preoccupied with the olive groves and the maritime trade of the Athenian city-state. But if we begin to apologize and advertise our inadequacies, we shall never move at all. Pushing forward in the hope that this may help someone to grasp some relations and ultimately do a better job, we offer, as the reader will see as he looks at our chart, a sort of schema of Western European history just insofar as it may make more intelligible the movement toward a scientific psychology. The chart and the following essay are to be read down from top to bottom for each era. For example, we carry the 500 B.C. characterizations right through from economic to psychological, and then rise to the top of the next column. In the same way we take the period of Julius Caesar and the birth of Christ, defining the various stages insofar as they differ from those of the preceding era.

To begin, then, with the upper lefthand corner of our chart. The Greek civilization in the era of the great tragedians, architects, sculptors, and philosophers was founded on relatively stable and efficient agriculture; trade through the Mediterranean world, often supported by conquest and tribute; and a tough and competent military organization. This required politically a stable city-state, as represented notably by Athens, Sparta, and Thebes, and a disciplined infantry, as represented notably by Sparta, but when the occasion demanded, expressing itself likewise wherever Greeks were Greeks, even an exportable surplus of mercenaries, as is evident in Xenophon's record of the march led by Cyrus the Younger. The religious life of such men was a composite, with the Olympian pantheon of gods and goddesses whom we know from the Homeric poems (see page 19), and the mystery religions, like the Orphic mysteries, derived rather largely from the Minoan civilization of the Mediterranean islands and Asia Minor (page 12). Both of these religious systems tended to disintegrate as men became more thoughtful and skeptical. In the era now being considered, from 500 B.C. onward, science, hardly distinguishable from philosophy, was beginning to appear, as evidenced in the increasing care with which astronomical and medical observations were made, and notably with the great outburst of scientific activity in Syracuse and in Alexandria shortly after the 500-year mark which we have just drawn. These Greeks were obviously men of many interests, many cultural passions, whose philosophy was essentially an attempt to answer the perennial *why* questions about the universe and about man. It is because of the economic prosperity, the relative political stability, the military competence, the freedom from religious dogmatism, and the beginning of the scientific spirit that philosophy is able to arise and shine upon a civilization of remarkable richness.

The psychology of such people in such an era reflects not only its philosophy, its perennial questions about the universe and man, but something of all the attributes of the civilization just described. The extraordinary range of the interests of the great historian, Herodotus, for example, his interest in understanding the religions of other peoples whom the Greeks encountered to the east and west, as they carry out their travels, their trade, and their wars, makes for a cultural relativity, almost a "social science" spirit in the study of religion and of philosophy and psychology. The uncertainties which arise when the different dominant ideas of the different city-states are compared, and when objectively-minded merchants and warriors encounter mystics and doubters, lead into questions about the nature of the soul which become in time truly psychological. They lead into questions as to how we can really know what we think we know, and what sort of a thing the mind really is. They were not likely to make discoveries that depended upon instruments, for it was the slaves, not the free men, who worked with their hands and understood instruments; but it was still possible for the medical men to observe physical realities and to think in quantitative terms about both the soul and the body of their patients; indeed, there is nearly as much psychology in the work of Hippocrates and his intellectual descendants as there is in the great schools of philosophy.

Let the eye now travel to the top of the second column. We note that agriculture is still dominant. Commerce continues. The great wars between Carthage and Rome were largely wars between maritime-commercial empires, and the tax and tribute system is, despite much piracy, continuing and flourishing. In fact, the gradual domination by Rome of the other cities of central and north Italy, and finally of the cities of all the world west of the Black Sea, in which literate men were developing their civilizations, reached its consummate expression in the Roman Empire, essentially a late expression of a trend to political centralization and military power which had been gaining for centuries. Here, borrowing right and left from Greek civilization and administering effectively a vast area under one political system, there was need for a large and highly disciplined infantry, but after initial conquests (like Caesar's conquest of Gaul) actually not very much fighting. Indeed, a relative *pax Romana* prevailed, in which Roman law and Roman bridges and roads expressed a unity which the Latin language and official codes of public and private conduct stamped upon Europe, and to this day it forms a major basis for the essential oneness of Western civilization.

It would not be quite correct to say that religion was disintegrating, but both in the Greek and in the Roman world the local deities of hearth and city represented symbols of continuity with the past rather than dynamic guides to contemporary living. In fact, thoughtful people in both Greece and Rome were tending to belittle or even openly to mock the childishness and low moral tone of the traditional gods. Science was holding up its head, notably in the Greek centers of learning at Alexandria. Indeed, even up to 200 or 100 B.C. medical and astronomical observations and the successful collation of scientific principles were moving forward, while geometry and mechanics achieved an essentially modern spirit, as reflected in sharp definitions and highly disciplined deductive reasoning.

But the light of fresh inventiveness had gone out of the eyes of the great Greek philosophical effort, which had reached its peak at about the same time as Greek economic and political supremacy, while two great systems became dominant which provided comfort and protection in a less confident age, namely Stoicism and Epicureanism. Such psychology as there was in this period was largely a direct expression of these two doctrines. For the Stoic the primary psychological principle was: accept nature. For the Epicurean it was: aim at well-being.

As the eye rises again to the half-millennium period with the designation A.D. 500, we must recognize the decline of much of the commercial, especially the maritime, successes of the preceding period. The ravages of the Barbarians broke through the imperial bulwarks, Rome itself being repeatedly sacked, and it was mainly in the monasteries that an asylum was offered from a chaos often expressed in local wars and banditry. The disintegration of the Empire went on apace until in the eighth century the Franks created some political unity, repelled the invading Moors, and established, with Charlemagne, a Holy Roman Empire. Despite the general destruction of the period from about A.D. 300 to a period some five hundred years later, it must be remembered that the Eastern Empire, pivoted at Constantinople (Byzantium), maintained itself and Greek philosophy and psychology are among the gems kept alive, while in the West some familiarity with Plato and with Aristotle's logic was kept alive within the monastic system. From the point of view of a Western historian, the spread of Christianity and its successful encounters not only with paganism, but with competing religious systems, gave this monastic system its power and symbolic meaning. And for the first time we have a single religious system dominating the minds of the men of the West. Utilizing, as they did, some remnants from Greek science and mathematics, they nevertheless depended very much more upon Hebrew and early Christian thought, and a psychology which was to have any relation to life at all had to be, so to speak, a psychology of God, man, and the relation of the two. It had to derive from theological problems. The psychology of such a period was therefore inevitably a psychology dealing with the ultimate questions of man's nature, such as his memory and reasoning powers, and most of all his capacity for free choice, or acts of will.

As we turn to the yearmark A.D. 1000, we find that the stability offered by the Holy Roman Empire (and the settling down of the Norsemen and the other erstwhile disturbers of the peace) gave some possibility for the development of better routes of travel by land and sea. Before long the Crusades and even an increase in rich intercultural exchange with the Middle East became possible. The Holy Roman Empire is dominant, but there are many independent kingdoms and frequent wars, falling short, however, of the universal destructiveness of the later years of the system of Rome itself. The power of the warrior, whether king or knight, depends upon his own toughness, courage, and skill, and the toughness and competence of the men at arms of higher or lower levels which he has established around him. It is the knight and his castle which symbolize the Western system, just as the Greek soldiers, in continuing the great tradition, long maintained the fortress of Byzantium and the Eastern Empire against the followers of Mohammed.

We have seen the Eastern and Western systems drawing apart since the heyday of Rome and notably since the time of Constantine, A.D. 325; and with the development of Russian civilization the Eastern church has finally virtually separated itself from the Western, the final date of breakup being 1052. It was here in the East, especially in Byzantium itself, that the Greek tradition was mainly continued, but by the twelfth and thirteenth centuries the Western world had begun to make more and more discoveries of the classical world, to dig up and study more adequately the Greco-Roman civilization which had been to some degree forgotten. We may speak of the "revival of learning" which, at an accelerated pace, expressed itself in the literature and philosophy of the Western world and in many cases initiated startlingly new cultural achievements, such as Italian painting. The theological preoccupations of philosophy continued, but the revival of learning meant a deeper interest in Plato and an enormous expansion of interest in many works of Aristotle previously lost to the West, so that by the thirteenth century Aristotle had become, by a wide margin, the dominant component in Western philosophy. This, of course, carried over for psychology, too, and it is in the systematic theology of Thomas Aquinas that we are confronted with a reconciliation of Aristotelian and Christian concepts, notably about the nature of reasoning, especially the process of conceptualizing, and the nature of the will.

As we turn to the column headed A.D. 1500, we note for the first time in many centuries a radically new and tremendously significant change in basic economic realities. The improvements in transportation already noted and the relative political and military stability permitted the simultaneous development of maritime endeavors on a world-wide scale, including journeys to the Middle East, to India, and even to the Western hemisphere, the commerce which used the new routes, and the banking facilities which facilitated the enormous new profitable adventures. Kings had their part in these far-reaching adventures and so did their nobles and, in time, their commoners. The availability of military power to the kings and their nobles was expressed in a rising nationalism; land and economic opportunities in far corners of the earth became the property of national states and of their dominant classes and individuals. Simultaneously, new weapons developed. More powerful archery and, pressing upon its heels, gunpowder and cannon destroyed the world of armored knights and their castles, as wars of national conquest dominated sixteenth- and seventeenth-century commercial developments. The Eastern Empire fell in the meantime (1453) to the Turks, and from that time forth it will be in the West, not in the East, that the Greek tradition will be maintained.

The same whirlwind of economic, political, military, and moral components which were expressed in the fifteenth, sixteenth, and seventeenth centuries in the West produced economic, political, and moral tensions between northern and southern Europe, and a good deal of northern Europe began to break away from the ideological control of the Papacy.

This era is likewise an era of tremendous acceleration of scientific growth, based on the mathematics of Plato and of the Arabs in its application to astronomy, and on the importation of philosophical and scientific ideas from the Middle East and even from India. This was rapidly followed by the development of mechanics and medicine and by the devising of instruments of observation, such as telescopes and microscopes. These developments threw science in an empirical direction. It was not just the revival of Plato's faith that the world was rational and could be mathematically understood; it was likewise the availability of tools by which vast new reaches of reality could be discovered. Galileo, professor of mathematics at Padua, combined a Platonist mathematical approach with a genius for observation. At last came the majestic mathematical system of Newton.

The empirical spirit just mentioned led immediately to an empirical psychology, combining both everyday observations and a rich storehouse of ideas based on Aristotle's observations. At the same time, biological models suggested by the revival of Greek medicine, as well as by observations through the microscope, gave "natural philosophy" a concern with psychological questions.

Ruthlessly sticking to this half-millennium procedure, we have, of course, overcondensed the story and have looked forward a little too much beyond what the men of 1500 could see. The Commercial Revolution moved so fast that vast systems of trade were soon expressed in colonial enterprises, such as the conquest of India, while beginning in the eighteenth century the application of power —water power and especially steam power, notably in the textile industry—made possible enormous increases in productivity, and an upward cycling in capital available for investment in more and more giant enterprises. Science played some part even at the beginning of this Industrial Revolution, but it was not until the nineteenth century that the world was overhauled and remade by industrialization.

To the competitive system within the ranks of the entrepreneurs, political struggle was added, a struggle between those at various points in the new structure. Some of the lower elements became powerful enough politically to warrant our using the term *competitive democratic* for the political structure of the Western system. To this was added, after 1848, and especially after 1917, a Marxist definition of economic reality which actually succeeded in forcing fundamental political changes and paved the way to the present two-system kind of world. The primary military facts implementing such struggles as these are, of course, the rich science and technology, including now the availability of nuclear fuels, which make it uncertain whether economic struggles, as such, are as fundamental in the outcome as is the military power and potential on each side.

From the point of view taken here, the discovery of the scientific method—*discovering how to discover,* so to speak—pervades and is destined more and more intimately to pervade all of the life of modern man. The protests against overscientificism seem to be as unavailing as the effort to "appease" science by giving it a corner where it may enjoy its meal without disturbing others. As Whitman saw, poetry is not destroyed but given new dimensions by science. The same is true of all the arts and all the codes by which life is lived, and most of all by the religious effort to understand cosmic meanings. All contemporary religions, whether expressed in Unitarianism or Jehovah's Witnesses, or the Brahmin philosophers or Sadhus of India, the Buddhists of Japan, or the dervishes of the Islamic world, struggle with and through science even though at times they seem to struggle against science. Science has to find a common way to the observability and the analyzability of natural phenomena, and has to move toward a conceptualizing scheme which must comprise the relations of men to their cosmos.

The science of such an era, from becoming *one* aspect, becomes *the dominant* aspect of the civilization. At the moment it appears that its mathematical structure and method is even more important than its experimental method, but as we learn from nuclear physics, there is an endless cycle from observation to mathematics to observation again.

The first principles discovered in such a scientific age turn out to be universal principles, like those suggested by the early Greek philosophers, that is, principles which forced themselves into every nook and cranny of knowledge. They inevitably pervade the life sciences just as they have pervaded physics, chemistry, geology, astronomy. They are mercilessly hostile to basic dualisms.

It is very evident that the psychology of today is being recast by such a modality of thought. The process will take considerable time. There is so much unleavened knowledge about mankind which does not as yet lend itself to such conceptualization—so much about man as a social, historical suffering individual, whose experience does not lend itself easily to the physico-chemical scheme—that by the time we have digested and absorbed these unregenerate "unscientific" kinds of psychology, the temper of the scientific era will itself have changed. It is also possible, as was clear in the case of the impact of the Greek upon the Minoan civilization, that what appears to be the conquest of one by the other will actually be the hybridization or even the fusion of two systems. The more intimate personal views of humanity, which have carried such a tremendous weight of wisdom right into the modern era, may alter to some degree the current conception of reality, and may force a return to forms of thinking which transcend the mathematical and the physicalist methods so successful today. But to say anything about what will happen here is the privilege only of a visionary.

Economy Agriculture-commerce	Agriculture-tax tribute	Agriculture	Agriculture	Commercial revolution	Industry
Politics City-state	Empire	Disintegration of Empire	Holy Roman Empire plus independent kingdoms	Rising nationalism	(1) Competitive-democratic (2) Marxist
Military Disciplined infantry	Disciplined infantry	Barbarians destroy Roman power; Eastern Empire remains	Holy Roman Empire; Greek soldiers maintain Eastern Empire	New weapons in the West. Fall of Eastern Empire (1453).	Complex technology including atomic
Religion (1) Olympian (2) Mystery	Local deities	Christianity subduing paganism	Western and Eastern Churches drawn apart (1052)	Roman and Eastern Catholic Reformation in West beginning	(1) All religion influenced by science (2) Many groups tend away from religion
Science Medical and astronomical observations	Medical and astronomical principles Geometry Mechanics	Residues from Greek science	Beginning of revival of learning (accelerated 1200–1500)	Revival of Plato, especially mathematics applied to astronomy	Experiments and mathematics applied to nuclear and space
Philosophy First principles	(1) Stoicism (2) Epicureanism	Theological	Theological, with touch of Plato and much Aristotle	Trend to empirical	Attempt to conceptualize physical and life sciences
Psychology (1) Nature of soul (2) Perception	(1) Accept nature (2) Aim at well-being	Problems of man's nature, especially will	Nature of (a) Abstraction (b) Will	(1) Empirical (2) Tending to biological concepts	Becoming dominated by ideas from (a) Physics (b) Medicine (c) Public affairs

One

THE PSYCHOLOGY OF THE GREEKS

INTRODUCTION

About 500 B.C. a tidal wave of human self-discovery is visible in many parts of the world, with deep penetration into the nature of mind and heart. There are curious parallelisms of thought all the way from the later Hebrew through the Greek, Persian, Indian, and Chinese philosophies. The new force of human thought erupts almost like a volcano, as if somehow there had been much direct communication among them all. We do not believe actually that there was very much direct communication, although of course there must have been some contact through merchants and travelers, and later on we know of a good deal of well-planned contact likewise through priests and missionaries. We can in a certain sense speak of a "world psychology" of that era, or any era, and we shall try through frequent comments and footnotes to show that common problems led to common methods and common solutions.

Nevertheless, the contribution of the Greeks was highly distinctive, as distinctive in the West as the Indian approach was for Asia. There is a deep fascination about Greek thought, whether it takes the form of the plays of Aeschylus, Sophocles, Euripides, or Aristophanes; or the lyrics of Sappho or Simonides; the history of Herodotus or Thucydides; or the tremendous wisdom of the philosophers from before Thales (600 B.C.) through the heroic age of Socrates, Plato, and Aristotle, to the earnest affirmations of faith in human reason which persisted even after the desolation of the Peloponnesian War. Then came the enfoldment of philosophy with mathematics which resulted in the beginnings of Greek science at Alexandria and laid a foundation for mathematical astronomy in the Ptolemaic system. As it had interacted with Hebrew thought in the Hellenistic period, Greek thought interacted with the much less profound thought of the Romans, and later with the thinking of the Church fathers, who were themselves, as successors to the Hebrew as well as to the Greek tradition, ready for thought about the nature of the soul, mind, will, and everything upon which human destiny, here and hereafter, depended. Greek psychology is thus one of the great fountains of Western thought.

Greek philosophy is a labor to which one may devote years. Typically one takes it in stride while pursuing a year's course in the history of philosophy, giving it a couple of months with special emphasis upon Plato and Aristotle. The psychologist, admitting his sins and derelictions, usually gives it only a cursory glance, though today psychologists are rapidly becoming more sophisticated with respect to their history and the place of the history of psychology in the broader history of thought. The task of doing justice to Greek psychology, however, is very much too big for us as editors. Just as in *Asian Psychology* we drew on our friend Professor Kuppuswamy for interpretations of the thought of India, upon Professor Hsu for China, and Koji Sato and Tadashi Tsushima for Japan, so for the huge responsibility of mature perspective on the Greek psychology we have turned to Professor Richard P. McKeon of the University of Chicago.

GREEK PSYCHOLOGY

by Richard P. McKeon

THE PRE-SOCRATICS; THE "FIRST PRINCIPLES"

There is no simple formula to relate the history of the world to the history of man's consciousness and knowledge of himself. The history of civilization and of the arts and the sciences, including psychological insights and knowledge, is part of the history of man's development and response to his environment; the history of the world and of man, in all his diversified activities and institutions, is a reflection of his altering and developing conception of himself. A generation ago these two interrelated inquiries were usually focused on the study of the contacts of the cultures of a thousand years B.C. and on the reconstruction from records, legends, and archeological remains of military, commercial, and political contacts which prepared for the emergence of "the glory that was Greece" after the semi-legendary Trojan war. The study of the remains of earlier civilizations in the islands of the Aegean and western Asia Minor and the decipherment of their records during the recent past have uncovered a more diversified background for Greek thought, in which the emergence of the world of mind is no longer the abrupt and unprecedented innovation of the Greeks that many of the Greeks themselves thought it had been. Mathematics, astronomy, mythical explanations, religious convictions, visual arts, and poetry had had beginnings before the mingling of peoples from which the Greeks emerged and the contacts of cultures which stimulated their creative genius.

Man's consciousness and conception of himself is recorded at each stage of his history in every record and remain he has left. The science of psychology emerges as a restatement of what he has already formulated in the world of mind as it evolved in his practical, religious, and artistic life. What he saw and felt, what he aspired to and thought, how he formed habits and virtues, yielded to terror, was appeased by repentance, and acted for love are set forth with insight and truth in his ritual and stories, his utensils, ornaments, and poetry. Later Greeks studied Homer for basic insights and knowledge of human character and psychology, and modern psychology preserves terms and distinctions borrowed from Greek religion, history, and drama. In much the same fashion, man's conception of the world and of himself is found in man's earliest philosophical speculations. Notions of human nature and psychological processes do not depend on supposing that human nature is sharply separated from nature or that mind is antithetical to matter.

Early Greek philosophy arose in a context of speculations concerning cosmology, medicine, and mathematics and of operations concerning politics, religion, and poetry. From beginnings in Asia Minor and southern Italy in the seventh century B.C., philosophic thought moved to Athens in the fifth century. The Ionian philosophers have been called "natural philosophers," since according to Aristotle they sought a single material principle for all things and processes. Thales, the originator of this tradition, found the principle in water, Anaximenes in air, Heraclitus in fire, and Empedocles in the four elements, adding earth to the three.

The Italian philosophers were the Pythagoreans, who found the principles of things in numbers, and the Eleatics, who sought the principle in unity rather than in the pluralities posited by their predecessors. After these explorations of plurality and unity for principles, Empedocles added Love and Strife as motive forces to the four elements, Anaxagoras postulated an infinity of "elements" ordered by Mind, and the Atomists constructed the world and man from an infinity of indivisible bodies moving in the void. Finally, the Sophists embodied, in their enterprise to teach virtue, the conviction that man is the measure of all things and that knowledge is sensation, and so strengthened the tendencies of operationalism and skepticism in Greece much as similar reactions to dogmatisms had emerged in India.

The world of man emerged in these speculations concerning the world, for justice, love, and mind were thought to be principles of the world, or the world was conceived as a living intelligent animal, or schematized as an intelligible order of bodies in which thought and sensations are motions; or it was a projection which man constructed from his phenomenal experiences. As oppositions developed among these traditions of inquiry and schools of philosophy and science, specifically psychological problems made their appearance, such as the relation between motion and thought, between feeling and knowledge, between justice and disorder, between love and strife, and between sense and understanding. Thought was conceived as a motion similar to the other motions of the elements, or it was set up as the antithesis of action; knowledge was explained as a reaction, passion, or feeling, or it was opposed to passivity as creation, action, or intuition; the origin of the world and of the world of mind was found in the interaction or succession of justice and chaos, love and strife, or in the identification of justice with strife;

understanding was explained by sensation, or set in opposition to sense.

Among the first principles which were found to explain man and his problems in the world, six are represented briefly below. Heraclitus, whose theory is presented first, found no fixed unchanging character for being, but held that all things are in a flux in which opposites are united—"strife is the father of all things"—and the unity of the world is constituted by conflict and contradiction. Second, Parmenides based knowledge on unchanging being, and found in the flux of becoming the uncertainties and contradictions of opinion. Third, the Pythagoreans held that the principles of nature are numbers, which they conceived as sensible entities rather than abstractions, and that the elements of numbers and therefore of all things are basic contraries like odd and even, limited and unlimited, one and many. Fourth, Anaxagoras turned from both finite sensible principles and a single intelligible principle to seek infinite sensible principles ordered by mind in a universe of change. Fifth, Democritus also sought infinite principles in the atoms, which move, congregate into larger composites, and collide with each other in the void. Sixth, the Sophists placed thought in the phenomenal framework of the experience of the individual man as it is conditioned by his perspectives and emotions, and they exprcssed skepticism concerning changeless being, eternal truths, and in general whatever is alleged to transcend experience.

A universe of flux or a changeless universe, a universe of mathematical relations, or qualitative mixtures, or congregated particles, raises questions of cognition, motion, feeling, and will—how the human mind perceives and thinks in an intelligible universe, how the human body moves and functions, undergoes influences, and acts on desires in a universe of changing things, how man deliberates and chooses in a universe which offers a variety of objectives. Philosophy, science, literature, and religion were already engaged in exploring these questions when the Sophists became traveling teachers of virtue and of the applied arts, and investigated man as the measure of all things; and in the same intellectual climate Socrates turned philosophy from speculation on nature to the examination of man and of knowledge, and of the use of knowledge in the virtues man acquires in action and in the communities he forms with other men.

Only fragments of the works of the Pre-Socratic philosophers have been preserved in the quotations made from their works by later writers. The fragments which follow are translations from Diels and Kranz, *Die Fragmente der Vorsokratiker.** The number which precedes the fragment is the number given to it in Diels' collection; the author and work cited in parentheses following the fragment represent the source of the fragment.

Heraclitus: The Flowing Philosophy

8. "What is in opposition is useful," and "from different things is the fairest harmony" [and "all things arise from strife"]. (Aristotle, *Nicomachean Ethics* viii. 1. 1155a4.)

30. Neither gods nor men made this world-order, which is the same for all, but it always was, and is, and will be an ever-living fire, kindling in measures and going out in measures. (Clement of Alexandria, *Stromateis* v. 104. 1.)

51. They do not grasp how what is at variance with itself is in accord: harmony is stretched tension, like that of the bow and the lyre. (Hippolytus of Rome, *Refutatio omnium Haeresium* ix. 9. 1.)

53. War is the father of all and the king of all, and it shows some to be gods, others to be men; it makes some slaves, others free. (*Ibid.* ix. 9. 4.)

55. I prefer things which can be seen, heard, learned. (*Ibid.* ix. 9. 5.)

67. God is day night, winter summer, war peace, satiety famine [this means all the contraries], but he alters, as fire when it is mixed with incenses is named according to the scent of any of them. (*Ibid.* ix. 10. 8.)

80. It should be known that war is general and justice is strife, and that everything happens by strife and necessity. (Origen, *Contra Celsum* vi. 42.)

85. It is hard to fight against basic impulse, for whatever it wishes it bribes from the soul. (Plutarch, *Coriolanus* 22.)

90. All things are exchanged for fire and fire for all things recipro-

* H. Diels and W. Kranz, *Die Fragmente der Vorsokratiker,* 6th ed., 3 vols. (Berlin, 1951–1952).

cally, as goods are exchanged for gold and gold for goods. (Plutarch, *De E.* 8. 388E.)

91. It is not possible to step twice in the same river. . . . It scatters and again combines (or rather, neither "again" nor "later," at once comes together and flows away) and approaches and departs. (*Ibid.* 18. 392B.)

110. It is not better for men to get whatever they wish. (Stobaeus, *Florilegium* iii. 1. 176.)

111. Disease makes health pleasant and good, hunger satiety, weariness rest. (*Ibid.* iii. 1. 177.)

Parmenides: The Philosophy of the One

2. . . . for you could neither know that which is not (that is impossible) nor express it. (Proclus, *On the Timaeus* i. 345.)

3. . . . for the same thing can be thought as can be. (Clement of Alexandria, *Stromateis* vi. 23.)

6. That which can be said and thought must be, for it is possible for it, but not for nothing, to be . . . (Simplicius, *On the Physics* 117. 4.)

Two opposed theories of sensation were found, according to Theophrastus (*De sensu* 1), that sensation is of like by like, and that it is of opposite by opposite. Parmenides, Empedocles, and Plato held the first theory, and the followers of Anaxagoras and Heraclitus the second. The theory of Parmenides was (*ibid.* 3) that there are two elements and that our knowledge depends on the excess of one or the other. Understanding varies as the hot or the cold predominates, a better and purer understanding being derived from the hot, but even in such knowledge there is a certain proportion. In this context, Theophrastus quotes Parmenides:

16. According to the mixture that each man has in his wandering limbs, mind comes to men; for that which thinks in each and every man is the same thing, namely, the substance of their limbs; for that of which there is more is thought. (*De Sensu* 3.)

The Pythagoreans: The Philosophy of Numbers

Early scientific investigations took two directions, according to Aristotle, in the effort of the Ionian inquirers to explain all things by material principles, and in the contemporary interest of the Pythagoreans or the Italian school in mathematics, which led them to the position that numbers are the first things in the whole of nature and that the elements of numbers are the elements of all things. The elements of numbers are the even and the odd, the first being limited, the second unlimited, and the universe is derived from these. The numbers of the Pythagoreans were not abstractions or things apart from sensible things, but the things themselves are numbers. Some Pythagoreans said there are ten principles which they arranged in two columns—limited and unlimited, odd and even, one and plurality, right and left, male and female, resting and moving, straight and curved, light and darkness, good and bad, square and oblong. (Aristotle, *Metaphysics* i. 5. 985b23–986b2.)

In like fashion, the early writers who studied psychological phenomena considered the soul to be either the principle of motion or the principle of sensation and cognition. The Pythagoreans were classified among the first (*De Anima* 1. 2. 404a16–19), "since some of them said that the soul is the motes in the air, others that it is what moved them. They referred to motes since they are seen to be in continual motion, even in a complete calm."

They were probably also among the protagonists of "another theory of the soul" (*ibid.* i. 4. 407b27–33) according to which it is "a kind of harmony, for (a) harmony is a blend or composition of opposites, and (b) the body is compounded out of opposites."

Anaxagoras: The Philosophy of Infinite Elements and Mind

1. All things were together infinite in number and in smallness, for the small also was infinite. And while all things were together, none was clear because of its smallness; for air and aither covered all things, both being infinite; for these are the greatest components in the mixture of all things, both in number and in size. (Simplicius, *On the Physics* 155. 26.)

2. For air and aither are separated from the surrounding mass, which is infinite in number. (Simplicius, *On the Physics* 155. 31.)

4. And since these things are so, one must hold that there are many things of all sorts in all composite things, and seeds of all things with all

kinds of shapes and colors; and that men too have been put together and all other animals which have life; that the men possess inhabited cities and constructed works, as we do, and sun and moon and the rest, as we have; and that the earth produces for them many things of all sorts, of which they gather into their houses and use the best. This I say concerning the process of separating off, that it must have taken place not only with us but elsewhere too.

But before these things were separated off, while all things were together, not even any color was clear; for the mixture of all things prevented it, the mixture of moist and dry, and of hot and cold, and of bright and dark, and there was much earth in the mixture and seeds infinite in number and in no way like one another. For none of the other things either is like any other. And since these things are so, one must hold that all things are present in the whole. (*Ibid.* 34. 29.)

9. Thus these things rotate and are separated off by the force and the speed. The speed produces the force. Their speed is like the speed of nothing that now exists among men, but altogether many times as fast. (*Ibid.* 35. 14.)

11. In everything there is a portion of everything except mind; and there are some things in which there is mind as well. (*Ibid.* 164. 23.)

12. All other things contain a portion of everything, but mind is infinite and self-ruling and mixed with nothing, but is alone by itself. For if it were not by itself, but were mixed with anything else, it would have had a share of all things, if it were mixed with anything; for in everything there is a portion of everything, as I have said before; and the things mixed with it would have interfered with it so that it would have power over nothing in the same way as it does being alone by itself. For it is the finest of all things and the purest, and it has all knowledge of everything and the greatest power; and mind controls all things that have life, both the greater and the smaller. Mind controlled the whole rotation, so that it started the rotation in the beginning. First it began the rotation from a small beginning, but now it extends further, and it will extend even further. And the things which were mixed together, and separated off, and divided, were all known by mind. And whatever things were to be, and whatever things were but are not now, and whatever things are now and whatever things shall be, mind arranged them all, as well as this rotation now developed by the stars, the sun, and the moon, and the air and aither which were separated off. It was this rotation which caused the separating off, and dense is separated off from rare, and hot from cold, and bright from dark, and dry from moist. But there are many portions of many things, and nothing is absolutely separated off or divided, one from another, except mind. Mind is all

alike, both the greater and the smaller, while nothing else is like anything else, but each individual thing is and was most clearly that of which it contains the most. (*Ibid.* 164. 24 and 156. 13.)

13. And when mind began the motion there was a separating off from all that was moved, and all that mind set in motion was separated off; and as things moved and were separated off, the rotation greatly increased this process of separating. (*Ibid.* 300. 31.)

14. But mind, which always is, is certainly now where all other things are, in the surrounding mass and in the things that were separated off and in the things that are being separated off. (*Ibid.* 157. 7.)

15. The dense and the moist and the cold and the dark collected here, where the earth is now, while the rare and the hot and the dry went outwards to the farther part of the aither. (*Ibid.* 179. 3.)

16. From these things, as they separated off, earth is solidified; for water is separated off from the clouds, earth from water, and stones are solidified from earth by the cold; and stones tend to move outward more than water. (*Ibid.* 179. 8 and 155. 21.)

Democritus: The Philosophy of Infinite Atoms and Motion

117. We know nothing is reality; for truth lies in the depths. (Diogenes Laertius, *Lives of the Philosophers* ix. 17.)

9. Sweet is by convention, bitter by convention, hot and cold are by convention, color is by convention; atoms and void in reality. . . . We know nothing accurately in reality, but only as it changes according to the condition of our body and of the things that impinge and press upon it. (Sextus Empiricus, *Adversus Mathematicos* vii. 135.)

11. There are two forms of knowledge, one genuine, one obscure. To the obscure knowledge belong all the following: sight, hearing, smell, taste, touch. The other form is genuine knowledge and is quite distinct from this. . . . When the obscure form can go no further—when one cannot see more minutely, nor hear, nor smell, nor perceive by touch—and a finer [investigation is needed, then the genuine way of knowing comes into play, possessed of a finer tool of inquiry]. (*Ibid.* vii. 139.)

154. We are pupils of the animals in the most important things: the spider for spinning and mending, the swallow for building, and the song-birds, swan and nightingale, by way of imitation. (Plutarch, *De Sollert. Anim.* 20. 974A.)

174. The cheerful man, who is impelled to just and lawful acts, rejoices by day and by night, and is strong and free from care; but the man who neglects justice and does not do what ought to be done, finds

all such things disagreeable when he remembers them, and he is afraid and torments himself. (Stobaeus, ii *Eclogae Ethicae* 9. 3.)

The doctrines of Democritus as stated by Diogenes Laertius, *Lives of the Philosophers* ix. 44–45:

He thought that the principles of all things are the atoms and the void and that all other things are conventions. He also thought that there are infinite worlds which come into being and pass away; that nothing can come into being from that which is not or pass away into that which is not; and that the atoms are infinite in sizes and in number, and move together in a vortex and from that all composite things are generated, fire, water, air, earth, for these too are combinations of certain atoms, and because of their solidity the atoms are not subject to alteration or dissolution; that the sun and the moon are formed by such masses in rotation and revolution; and that the soul (*psyche*), which he says is the same as reason (*nous*), is formed in the same way; that we perceive by the impact of images (or idols) on us; that all things happen by necessity, since the cause of the generation of all things is the vortex, which he calls necessity; that the end of actions is cheerfulness (*euthumia*), which is not the same as pleasure, as some have mistakenly held, but in which the soul continues in tranquility and security, undisturbed by fear, or superstition, or any other perturbation of the mind. This he calls *well-being* and many other names. He thought, however, that things which are done are conventions, but the atoms and the void are natural. These are the doctrines he held.

The Sophists: The Philosophy of Behavior and Actions

Protagoras

Under the questioning of Socrates, the young man Theaetetus developed a theory that knowledge is perception. This, Socrates remarked, is Protagoras' conception of knowledge, and he quoted from Protagoras' work "Truth or Refutatory Arguments" to make his point. This citation is one of the few fragments preserved from Protagoras' work:

1. Man is the measure of all things, of the being of things which are and of the not-being of things which are not. (Plato, *Theaetetus* 152A.)

Socrates went on to classify this analysis of knowledge with other theories which maintain that nothing "is" but all things "become" in continuous processes of production, motion, or mixture. Among the protagonists of "becoming" are Protagoras, Heraclitus, and Empedocles as well as the poets Epicharmus and Homer, while only Parmenides is ranged on the side of "being." Socrates then refuted the theory, arguing that perception and feeling are impressions of bodies on our bodies, while knowledge is concerned with the common properties of sensible things and of all other things and with truth.

Scholars are not agreed that the sentence of Protagoras is susceptible of the interpretation which Socrates gives it in his half-playful discussion with the brilliant young mathematician, but there is more reliable evidence that Protagoras held that the perceptions, judgments, and convictions of individual men are conditioned by their circumstances and perspectives, and that he denied the law of contradiction according to which it is impossible for the same property to belong and not belong to the same thing in the same respect.

Gorgias

More considerable portions of the works of Gorgias survive, and his position, which also expresses the Sophist effort to take into account the circumstances and behavior which affect the thought and action of individual men, is easier to reconstruct. Like Protagoras, he was skeptical of dogmatisms, whether they had a learned or a propaganda basis, and he was interested in the theory and arts of communication. We have fragments (*Fragments* 1 to 5) from a book of his called "On Not-being or on Nature," which demonstrated in its three parts that (1) nothing is, (2) if anything were, it could not be known, and (3) if anything were known, it could not be communicated. Gorgias' theories of communication and his elaboration of the arts of rhetoric and of the devices of persuasion are expressed less paradoxically and skeptically, and are based on shrewd psychological observation.

11 (8). Speech is a great power, which accomplishes the most divine labors by means of the smallest and least visible efforts, for it can

stop fear, wipe out grief, create joy, and increase pity. (*Encomium on Helen.*)

11 (13). That persuasion, when added to speech, can also impress the soul in any way it wishes, can be learned, first, from the arguments of the natural scientists, who by removing one opinion and implanting another, cause what is incredible and invisible to appear before the eyes of opinion; second, from the pressures operative in political arguments, in which a speech can move and persuade a crowd by the art of its composition, not by the truth of its statements; third, from the conflict of philosophical arguments in which quickness of judgment is shown to alter easily the conviction of opinion. (*Ibid.*)

23. Tragedy, by means of myths and emotions, creates a deception such that the deceiver is more correct than one who does not deceive and the man who is deceived is wiser than one who is not. For the deceiver is more correct because having promised this result he has accomplished it; and he who is deceived is wiser, because anyone not lacking in sensibility allows himself to be won by the pleasure of speech. (Plutarch, *De Glor. Ath.* 5. 348C.)

SOCRATES

According to Aristotle, who set the fashion for later accounts of the history of earlier thought, Socrates introduced two important changes in speculative inquiry: he turned his attention from the world of nature to ethical matters and he examined the processes and grounds of inductive argument and definition. This judgment is given vivid exemplification in the account which Plato puts into the mouth of Socrates of his reaction to the theory of mind developed by Anaxagoras: if mind is the cause of all things, the operation of mind should be discernible in the marks of perfection found in its effects, and not simply in the motions of the material elements.

Phaedo *

Then one day I heard a man reading from a book, as he said, by Anaxagoras, that it is the mind that arranges and causes all things. I was pleased with this theory of cause, and it seemed to me to be somehow

* From Plato, *Phaedo* 97B–99A, trans. by H. N. Fowler, Loeb Classical Library (Cambridge, Mass., Harvard University Press). Reprinted by permission of the publishers.

right that the mind should be the cause of all things, and I thought, "If this is so, the mind in arranging things arranges everything and establishes each thing as it is best for it to be. So if anyone wishes to find the cause of the generation or destruction or existence of a particular thing, he must find out what sort of existence, or passive state of any kind, or activity is best for it. And therefore in respect to that particular thing, and other things too, a man need examine nothing but what is best and most excellent; for then he will necessarily know also what is inferior, since the science of both is the same." As I considered these things I was delighted to think that I had found in Anaxagoras a teacher of the cause of things quite to my mind, and I thought he would tell me whether the earth is flat or round, and when he had told me that, would go on to explain the cause and the necessity of it, and would tell me the nature of the best and why it is best for the earth to be as it is; and if he said the earth was in the centre, he would proceed to show that it is best for it to be in the centre; and I had made up my mind that if he made those things clear to me, I would no longer yearn for any other kind of cause. And I had determined that I would find out in the same way about the sun and the moon and the other stars, their relative speed, their revolutions, and their other changes, and why the active or passive condition of each of them is for the best. For I never imagined that, when he said they were ordered by intelligence, he would introduce any other cause for these things than that it is best for them to be as they are. So I thought when he assigned the cause of each thing and of all things in common he would go on and explain what is best for each and what is good for all in common. I prized my hopes very highly, and I seized the books very eagerly and read them as fast as I could, that I might know as fast as I could about the best and the worst.

My glorious hope, my friend, was quickly snatched away from me. As I went on with my reading I saw that the man made no use of intelligence, and did not assign any real causes for the ordering of things, but mentioned as causes air and ether and water and many other absurdities. And it seemed to me it was very much as if one should say that Socrates does with intelligence whatever he does, and then, in trying to give the causes of the particular thing I do, should say first that I am now sitting here because my body is composed of bones and sinews, and the bones are hard and have joints which divide them and the sinews can be contracted and relaxed and, with the flesh and the skin which contains them all, are laid about the bones; and so, as the bones are hung loose in their ligaments, the sinews, by relaxing and contracting, make me able to bend my limbs now, and that is the cause of my sitting here with my legs bent. Or as if in the same way he should give voice and air and hearing and countless other things of the sort as causes for our talking with each other, and should fail to mention the real causes, which are, that the Athenians decided that it was best to condemn me, and therefore I have decided that it was best for me to sit here and that it is right for me to stay and undergo whatever penalty they order. For, by Dog, I fancy these bones and sinews of mine would have been in Megara or Boeotia long ago, carried thither by an opinion of what was best, if I did not think it was better and nobler to endure any penalty the city may inflict rather than to escape and run away. But it is most absurd to call things of that sort causes. If anyone were to say that I could not have done what I thought proper if I had not bones and sinews and other things that I have, he would be right. But to say that those things are the cause of my doing what I do, and that I act with intelligence but not from the choice of what is best, would be an extremely careless way of talking. Whoever talks in that way is unable to make a distinction and to see that in reality a cause is one thing, and the thing without which the cause could never be a cause is quite another thing. And so it seems to me that most people, when they give the name of cause to the latter, are groping in the dark, as it were, and are giving it a name that does not belong to it. And so one man makes the earth stay below the heavens by putting a vortex about it, and another regards the earth as a flat trough supported on a foundation of air; but they do not look for the power which causes things to be now placed as it is best for them to be placed, nor do they think it has any divine force, but they think they can find a new Atlas more powerful and more immortal and more all-embracing than this, and in truth they give no thought to the good, which must embrace and hold together all things. Now I would gladly be the pupil of anyone who would teach me the nature of such a cause; but since that was denied me and I was not able to discover it myself or to learn of it from anyone else, do you wish me, Cebes (said he), to give you an account of the way in which I have conducted my second voyage in quest of the cause?

Plato also presents Socrates elaborating a theory of the soul in analogy with the theory of the state in the *Republic.* This theory is concerned with human powers and reason rather than with cosmic order and harmony, and it depends on the differentiation and interrelation of rational, desiderative, and spirited functions in man.

Republic *

"The soul of the thirsty then, in so far as it thirsts, wishes nothing else than to drink, and yearns for this and its impulse is towards this." "Obviously." "Then if anything draws it back when thirsty it must be something different in it from that which thirsts and drives it like a beast to drink. For it cannot be, we say, that the same thing with the same part of itself at the same time acts in opposite ways about the same thing." "We must admit that it does not." "So I fancy it is not well said of the archer that his hands at the same time thrust away the bow and draw it nigh, but we should rather say that there is one hand that puts it away and another that draws it to." "By all means," he said. "Are we to say, then, that some men sometimes though thirsty refuse to drink?" "We are indeed," he said, "many and often." "What then," said I, "should one affirm about them? Is it not that there is a something in the soul that bids them drink and a something that forbids, a different something that masters that which bids?" "I think so." "And is it not the fact that that which inhibits such actions arises when it arises from the calculations of reason, but the impulses which draw and drag come through affections and diseases?" "Apparently." "Not unreasonably," said I, "shall we claim that they are two and different from one another, naming that in the soul whereby it reckons and reasons the rational and that with which it loves, hungers, thirsts, and feels the flutter and titillation of other desires, the irrational and appetitive—companion of various repletions and pleasures." "It would not be unreasonable but quite natural," he said, "for us to think this." "These two forms, then, let us assume to have been marked off as actually existing in the soul. But now the Thumos or principle of high spirit, that with which we feel anger, is it a third, or would it be identical in nature with one of these?" "Perhaps," he said, "with one of these, the appetitive." "But," I said, "I once heard a story which I believe, that Leontius the son of Aglaion, on his way up from the Peiraeus under the outer side of the northern wall, becoming aware of dead bodies that lay at the place of public execution at the same time felt a desire to see them and a repugnance and aversion, and that for a time he resisted and veiled his head, but overpowered in despite of all by his desire, with wide staring eyes he rushed up to the corpses and cried, 'There, ye wretches, take your fill of the fine spectacle!' " "I too," he said, "have heard the story." "Yet, surely this

* From Plato, *Republic* IV, 439A–441C, trans. by Paul Shorey, Loeb Classical Library (Cambridge, Mass., Harvard University Press). Reprinted by permission of the publishers.

anecdote," I said, "signifies that the principle of anger sometimes fights against desires as an alien thing against an alien." "Yes, it does," he said.

"And do we not," said I, "on many other occasions observe when his desires constrain a man contrary to his reason that he reviles himself and is angry with that within which masters him; and that as it were in a faction of two parties the high spirit of such a man becomes the ally of his reason? But its making common cause with the desires against the reason when reason whispers low 'Thou must not'—that, I think, is a kind of thing you would not affirm ever to have perceived in yourself, nor, I fancy, in anybody else either." "No, by heaven," he said. "Again, when a man thinks himself to be in the wrong, is it not true that the nobler he is the less is he capable of anger though suffering hunger and cold and whatsoever else at the hands of him whom he believes to be acting justly therein, and as I say his spirit refuses to be aroused against such a one?" "True," he said. "But what when a man believes himself to be wronged, does not his spirit in that case seethe and grow fierce (and also because of his suffering hunger, cold and the like) and make itself the ally of what he judges just, and in noble souls it endures and wins the victory and will not let go until either it achieves its purpose, or death ends all, or, as a dog is called back by a shepherd, it is called back by the reason within and calmed." "Your similitude is perfect," he said, "and it confirms our former statements that the helpers are as it were dogs subject to the rulers who are as it were the shepherds of the city." "You apprehend my meaning excellently," said I. "But do you also take note of this?" "Of what?" "That what we now think about the spirited element is just the opposite of our recent surmise. For then we supposed it to be a part of the appetitive, but now, far from that, we say that, in the factions of the soul, it much rather marshals itself on the side of the reason." "By all means," he said. "Is it then distinct from this too, or is it a form of the rational, so that there are not three but two kinds in the soul, the rational and the appetitive, or just as in the city there were three existing kinds that composed its structure, the money-makers, the helpers, the counsellors, so also in the soul there exists a third kind, this principle of high spirit, which is the helper of reason by nature unless it is corrupted by evil nurture?" "We have to assume it as a third," he said. "Yes," said I, "provided it shall have been shown to be something different from the rational, as it has been shown to be other than the appetitive." "That is not hard to be shown," he said; "for that much one can see in children, that they are from their very birth chock-full of rage and high spirit, but as for reason, some of them, to my thinking, never participate in it, and the majority quite late." "Yes, by heaven, excellently said," I replied; "and further, one could see in animals that what you say is true. And to these instances we may add the testimony of Homer quoted above:

He smote his breast and chided thus his heart.

For there Homer has clearly represented that in us which has reflected about the better and the worse as rebuking that which feels unreasoning anger as if it were a distinct and different thing." "You are entirely right," he said.

PLATO

Plato continued Socrates' inquiry into the nature and processes of scientific investigation, and he employed the method of dialectic, which he evolved, on the problems of man and of human and social action. His philosophy laid the foundations and provided the principles for much of the later study of psychological forces and functions. The world of the mind is explored in his work in two related dimensions: he presents the operations of the universe and its parts as organically interdependent and as intelligible or rational because they are intelligent, and he makes shrewd and profound observations concerning human perception and understanding, feelings and purposes, skills and derangements, passions and character, deformations and therapy in this universe of intelligible relations and proportions. The world of mind revealed in the insights of poets comes into contact with the critical distinctions of the scientific inquirer in the problems raised by Plato's persistent inquiries concerning virtue, science, and wisdom.

Timaeus *

For Him who is most good it neither was nor is permissible to perform any action save what is most fair. As He reflected, therefore, He perceived that of such creatures as are by nature visible, none that is irrational will be fairer, comparing wholes with wholes, than the ra-

* From Plato, *Timaeus* 30A–C, trans. by R. G. Bury, Loeb Classical Library (Cambridge, Mass., Harvard University Press). Reprinted by permission of the publishers.

tional; and further, that reason cannot possibly belong to any apart from Soul. So because of this reflexion He constructed reason within soul and soul within body as he fashioned the All, that so the work He was executing might be of its nature most fair and most good. Thus, then, in accordance with the likely account, we must declare that this Cosmos has verily come into existence as a Living Creature endowed with soul and reason owing to the providence of God.

And when the construction of the Soul had been completed to the satisfaction of its Constructor, then He fabricated within it all the Corporeal, and uniting them centre to centre He made them fit together. And the Soul, being woven throughout the Heaven every way from the centre to the extremity, and enveloping it in a circle from without, and herself revolving within herself, began a divine beginning of unceasing and intelligent life lasting throughout all time. And whereas the body of the Heaven is visible, the Soul is herself invisible but partakes in reasoning and in harmony, having come into existence by the agency of the best of things intelligible and ever-existing as the best of things generated. Inasmuch, then, as she is a compound, blended of the natures of the Same and the Other and Being, these three portions, and is proportionately divided and bound together, and revolves back upon herself, whenever she touches anything which has its substance dispersed or anything which has its substance undivided she is moved throughout her whole being and announces what the object is identical with and from what it is different, and in what relation, where and how and when, it comes about that each thing exists and is acted upon by others both in the sphere of Becoming and in that of the ever-uniform. And her announcement, being identically true concerning both the Other and the Same, is borne through the self-moved without speech or sound; and whenever it is concerned with the sensible, and the circle of the Other moving in straight course proclaims it to the whole of its Soul, opinions and beliefs arise which are firm and true; and again, when it is concerned with the rational, and the circle of the Same, spinning truly, declares the facts, reason and knowledge of necessity result. But should anyone assert that the substance in which these two states arise is something other than Soul, his assertion will be anything rather than the truth.

The motions of the Soul of the World are cognitions and emotions, and these motions direct or influence the physical motions of bodies.

Laws *

Soul drives all things in Heaven and earth and sea by its own motions, of which the names are wish, reflection, forethought, counsel, opinion true and false, joy, grief, confidence, fear, hate, love, and all the motions that are akin to these or are prime-working motions; these, when they take over the secondary motions of bodies, drive them all to increase and decrease and separation and combination, and, supervening on these, to heat and cold, heaviness and lightness, hardness and softness, whiteness and blackness, bitterness and sweetness, and all those qualities which soul employs, both when it governs things rightly and happily as a true goddess, in conjunction with reason, and when, in converse with unreason, it produces results which are in all respects the opposite.

The transition from the World-Soul to the human soul is made by discovering identical elements in both and by virtue of that identity the human faculties are effective and relevant to the environing world. Plato distinguishes four such components: the infinite (more and less, hotter and colder, quicker and slower, greater and smaller), the finite (equal and double, and everything which puts an end to differences between opposites and makes them commensurable by means of number), the mixture of the infinite and the finite (health, beauty, and strength of body and beauties of the soul), and the cause of the mixture (mind and wisdom). In the *Philebus* he makes use of these distinctions to investigate the nature of *pleasure.*

Philebus †

SOCRATES. Shall we not say that our body has a soul?

PROTARCHUS. Clearly we shall.

SOC. Where did it get it, Protarchus, unless the body of the universe had a soul, since that body has the same elements as ours, only in every way superior?

* From Plato, *Laws* X, 896E–897B, trans. by R. G. Bury, Loeb Classical Library (Cambridge, Mass., Harvard University Press). Reprinted by permission of the publishers.

† From Plato, *Philebus* 30A–34C, trans. by W. R. M. Lamb, Loeb Classical Library (Cambridge, Mass., Harvard University Press). Reprinted by permission of the publishers.

PRO. Clearly it could get it from no other source.

SOC. No; for we surely do not believe, Protarchus, that of those four elements, the finite, the infinite, the combination, and the element of cause which exists in all things, this last, which gives to our bodies souls and the art of physical exercise and medical treatment when the body is ill, and which is in general a composing and healing power, is called the sum of all wisdom, and yet, while these same elements exist in the entire heaven and in great parts thereof, and are, moreover, fair and pure, there is no means of including among them that nature which is the fairest and most precious of all.

PRO. Certainly there would be no sense in that.

SOC. Then if that is not the case, it would be better to follow the other line of thought and say, as we have often said, that there is in the universe a plentiful infinite and a sufficient limit, and in addition a by no means feeble cause which orders and arranges years and seasons and months, and may most justly be called wisdom and mind.

PRO. Yes, most justly.

SOC. Surely reason and mind could never come into being without soul.

PRO. No, never.

SOC. Then in the nature of Zeus you would say that a kingly soul and a kingly mind were implanted through the power of the cause, and in other deities other noble qualities from which they derive their favourite epithets.

PRO. Certainly.

SOC. Now do not imagine, Protarchus, that this is mere idle talk of mine; it confirms the utterances of those who declared of old that mind always rules the universe.

PRO. Yes, certainly.

SOC. And to my question it has furnished the reply that mind belongs to that one of our four classes which was called the cause of all. Now, you see, you have at last my answer.

PRO. Yes, and a very sufficient one; and yet you answered without my knowing it.

SOC. Yes, Protarchus, for sometimes a joke is a restful change from serious talk.

PRO. You are right.

SOC. We have now, then, my friend, pretty clearly shown to what class mind belongs and what power it possesses.

PRO. Certainly.

SOC. And likewise the class of pleasure was made clear some time ago.

PRO. Yes, it was.

SOC. Let us, then, remember concerning both of them that mind was akin to cause and belonged more or less to that class, and that pleasure was itself infinite and belonged to the class which, in and by itself, has not and never will have either beginning or middle or end.

PRO. We will remember that, of course.

SOC. Our next task is to see in what and by means of what feeling each of them comes into being whenever they do come into being. We will take pleasure first and discuss these questions in relation to pleasure, as we examined its class first. But we cannot examine pleasure successfully apart from pain.

PRO. If that is our proper path, let us follow it.

SOC. Do you agree with us about the origin of pleasure?

PRO. What do you think it is?

SOC. I think pain and pleasure naturally originate in the combined class.

PRO. Please, my dear Socrates, remind us which of the aforesaid classes you mean by the combined class.

SOC. I will do so, as well as I can, my brilliant friend.

PRO. Thank you.

SOC. By combined class, then, let us understand that which we said was the third of the four.

PRO. The one you mentioned after the infinite and the finite, and in which you put health and also, I believe, harmony?

SOC. You are quite right. Now please pay very close attention.

PRO. I will. Say on.

SOC. I say, then, that when, in us living beings, harmony is broken up, a disruption of nature and a generation of pain also take place at the same moment.

PRO. What you say is very likely.

SOC. But if harmony is recomposed and returns to its own nature, then I say that pleasure is generated, if I may speak in the fewest and briefest words about matters of the highest import.

PRO. I think you are right, Socrates; but let us try to be more explicit.

SOC. It is easiest to understand common and obvious examples, is it not?

PRO. What examples?

SOC. Is hunger a kind of breaking up and a pain?

PRO. Yes.

SOC. And eating, which is a filling up again, is a pleasure?

PRO. Yes.

SOC. Thirst again is a destruction and a pain, but the filling with moisture of that which was dried up is a pleasure. Then, too, the unnatural dissolution and disintegration we experience through heat are a pain, but the natural restoration and cooling are a pleasure.

PRO. Certainly.

SOC. And the unnatural hardening of the moisture in an animal through cold is pain; but the natural course of the elements returning to their place and separating is a pleasure. See, in short, if you think it is a reasonable statement that whenever in the class of living beings, which, as I said before, arises out of the natural union of the infinite and the finite, that union is destroyed, the destruction is pain, and the passage and return of all things to their own nature is pleasure.

PRO. Let us accept that; for it seems to me to be true in its general lines.

SOC. Then we may assume this as one kind of pain and pleasure arising severally under the conditions I have described?

PRO. Let that be assumed.

SOC. Now assume within the soul itself the anticipation of these conditions, the sweet and cheering hope of pleasant things to come, the fearful and woeful expectation of painful things to come.

PRO. Yes, indeed, this is another kind of pleasure and pain, which belongs to the soul itself, apart from the body, and arises through expectation.

SOC. You are right. I think that in these two kinds, both of which are, in my opinion, pure, and not formed by mixture of pain and pleasure, the truth about pleasure will be made manifest, whether the entire class is to be desired or such desirability is rather to be attributed to some other class among those we have mentioned, whereas pleasure and pain, like heat, cold, and other such things, are sometimes desirable and sometimes undesirable, because they are not good in themselves, though some of them sometimes admit on occasion the nature of the good.

PRO. You are quite right in saying that we must track our quarry on this trail.

SOC. First, then, let us agree on this point: If it is true, as we said, that destruction is pain and restoration is pleasure, let us consider the case of living beings in which neither destruction nor restoration is going on, and what their state is under such conditions. Fix your mind on my question: Must not every living being under those conditions necessarily be devoid of any feeling of pain or pleasure, great or small?

PRO. Yes, necessarily.

SOC. Have we, then, a third condition, besides those of feeling pleasure and pain?

PRO. Certainly.

SOC. Well then, do your best to bear it in mind; for remembering or forgetting it will make a great difference in our judgement of pleasure. And I should like, if you do not object, to speak briefly about it.

PRO. Pray do so.

SOC. You know that there is nothing to hinder a man from living the life of wisdom in this manner.

PRO. You mean without feeling pleasure or pain?

SOC. Yes, for it was said, you know, in our comparison of the lives that he who chose the life of mind and wisdom was to have no feeling of pleasure, great or small.

PRO. Yes, surely, that was said.

SOC. Such a man, then, would have such a life; and perhaps it is not unreasonable, if that is the most divine of lives.

PRO. Certainly it is not likely that gods feel either joy or its opposite.

SOC. No, it is very unlikely; for either is unseemly for them. But let us reserve the discussion of that point for another time, if it is appropriate, and we will give mind credit for it in contending for the second place, if we cannot count it for the first.

PRO. Quite right.

SOC. Now the other class of pleasure, which we said was an affair of the soul alone, originates entirely in memory.

PRO. How is that?

SOC. We must, apparently, first take up memory, and perception even before memory, if these matters are to be made clear to us properly.

PRO. What do you mean?

SOC. Assume that some of the affections of our body are extinguished in the body before they reach the soul, leaving the soul unaffected, and that other affections permeate both body and soul and cause a vibration in both conjointly and in each individually.

PRO. Let us assume that.

SOC. Shall we be right in saying that the soul forgets those which do not permeate both, and does not forget those which do?

PRO. Yes, certainly.

SOC. Do not in the least imagine that when I speak of forgetting I mean that forgetfulness arises in this case; for forgetfulness is the departure of memory, and in the case under consideration memory has not yet come into being; now it is absurd to speak of the loss of that which does not exist and has not yet come into being, is it not?

PRO. Certainly.

SOC. Then just change the terms.

PRO. How?

SOC. Instead of saying that the soul forgets, when it is unaffected by the vibrations of the body, apply the term want of perception to that which you are now calling forgetfulness.

PRO. I understand.

SOC. And the union of soul and body in one common affection and one common motion you may properly call perception.

PRO. Very true.

SOC. Then do we now understand what we mean by perception?

PRO. Certainly.

SOC. I think, then, that memory may rightly be defined as the preservation of perception.

PRO. Quite rightly.

SOC. But do we not say that memory differs from recollection?

PRO. Perhaps.

SOC. And is this the difference?

PRO. What?

SOC. When the soul alone by itself, apart from the body, recalls completely any experience it has had in company with the body, we say that it recollects, do we not?

PRO. Certainly.

SOC. And again when the soul has lost the memory of a perception or of something it has learned and then alone by itself regains this, we call everything of that kind recollection.

PRO. You are right.

SOC. Now my reason for saying all this is—

PRO. What?

SOC. That henceforth we may comprehend as completely and clearly as possible the pleasure of the soul, and likewise its desire, apart from the body; for both of these appear to be made plain by what has been said about memory and recollection.

The same basic distinctions are used to examine the differences between sensation and thought and the transition from the data of sense experience to the calculations of reason, from the infinites of "greater and smaller" to the finitudes of number.

Republic *

. . ."Do you observe then," said I, "in this study what I do?" "What?" "It seems likely that it is one of those studies which we are seeking that naturally conduce to the awakening of thought, but that no one makes the right use of it, though it really does tend to draw the mind

* From Plato, *Republic* VII, 522E–525B, trans. by Paul Shorey, Loeb Classical Library (Cambridge, Mass., Harvard University Press). Reprinted by permission of the publishers.

to essence and reality." "What do you mean?" he said. "I will try," I said, "to show you at least my opinion. Do you keep watch and observe the things I distinguish in my mind as being or not being conducive to our purpose, and either concur or dissent, in order that here too we may see more clearly whether my surmise is right." "Point them out," he said. "I do point them out," I said, "if you can discern that some reports of our perceptions do not provoke thought to reconsideration because the judgement of them by sensation seems adequate, while others always invite the intellect to reflection because the sensation yields nothing that can be trusted." "You obviously mean distant appearances," he said, "and shadow-painting." "You have quite missed my meaning," said I. "What do you mean?" he said. "The experiences that do not provoke thought are those that do not at the same time issue in a contradictory perception. Those that do have that effect I set down as provocatives, when the perception no more manifests one thing than its contrary, alike whether its impact comes from nearby or afar. An illustration will make my meaning plain. Here, we say, are three fingers, the little finger, the second and the middle." "Quite so," he said. "Assume that I speak of them as seen near at hand. But this is the point that you are to consider." "What?" "Each one of them appears to be equally a finger, and in this respect it makes no difference whether it is observed as intermediate or at either extreme, whether it is white or black, thick or thin, or of any other quality of this kind. For in none of these cases is the soul of most men impelled to question the reason and to ask what in the world is a finger, since the faculty of sight never signifies to it at the same time that the finger is the opposite of a finger." "Why, no, it does not," he said. "Then," said I, "it is to be expected that such a perception will not provoke or awaken reflection and thought." "It is." "But now, what about the bigness and the smallness of these objects? Is our vision's view of them adequate, and does it make no difference to it whether one of them is situated outside or in the middle; and similarly of the relation of touch, to thickness and thinness, softness and hardness? And are not the other senses also defective in their reports of such things? Or is the operation of each of them as follows? In the first place, the sensation that is set over the hard is of necessity related also to the soft, and it reports to the soul that the same thing is both hard and soft to its perception." "It is so," he said. "Then," said I, "is not this again a case where the soul must be at a loss as to what significance for it the sensation of hardness has, if the sense reports the same thing as also soft? And, similarly, as to what the sensation of light and heavy means by light and heavy, if it reports the heavy as light, and the light as heavy?" "Yes, indeed," he said, "these communications to the soul are strange and invite reconsideration." "Naturally, then," said I, "it is in such cases as these that the soul first summons to its aid the calculating reason and tries to consider whether each of the things reported to it is one or two." "Of course." "And if it appears to be two, each of the two is a distinct unit." "Yes." "If, then, each is one and both two, the very meaning of 'two' is that the soul will conceive them as distinct. For if they were not separable, it would not have been thinking of two, but of one." "Right." "Sight too saw the great and the small, we say, not separated but confounded. Is not that so?" "Yes." "And for the clarification of this, the intelligence is compelled to contemplate the great and small, not thus confounded but as distinct entities, in the opposite way from sensation." "True." "And is it not in some such experience as this that the question first occurs to us, what in the world, then, is the great and the small?" "By all means." "And this is the origin of the designation *intelligible* for the one, and *visible* for the other." "Just so," he said.

"This, then, is just what I was trying to explain a little while ago when I said that some things are provocative of thought and some are not, defining as provocative things that impinge upon the senses together with their opposites, while those that do not I said do not tend to awaken reflection." "Well, now I understand," he said, "and agree." "To which class, then, do you think number and the one belong?" "I cannot conceive," he said. "Well, reason it out from what has already been said. For, if unity is adequately seen by itself or apprehended by some other sensation, it would not tend to draw the mind to the apprehension of essence, as we were explaining in the case of the finger. But if some contradiction is always seen coincidentally with it, so that it no more appears to be one than the opposite, there would forthwith be need of something to judge between them, and it would compel the soul to be at a loss and to inquire, by arousing thought in itself, and to ask, whatever then is the one as such, and thus the study of unity will be one of the studies that guide and convert the soul to the contemplation of true being." "But surely," he said, "the visual perception of it does especially involve this. For we see the same thing at once as one and as an indefinite plurality." "Then if this is true of the one," I said, "the same holds of all number, does it not?" "Of course." "But, further, reckoning and the science of arithmetic are wholly concerned with number." "They are, indeed." "And the qualities of number appear to lead to the apprehension of truth." "Beyond anything," he said. . . .

When Plato turns to the consideration of psychic derangement, the same distinctions lead him to differentiate two kinds, one of which is a disruption of the relations among the functions of man which is like a disease of the body, while the other is ignorance which is like a deformity of the body.

Sophist *

ELEAN STRANGER. We must say that there are two kinds of evil in the soul.

THEAETETUS. What kinds?

STR. The one comparable to a disease in the body, the other to a deformity.

THEAET. I do not understand.

STR. Perhaps you have not considered that disease and discord are the same thing?

THEAET. I do not know what reply I ought to make to this, either.

STR. Is that because you think discord is anything else than the disagreement of the naturally related, brought about by some corruption?

THEAET. No; I think it is nothing else.

STR. But is deformity anything else than the presence of the quality of disproportion, which is always ugly?

THEAET. Nothing else at all.

STR. Well then; do we not see that in the souls of worthless men opinions are opposed to desires, anger to pleasures, reason to pain, and all such things to one another?

THEAET. Yes, they are, decidedly.

STR. Yet they must all be naturally related.

THEAET. Of course.

STR. Then we shall be right if we say wickedness is a discord and disease of the soul.

THEAET. Yes, quite right.

STR. But if things which partake of motion and aim at some particular mark pass beside the mark and miss it on every occasion when they try to hit it, shall we say that this happens to them through right proportion to one another or, on the contrary, through disproportion?

THEAET. Evidently through disproportion.

STR. But yet we know that every soul, if ignorant of anything, is ignorant against its will.

THEAET. Very much so.

STR. Now being ignorant is nothing else than the aberration of a soul

* From Plato, *Sophist* 277E–228E, trans. by H. N. Fowler, Loeb Classical Library (Cambridge, Mass., Harvard University Press). Reprinted by permission of the publishers.

that aims at truth, when the understanding passes beside the mark.

THEAET. Very true.

STR. Then we must regard a foolish soul as deformed and ill-proportioned.

THEAET. So it seems.

STR. Then there are, it appears, these two kinds of evils in the soul, one, which people call wickedness, which is very clearly a disease.

THEAET. Yes.

STR. And the other they call ignorance, but they are not willing to acknowledge that it is a vice, when it arises only in the soul.

THEAET. It must certainly be admitted, though I disputed it when you said it just now, that there are two kinds of vice in the soul, and that cowardice, intemperance, and injustice must all alike be considered a disease in us, and the widespread and various condition of ignorance must be regarded as a deformity.

The causes of evil-doing and sin are important considerations in the treatment of problems of law and justice, since they bear on the distinction between voluntary and involuntary actions and between injuries and injustices, torts and crimes.

Laws *

CLINIAS. What you have said seems very reasonable; but we should be glad to hear a still clearer statement respecting the difference between injury and injustice, and how the distinction between the voluntary and the involuntary applies in these cases.

ATHENIAN STRANGER. I must endeavour to do as you bid me, and explain the matter. No doubt in conversing with one another you say and hear said at least thus much about the soul, that one element in its nature (be it affection or part) is "passion," which is an inbred quality of a contentious and pugnacious kind, and one that overturns many things by its irrational force.

CLIN. Of course.

ATH. Moreover, we distinguish "pleasure" from passion, and we assert that its mastering power is of an opposite kind, since it effects all that its intention desires by a mixture of persuasion and deceit.

CLIN. Exactly.

ATH. Nor would it be untrue to say that the third cause of sins is

* From Plato, *Laws* IX, 863A–864C. trans. by R. G. Bury, Loeb Classical Library (Cambridge, Mass., Harvard University Press). Reprinted by permission of the publishers.

ignorance. This cause, however, the lawgiver would do well to subdivide into two, counting ignorance in its simple form to be the cause of minor sins, and in its double form—where the folly is due to the man being gripped not by ignorance only, but also by a conceit of wisdom as though he had full knowledge of things he knows nothing at all about,—counting this to be the cause of great and brutal sins when it is joined with strength and might, but the cause of childish and senile sins when it is joined with weakness; and these last he will count as sins and he will ordain laws, as for sinners, but laws that will be, above all others, of the most mild and merciful kind.

CLIN. That is reasonable.

ATH. And pretty well everyone speaks of one man being "superior," another "inferior," to pleasure or to passion; and they are so.

CLIN. Most certainly.

ATH. But we have never heard it said that one man is "superior," another "inferior," to ignorance.

CLIN. Quite true.

ATH. And we assert that all these things urge each man often to go counter to the actual bent of his own inclination.

CLIN. Very frequently.

ATH. Now I will define for you, clearly and without complication, my notion of justice and injustice. The domination of passion and fear and pleasure and pain and envies and desires in the soul, whether they do any injury or not, I term generally "injustice"; but the belief in the highest good—in whatsoever way either States or individuals think they can attain to it,—if this prevails in their souls and regulates every man, even if some damage be done, we must assert that everything thus done is just, and that in each man the part subject to this governance is also just, and best for the whole life of mankind, although most men suppose that such damage is an involuntary injustice. But we are not now concerned with a verbal dispute. Since, however, it has been shown that there are three kinds of sinning, we must first of all recall these still more clearly to mind. Of these, one kind, as we know, is painful; and that we term passion and fear.

CLIN. Quite so.

ATH. The second kind consists of pleasure and desires; the third, which is a distinct kind, consists of hopes and untrue belief regarding the attainment of the highest good. And when this last kind is subdivided into three, five classes are made, as we now assert; and for these five classes we must enact distinct laws, of two main types.

CLIN. What are they?

ATH. The one concerns acts done on each occasion by violent and open means, the other acts done privily under cover of darkness and deceit, or sometimes acts done in both these ways,—and for acts of this last kind the laws will be most severe, if they are to prove adequate.

CLIN. Naturally.

ARISTOTLE *

Aristotle's *De Anima* (*On the Soul*) is in significant respects the beginning of the history of scientific statements and treatment of problems of psychology. The beginning is far from abrupt, as is apparent from the fact that the first of the three books of that work is devoted to the examination of earlier doctrines of the soul propounded by the Pythagoreans, Democritus, Anaxagoras, Heraclitus, Empedocles, and Plato. After his review of his predecessors, Aristotle professes to make a "fresh start." His approach separates the problems of animate life and human thought from the problems of cosmological and corporeal motions: he argues against the separated ideas and world soul of his master Plato and against the soul atoms of Democritus. In his theory the soul is conceived, not as a spirit imprisoned in a body nor as a body moving a body, but as a function related to the body, as cutting is related to the ax or seeing to the eye. The study of the soul is therefore a part of "natural science" or "physics," which is the study of the motions of bodies, since the soul is the principle of the motions of all animate beings—plants and animals as well as men.

There is no need to demonstrate the existence of the soul so understood: living things are distinct from dead, and the study of the soul is the study of the movements and functions which characterize living things. In plants these movements subserve three general functions—reproduction, growth, and nutrition. Animals possess these functions and add to them powers of locomotion and sense perception. The lines are not sharply drawn; on the contrary, in his biological works Aristotle examines in great detail numerous bor-

* All translations of Aristotle on the following pages follow *The Oxford Translation of Aristotle* (Oxford, The Clarendon Press). Reprinted by permission of the publishers. Selections and annotations are from Richard McKeon (ed.), *The Basic Writings of Aristotle* (New York: Random House, 1941).

derline cases of organisms possessing some functions of plants and some of animals. Memory, common sense, and imagination accompany the five senses in some of the higher animals, and they in turn prepare for the operation of reason, which in its full development is peculiar to man.

The problems of the world of the mind are distributed, therefore, through the various sciences which Aristotle treated. He distinguished three kinds of sciences according to the purposes they were suited to serve: theoretical sciences for knowing, practical sciences for doing, and productive or poetic sciences for making. The theoretical sciences—physics, mathematics, and metaphysics—themselves embody his conception of the nature of inquiry and knowledge, and several of the biological sciences, which include biology and psychology, investigate the functions of the soul—reproduction, growth, nutrition, self-locomotion, sensation, and understanding. The practical sciences—ethics and politics—build on the basis of psychological knowledge: the distinction between moral and intellectual virtues corresponds to the distinction between two parts of the soul (for there are no virtues in the third, the vegetative, part) and the intellectual virtues include science, intuition, and wisdom, while the institutions of states depend on human actions, passions, customs, and purposes. The fullest examination of the passions, finally, is found in the productive sciences and in rhetoric, for the effects of art and persuasion are marked by pleasure and emotions and they exhibit characters in action and speech. Many of the distinctions which continued to be used, and many which provoked alternative distinctions in later investigations of the world of the mind, were first made in the technical vocabulary of this comprehensive exploration of functions, habits, and characters, and their evolution has been the history of the technical terms of psychology.

De Anima

BOOK I

Holding as we do that, while knowledge of any kind is a thing to be honoured and prized, one kind of it may, either by reason of its greater exactness or of a higher dignity and greater wonderfulness in its objects, be more honourable and precious than another, on both accounts we should naturally be led to place in the front rank the study of the soul. The knowledge of the soul admittedly contributes greatly to the advance of truth in general, and, above all, to our understanding of Nature, for the soul is in some sense the principle of animal life. Our aim is to grasp and understand, first its essential nature, and secondly its properties; of these some are thought to be affections proper to the soul itself, while others are considered to attach to the animal [1] owing to the presence within it of soul.

To attain any assured knowledge about the soul is one of the most difficult things in the world. As the form of question which here presents itself, viz. the question "What is it?", recurs in other fields, it might be supposed that there was some single method of inquiry applicable to all objects whose essential nature we are endeavouring to ascertain (as there *is* for derived properties the single method of demonstration); in that case what we should have to seek for would be this unique method. But if there is no such single and general method for solving the question of essence, our task becomes still more difficult; in the case of each different subject we shall have to determine the appropriate process of investigation. If to this there be a clear answer, e.g. that the process is demonstration or division, or some other known method, difficulties and hesitations still beset us—with what facts shall we begin the inquiry? For the facts which form the starting-points in different subjects must be different, as e.g. in the case of numbers and surfaces.

First, no doubt, it is necessary to determine in which of the *summa genera* soul lies, what it *is;* is it "a this-somewhat," a substance, or is it a quale or a quantum, or some other of the remaining kinds of predicates which we have distinguished? Further, does soul belong to the class of potential existents, or is it not rather an actuality? Our answer to this question is of the greatest importance.

We must consider also whether soul is divisible or is without parts, and whether it is everywhere homogeneous or not; and if not homogeneous, whether its various forms are different specifically or generically: up to the present time those who have discussed and investigated soul seem to have confined themselves to the human soul. We must be careful not to ignore the question whether soul can be defined in a single unambiguous formula, as is the case with animal, or whether we must not give a separate formula for each sort of it, as we do for horse, dog, man, god (in the latter case the "universal" animal—and so too every other "common predicate"—being treated either as nothing at all or as a

[1] That is, the complex of soul and body.

later product [2]). Further, if what exists is not a plurality of souls, but a plurality of parts of one soul, which ought we to investigate first, the whole soul or its parts? (It is also a difficult problem to decide which of these parts are in nature distinct from one another.) Again, which ought we to investigate first, these parts or their functions, mind or thinking, the faculty or the act of sensation, and so on? If the investigation of the functions precedes that of the parts, the further question suggests itself: ought we not before either to consider the correlative objects, e.g. of sense or thought? It seems not only useful for the discovery of the causes of the derived properties of substances to be acquainted with the essential nature of those substances (as in mathematics it is useful for the understanding of the property of the equality of the interior angles of a triangle to two right angles to know the essential nature of the straight and the curved or of the line and the plane) but also conversely, for the knowledge of the essential nature of a substance is largely promoted by an acquaintance with its properties: for, when we are able to give an account conformable to experience of all or most of the properties of a substance, we shall be in the most favourable position to say something worth saying about the essential nature of that subject; in all demonstration a definition of the essence is required as a starting-point, so that definitions which do not enable us to discover the derived properties, or which fail to facilitate even a conjecture about them, must obviously, one and all, be dialectical and futile.

A further problem presented by the affections of soul is this: are they all affections of the complex of body and soul, or is there any one among them peculiar to the soul by itself? To determine this is indispensable but difficult. If we consider the majority of them, there seems to be no case in which the soul can act or be acted upon without involving the body; e.g. anger, courage, appetite, and sensation generally. Thinking seems the most probable exception; but if this too proves to be a form of imagination or to be impossible without imagination, it too requires a body as a condition of its existence. If there is any way of acting or being acted upon proper to soul, soul will be capable of separate existence; if there is none, its separate existence is impossible. In the latter case, it will be like what is straight, which has many properties arising from the straightness in it, e.g. that of touching a bronze sphere at a point, though straightness divorced from the other constituents of the straight thing cannot touch it in this way; it cannot be so divorced at all, since it is always found in a body. It therefore seems that all the affections of soul involve a body—passion, gentleness, fear, pity,

[2] That is, as presupposing the various sorts instead of being presupposed by them.

courage, joy, loving, and hating; in all these there is a concurrent affection of the body. In support of this we may point to the fact that, while sometimes on the occasion of violent and striking occurrences there is no excitement or fear felt, on others faint and feeble stimulations produce these emotions, viz. when the body is already in a state of tension resembling its condition when we are angry. Here is a still clearer case: in the absence of any external cause of terror we find ourselves experiencing the feelings of a man in terror. From all this it is obvious that the affections of soul are enmattered formulable essences.

Consequently their definitions ought to correspond, e.g. anger should be defined as a certain mode of movement of such and such a body (or part or faculty of a body) by this or that cause and for this or that end. That is precisely why the study of the soul must fall within the science of Nature, at least so far as in its affections it manifests this double character. Hence a physicist would define an affection of soul differently from a dialectician; the latter would define e.g. anger as the appetite for returning pain for pain, or something like that, while the former would define it as a boiling of the blood or warm substance surrounding the heart. The latter assigns the material conditions, the former the form of formulable essence; for what he states is the formulable essence of the fact, though for its actual existence there must be embodiment of it in a material such as is described by the other. Thus the essence of a house is assigned in such a formula as "a shelter against destruction by wind, rain, and heat"; the physicist would describe it as "stones, bricks, and timbers"; but there is a third possible description which would say that it was that form in that material with that purpose or end. Which, then, among these is entitled to be regarded as the genuine physicist? The one who confines himself to the material, or the one who restricts himself to the formulable essence alone? Is it not rather the one who combines both in a single formula? If this is so, how are we to characterize the other two? Must we not say that there is no type of thinker who concerns himself with those qualities or attributes of the material which are in fact inseparable from the material, and without attempting even in thought to separate them? The physicist is he who concerns himself with all the properties active and passive of bodies or materials thus or thus defined; attributes not considered as being of this character he leaves to others, in certain cases it may be to a specialist, e.g. a carpenter or a physician, in others (*a*) where they are inseparable in fact, but are separable from any particular kind of body by an effort of abstraction, to the mathematician, (*b*) where they are separate both in fact and in thought from body altogether, to the First Philosopher or metaphysician. But we must return from this digression, and repeat that the affections of soul are inseparable from the material substratum of animal life, to which we have seen that such affections, e.g. passion and fear, attach, and have not the same mode of being as a line or a plane.

BOOK II

Let the foregoing suffice as our account of the views concerning the soul which have been handed on by our predecessors; let us now dismiss them and make as it were a completely fresh start, endeavouring to give a precise answer to the question, What is soul? i.e. to formulate the most general possible definition of it.

We are in the habit of recognizing, as one determinate kind of what is, substance, and that in several senses, (*a*) in the sense of matter or that which in itself is not "a this," and (*b*) in the sense of form or essence, which is that precisely in virtue of which a thing is called "a this," and thirdly (*c*) in the sense of that which is compounded of both (*a*) and (*b*). Now matter is potentiality, form actuality; of the latter there are two grades related to one another as e.g. knowledge to the exercise of knowledge.

Among substances are by general consent reckoned bodies and especially natural bodies; for they are the principles of all other bodies. Of natural bodies some have life in them, others not; by life we mean self-nutrition and growth (with its correlative decay). It follows that every natural body which has life in it is a substance in the sense of a composite.

But since it is also a *body* of such and such a kind, viz. having life, the *body* cannot be soul; the body is the subject or matter, not what is attributed to it. Hence the soul must be a substance in the sense of the form of a natural body having life potentially within it. But substance[3] is actuality, and thus soul is the actuality of a body as above characterized. Now the word actuality has two senses corresponding respectively to the possession of knowledge and the actual exercise of knowledge. It is obvious that the soul is actuality in the first sense, viz. that of knowledge as possessed, for both sleeping and waking presuppose the existence of soul, and of these waking corresponds to actual knowing, sleeping to knowledge possessed but not employed, and, in the history of the individual, knowledge comes before its employment or exercise.

That is why the soul is the first grade of actuality of a natural body having life potentially in it. The body so described is a body which is organized. The parts of plants in spite of their extreme simplicity are "organs"; e.g. the leaf serves to shelter the pericarp, the pericarp to

[3] *Sc.* in the sense of form.

shelter the fruit, while the roots of plants are analogous to the mouth of animals, both serving for the absorption of food. If, then, we have to give a general formula applicable to all kinds of soul, we must describe it as the first grade of actuality of a natural organized body. That is why we can wholly dismiss as unnecessary the question whether the soul and the body are one: it is as meaningless as to ask whether the wax and the shape given to it by the stamp are one, or generally the matter of a thing and that of which it is the matter. Unity has many senses (as many as "is" has), but the most proper and fundamental sense of both is the relation of an actuality to that of which it is the actuality.

We have now given an answer to the question, What is soul?—an answer which applies to it in its full extent. It is substance in the sense which corresponds to the definitive formula of a thing's essence. That means that it is "the essential whatness" of a body of the character just assigned.[4] Suppose that what is literally an "organ," [5] like an axe, were a *natural* body, its "essential whatness," would have been its essence, and so its soul; if this disappeared from it, it would have ceased to be an axe, except in name. As it is,[6] it is just an axe; it wants the character which is required to make its whatness or formulable essence a soul; for that, it would have had to be a *natural* body of a particular kind, viz. one having *in itself* the power of setting itself in movement and arresting itself. Next, apply this doctrine in the case of the "parts" of the living body. Suppose that the eye were an animal—sight would have been its soul, for sight is the substance or essence of the eye which corresponds to the formula,[7] the eye being merely the matter of seeing; when seeing is removed the eye is no longer an eye, except in name—it is no more a real eye than the eye of a statue or of a painted figure. We must now extend our consideration from the "parts" to the whole living body; for what the departmental sense is to the bodily part which is its organ, that the whole faculty of sense is to the whole sensitive body as such.

We must not understand by that which is "potentially capable of living" what has lost the soul it had, but only what still retains it; but seeds and fruits are bodies which possess the qualification.[8] Consequently, while waking is actuality in a sense corresponding to the cutting and the seeing,[9] the soul is actuality in the sense corresponding to the

[4] Viz., organized, or possessed potentially of life.

[5] That is, instrument.

[6] Being an artificial, not a natural, body.

[7] That is, which states what it is to be an eye.

[8] Though only potentially, that is, they are at a further remove from actuality than the fully formed and organized body.

[9] That is, to the second grade of actuality.

power of sight and the power in the tool;[10] the body corresponds to what exists in potentiality; as the pupil *plus* the power of sight constitutes the eye, so the soul *plus* the body constitutes the animal.

From this it indubitably follows that the soul is inseparable from its body, or at any rate that certain parts of it are (if it has parts)—for the actuality of some of them is nothing but the actualities of their bodily parts. Yet some may be separable because they are not the actualities of any body at all. Further, we have no light on the problem whether the soul may not be the actuality of its body in the sense in which the sailor is the actuality[11] of the ship.

This must suffice as our sketch or outline determination of the nature of soul.

Since what is clear or logically more evident emerges from what in itself is confused but more observable by us, we must reconsider our results from this point of view. For it is not enough for a definitive formula to express as most now do the mere fact; it must include and exhibit the ground also. At present definitions are given in a form analogous to the conclusion of a syllogism; e.g. What is squaring? The construction of an equilateral rectangle equal to a given oblong rectangle. Such a definition is in form equivalent to a conclusion. One that tells us that squaring is the discovery of a line which is a mean proportional between the two unequal sides of the given rectangle discloses the ground of what is defined.

We resume our inquiry from a fresh starting-point by calling attention to the fact that what has soul in it differs from what has not in that the former displays life. Now this word has more than one sense, and provided any one alone of these is found in a thing we say that thing is living. Living, that is, may mean thinking or perception or local movement and rest, or movement in the sense of nutrition, decay and growth. Hence we think of plants also as living, for they are observed to possess in themselves an originative power through which they increase or decrease in all spatial directions; they grow up *and* down, and everything that grows increases its bulk alike in both directions or indeed in all, and continues to live so long as it can absorb nutriment.

This power of self-nutrition can be isolated from the other powers mentioned, but not they from it—in mortal beings at least. The fact is obvious in plants; for it is the only psychic power they possess.

This is the originative power the possession of which leads us to speak of things as *living* at all, but it is the possession of sensation that

[10] That is, to the first grade of actuality.
[11] That is, actuator.

leads us for the first time to speak of living things as animals; for even those beings which possess no power of local movement but do possess the power of sensation we call animals and not merely living things.

The primary form of sense is touch, which belongs to all animals. Just as the power of self-nutrition can be isolated from touch and sensation generally, so touch can be isolated from all other forms of sense. (By the power of self-nutrition we mean that departmental power of the soul which is common to plants and animals: all animals whatsoever are observed to have the sense of touch.) What the explanation of these two facts is, we must discuss later. At present we must confine ourselves to saying that soul is the source of these phenomena and is characterized by them, viz. by the powers of self-nutrition, sensation, thinking, and motivity.

Is each of these a soul or a part of a soul? And if a part, a part in what sense? A part merely distinguishable by definition or a part distinct in local situation as well? In the case of certain of these powers, the answers to these questions are easy; in the case of others we are puzzled what to say. Just as in the case of plants which when divided are observed to continue to live though removed to a distance from one another (thus showing that in *their* case the soul of each individual plant before division was actually one, potentially many), so we notice a similar result in other varieties of soul, i.e. in insects which have been cut in two; each of the segments possesses both sensation and local movement; and if sensation, necessarily also imagination and appetition; for, where there is sensation, there is also pleasure and pain, and, where these, necessarily also desire.

We have no evidence as yet about mind or the power to think; it seems to be a widely different kind of soul, differing as what is eternal from what is perishable; it alone is capable of existence in isolation from all other psychic powers. All the other parts of soul, it is evident from what we have said, are, in spite of certain statements to the contrary, incapable of separate existence though, of course, distinguishable by definition. If opining is distinct from perceiving, to be capable of opining and to be capable of perceiving must be distinct, and so with all the other forms of living above enumerated. Further, some animals possess all these parts of soul, some certain of them only, others one only (this is what enables us to classify animals); the cause must be considered later. A similar arrangement is found also within the field of the senses; some classes of animals have all the senses, some only certain of them, others only one, the most indispensable, touch.

Since the expression "that whereby we live and perceive" has two meanings, just like the expression "that whereby we know"—that may mean either (*a*) knowledge or (*b*) the soul, for we can speak of knowing *by* or *with* either, and similarly that whereby we are in health may be either (*a*) health or (*b*) the body or some part of the body; and since of the two terms thus contrasted knowledge or health is the name of a form, essence, or ratio, or if we so express it an actuality of a recipient matter—knowledge of what is capable of knowing, health of what is capable of being made healthy (for the operation of that which is capable of originating change terminates and has its seat in what is changed or altered); further, since it is the soul by or with which primarily we live, perceive, and think:—it follows that the soul must be a ratio or formulable essence, not a matter or subject. For, as we said, the word substance has three meanings—form, matter, and the complex of both —and of these three what is called matter is potentiality, what is called form actuality. Since then the complex here is the living thing, the body cannot be the actuality of the soul; it is the soul which is the actuality of a certain kind of body. Hence the rightness of the view that the soul cannot be without a body, while it cannot *be* a body; it is not a body but something relative to a body. That is why it is *in* a body, and a body of a definite kind. It was a mistake, therefore, to do as former thinkers did, merely to fit it into a body without adding a definite specification of the kind or character of that body. Reflection confirms the observed fact; the actuality of any given thing can only be realized in what is already potentially that thing, i.e. in a matter of its own appropriate to it. From all this it follows that soul is an actuality or formulable essence of something that possesses a potentiality of being besouled.

Of the psychic powers above enumerated some kinds of living things, as we have said, possess all, some less than all, others one only. Those we have mentioned are the nutritive, the appetitive, the sensory, the locomotive, and the power of thinking. Plants have none but the first, the nutritive, while another order of living things has this *plus* the sensory. If any order of living things has the sensory, it must also have the appetitive; for appetite is the genus of which desire, passion, and wish are the species; now all animals have one sense at least, viz. touch, and whatever has a sense has the capacity for pleasure and pain and therefore has pleasant and painful objects present to it, and wherever these are present, there is desire, for desire is just appetition of what is pleasant. Further, all animals have the sense for food (for touch is the sense for food); the food of all living things consists of what is dry, moist, hot, cold, and these are the qualities apprehended by touch; all other sensible qualities are apprehended by touch only indirectly. Sounds, colours, and odours contribute nothing to nutriment; flavours fall within the field of tangible qualities. Hunger and thirst are forms of desire, hunger a desire for what is dry and hot, thirst a desire for what is cold and moist; flavour is a sort of seasoning added to both. We must later clear up these points, but at present it may be enough to say that all animals that possess the sense of touch have also appetition. The case of imagination is obscure; we must examine it later. Certain kinds of animals possess in addition the power of locomotion, and still another order of animate beings, i.e. man and possibly another order like man or superior to him, the power of thinking, i.e. mind. It is now evident that a single definition can be given of soul only in the same sense as one can be given of figure. For, as in that case there is no figure distinguishable and apart from triangle, etc., so here there is no soul apart from the forms of soul just enumerated. It is true that a highly general definition can be given for figure which will fit all figures without expressing the peculiar nature of any figure. So here in the case of soul and its specific forms. Hence it is absurd in this and similar cases to demand an absolutely general definition, which will fail to express the peculiar nature of anything that *is,* or again, omitting this, to look for separate definitions corresponding to each *infima species.* The cases of figure and soul are exactly parallel; for the particulars subsumed under the common name in both cases—figures and living beings—constitute a series, each successive term of which potentially contains its predecessor, e.g. the square the triangle, the sensory power the self-nutritive. Hence we must ask in the case of each order of living things, What is its soul, i.e. What is the soul of plant, animal, man? Why the terms are related in this serial way must form the subject of later examination. But the facts are that the power of perception is never found apart from the power of self-nutrition, while —in plants—the latter is found isolated from the former. Again, no sense is found apart from that of touch, while touch *is* found by itself; many animals have neither sight, hearing, nor smell. Again, among living things that possess sense some have the power of locomotion, some not. Lastly, certain living beings—a small minority—possess calculation and thought, for (among mortal beings) those which possess calculation have all the other powers above mentioned, while the converse does not hold—indeed some live by imagination alone, while others have not even imagination. The mind that knows with immediate intuition presents a different problem.

It is evident that the way to give the most adequate definition of soul is to seek in the case of *each* of its forms for the most appropriate definition.

BOOK III

There are two distinctive peculiarities by reference to which we characterize the soul—(1) local movement and (2) thinking, discriminating, and perceiving. Thinking, both speculative and practical, is regarded as akin to a form of perceiving; for in the one as well as the other the soul discriminates and is cognizant of something which *is*. Indeed the ancients go so far as to identify thinking and perceiving; e.g. Empedocles says "For 'tis in respect of what is present that man's wit is increased," and again "whence it befalls them from time to time to think diverse thoughts," and Homer's phrase "For suchlike is man's mind" means the same. They all look upon thinking as a bodily process like perceiving, and hold that like is *known* as well as *perceived* by like, as I explained at the beginning of our discussion. Yet they ought at the same time to have accounted for error also; for it is more intimately connected with animal existence and the soul continues longer in the state of error than in that of truth. They cannot escape the dilemma: either (1) whatever seems is true (and there are some who accept this) or (2) error is contact with the unlike; for that is the opposite of the knowing of like by like.

But it is a received principle that error as well as knowledge in respect to contraries is one and the same.

That perceiving and practical thinking are not identical is therefore obvious; for the former is universal in the animal world, the latter is found in only a small division of it. Further, speculative thinking is also distinct from perceiving—I mean that in which we find rightness and wrongness—rightness in prudence, knowledge, true opinion, wrongness in their opposites; for perception of the special objects of sense is always free from error, and is found in all animals, while it is possible to think falsely as well as truly, and thought is found only where there is discourse of reason as well as sensibility. For imagination is different from either perceiving or discursive thinking, though it is not found without sensation, or judgement without it. That this activity is not the same kind of thinking as judgement is obvious. For imagining lies within our own power whenever we wish (e.g. we can call up a picture, as in the practice of mnemonics by the use of mental images), but in forming opinions we are not free: we cannot escape the alternative of falsehood or truth. Further, when we think something to be fearful or threatening, emotion is immediately produced, and so too with what is encouraging; but when we merely imagine we remain as unaffected as persons who are looking at a painting of some dreadful or encouraging scene. Again without the field of judgement itself we find varieties—knowledge, opinion, prudence, and their opposites; of the differences between these I must speak elsewhere.

Thinking is different from perceiving and is held to be in part imagination, in part judgement: we must therefore first mark off the sphere of imagination and then speak of judgement. If then imagination is that in virtue of which an image arises for us, excluding metaphorical uses of the term, is it a single faculty or disposition relative to images, in virtue of which we discriminate and are either in error or not? The faculties in virtue of which we do this are sense, opinion, science, intelligence.

That imagination is not sense is clear from the following considerations: (1) Sense is either a faculty or an activity, e.g. sight or seeing: imagination takes place in the absence of both, as e.g. in dreams. (2) Again, sense is always present, imagination not. If actual imagination and actual sensation were the same, imagination would be found in all the brutes: this is held not to be the case; e.g. it is not found in ants or bees or grubs. (3) Again, sensations are always true, imaginations are for the most part false. (4) Once more, even in ordinary speech, we do not, when sense functions precisely with regard to its object, say that we imagine it to be a man, but rather when there is some failure of accuracy in its exercise. And (5), as we were saying before, visions appear to us even when our eyes are shut. Neither is imagination *any* of the things that are never in error: e.g. knowledge or intelligence; for imagination may be false.

It remains therefore to see if it is opinion, for opinion may be either true or false.

But opinion involves belief (for without belief in what we opine we cannot have an opinion), and in the brutes though we often find imagination we never find belief. Further, every opinion is accompanied by belief, belief by conviction, and conviction by discourse of reason: while there are some of the brutes in which we find imagination, without discourse of reason. It is clear then that imagination cannot, again, be (1) opinion *plus* sensation, or (2) opinion mediated by sensation, or (3) a blend of opinion and sensation; this is impossible both for these reasons and because the content of the supposed opinion cannot be different from that of the sensation (I mean that imagination must be the blending of the perception of white with the opinion that it is white: it could scarcely be a blend of the opinion that it is good with the perception that it is white): to imagine is therefore (on this view) identical with the thinking of exactly the same as what one in the strictest sense perceives. But what we imagine is sometimes false though our contemporaneous judgement about it is true; e.g. we imagine the sun to be a foot in diameter though we are convinced that it is larger than the inhabited part of the earth, and the following dilemma presents itself. Either (*a*) while the fact has not changed and the observer has neither forgotten nor lost belief in the true opinion which he had, that opinion has disappeared, or (*b*) if he retains it then his opinion is at once true and false. A true opinion, however, becomes false only when the fact alters without being noticed.

Imagination is therefore neither any one of the states enumerated, nor compounded out of them.

But since when one thing has been set in motion another thing may be moved by it, and imagination is held to be a movement and to be impossible without sensation, i.e. to occur in beings that are percipient and to have for its content what can be perceived, and since movement may be produced by actual sensation and that movement is necessarily similar in character to the sensation itself, this movement must be (1) necessarily (*a*) incapable of existing apart from sensation, (*b*) incapable of existing except when we perceive, (2) such that in virtue of its possession that in which it is found may present various phenomena both active and passive, and (3) such that it may be either true or false.

The reason of the last characteristic is as follows. Perception (1) of the special objects of sense is never in error or admits the least possible amount of falsehood. (2) That of the concomitance of the objects concomitant with the sensible qualities comes next: in this case certainly we may be deceived; for while the perception that there is white before us cannot be false, the perception that what is white is this or that may be false. (3) Third comes the perception of the universal attributes which accompany the concomitant objects to which the special sensibles attach (I mean e.g. of movement and magnitude); it is in respect of these that the greatest amount of sense-illusion is possible.

The motion which is due to the activity of sense in these three modes of its exercise will differ from the activity of sense; (1) the first kind of derived motion is free from error while the sensation is present; (2) and (3) the others may be erroneous whether it is present or absent, especially when the object of perception is far off. If then imagination presents no other features than those enumerated and is what we have described, then imagination must be a movement resulting from an actual exercise of a power of sense.

As sight is the most highly developed sense, the name *phantasia* (imagination) has been formed from *phaos* (light) because it is not possible to see without light.

And because imaginations remain in the organs of sense and resemble sensations, animals in their actions are largely guided by them, some (i.e. the brutes) because of the non-existence in them of mind, others (i.e. men) because of the temporary eclipse in them of mind by feeling or disease or sleep.

About imagination, what it is and why it exists, let so much suffice.

Turning now to the part of the soul with which the soul knows and thinks (whether this is separable from the others in definition only, or spatially as well) we have to inquire (1) what differentiates this part, and (2) how thinking can take place.

If thinking is like perceiving, it must be either a process in which the soul is acted upon by what is capable of being thought, or a process different from but analogous to that. The thinking part of the soul must therefore be, while impassible, capable of receiving the form of an object; that is, must be potentially identical in character with its object without being the object. Mind must be related to what is thinkable, as sense is to what is sensible.

Therefore, since everything is a possible object of thought, mind in order, as Anaxagoras says, to dominate, that is, to know, must be pure from all admixture; for the co-presence of what is alien to its nature is a hindrance and a block: it follows that it too, like the sensitive part, can have no nature of its own, other than that of having a certain capacity. Thus that in the soul which is called mind (by mind I mean that whereby the soul thinks and judges) is, before it thinks, not actually any real thing. For this reason it cannot reasonably be regarded as blended with the body: if so, it would acquire some quality, e.g. warmth or cold, or even have an organ like the sensitive faculty: as it is, it has none. It was a good idea to call the soul "the place of forms," though (1) this description holds only of the intellective soul, and (2) even this is the forms only potentially, not actually.

Observation of the sense-organs and their employment reveals a distinction between the impassibility of the sensitive and that of the intellective faculty. After strong stimulation of a sense we are less able to exercise it than before, as e.g. in the case of a loud sound we cannot hear easily immediately after, or in the case of a bright colour or a powerful odour we cannot see or smell, but in the case of mind, thought about an object that is highly intelligible renders it more and not less able afterwards to think objects that are less intelligible: the reason is that while the faculty of sensation is dependent upon the body, mind is separable from it.

Once the mind has become each set of its possible objects, as a man of science has, when this phrase is used of one who is actually a man of science (this happens when he is now able to exercise the power on his own initiative), its condition is still one of potentiality, but in a different sense from the potentiality which preceded the acquisition of knowledge by learning or discovery: the mind too is then able to think *itself*.

Since we can distinguish between a spatial magnitude and what it is to be such, and between water and what it is to be water, and so in many other cases (though not in all; for in certain cases the thing and its form are identical), flesh and what it is to be flesh are discriminated either by different faculties, or by the same faculty in two different states: for flesh necessarily involves matter and is like what is snub-nosed, a *this* in a *this*.[12] Now it is by means of the sensitive faculty that we discriminate the hot and the cold, i.e. the factors which combined in a certain ratio constitute flesh: the essential character of flesh is apprehended by something different either wholly separate from the sensitive faculty or related to it as a bent line to the same line when it has been straightened out.

Again in the case of abstract objects what is straight is analogous to what is snub-nosed; for it necessarily implies a continuum as its matter: its constitutive essence is different, if we may distinguish between straitness and what is straight: let us take it to be two-ness. It must be apprehended, therefore, by a different power or by the same power in a different state. To sum up, in so far as the realities it knows are capable of being separated from their matter, so it is also with the powers of mind.

The problem might be suggested: if thinking is a passive affection, then if mind is simple and impassible and has nothing in common with anything else, as Anaxagoras says, how can it come to think at all? For interaction between two factors is held to require a precedent community of nature between the factors. Again it might be asked, is mind a possible object of thought to itself? For if mind is thinkable *per se* and what is thinkable is in kind one and the same, then either (*a*) mind will belong to everything, or (*b*) mind will contain some element common to it with all other realities which makes them all thinkable.

(1) Have not we already disposed of the difficulty about interaction involving a common element, when we said that mind is in a sense potentially whatever is thinkable, though actually it is nothing until it has thought? What it thinks must be in it just as characters may be said to be on a writing-tablet on which as yet nothing actually stands written: this is exactly what happens with mind.

(2) Mind is itself thinkable in exactly the same way as its objects are. For (*a*) in the case of objects which involve no matter, what thinks and what is thought are identical; for speculative knowledge and its

[12] That is, a particular form in a particular matter.

object are identical. (Why mind is not always thinking we must consider later.) (*b*) In the case of those which contain matter each of the objects of thought is only potentially present. It follows that while *they* will not have mind in them (for mind is a potentiality of them only in so far as they are capable of being disengaged from matter) mind may yet be thinkable.

Since in every class of things, as in nature as a whole, we find two factors involved, (1) a matter which is potentially all the particulars included in the class, (2) a cause which is productive in the sense that it makes them all (the latter standing to the former, as e.g. an art to its material), these distinct elements must likewise be found within the soul.

And in fact mind as we have described it is what it is by virtue of becoming all things, while there is another which is what it is by virtue of making all things: this is a sort of positive state like light; for in a sense light makes potential colours into actual colours.

Mind in this sense of it is separable, impassible, unmixed, since it is in its essential nature activity (for always the active is superior to the passive factor, the originating force to the matter which it forms).

Actual knowledge is identical with its object: in the individual, potential knowledge is in time prior to actual knowledge, but in the universe as a whole it is not prior even in time. Mind is not at one time unknowing and at another not. When mind is set free from its present conditions it appears as just what it is and nothing more: this alone is immortal and eternal (we do not, however, remember its former activity because, while mind in this sense is impassible, mind as passive is destructible), and without it nothing thinks.

Parva Naturalia (The Short Physical Treatises)

MEMORY AND REMINISCENCE

. . . The process of movement [sensory stimulation] involved in the act of perception stamps in, as it were, a sort of impression of the percept, just as persons do who make an impression with a seal. This explains why, in those who are strongly moved owing to passion, or time of life, no mnemonic impression is formed; just as no impression would be formed if the movement of the seal were to impinge on running water; while there are others in whom, owing to the receiving surface being frayed, as happens to [the stucco on] old [chamber] walls, or owing to the hardness of the receiving surface, the requisite impression is not implanted at all. Hence both very young and very old persons are defective in memory; they are in a state of flux, the former because of their growth, the latter, owing to their decay. In like manner, also, both those who are too quick and those who are too slow have bad memories. The former are too soft, the latter too hard [in the texture of their receiving organs], so that in the case of the former the presented image [though imprinted] does not remain in the soul, while on the latter it is not imprinted at all.

ON DREAMS

. . . In order to answer our original question, let us now, therefore, assume one proposition, which is clear from what precedes, viz. that even when the external object of perception has departed, the impressions it has made persist, and are themselves objects of perception; and [let us assume] besides, that we are easily deceived respecting the operations of sense-perception when we are excited by emotions, and different persons according to their different emotions; for example, the coward when excited by fear, the amorous person by amorous desire; so that, with but little resemblance to go upon, the former thinks he sees his foes approaching, the latter, that he sees the object of his desire; and the more deeply one is under the influence of the emotion, the less similarity is required to give rise to these illusory impressions. Thus too, both in fits of anger, and also in all states of appetite, all men become easily deceived, and more so the more their emotions are excited. This is the reason too why persons in the delirium of fever sometimes think they see animals on their chamber walls, an illusion arising from the faint resemblance to animals of the markings thereon when put together in patterns; and this sometimes corresponds with the emotional states of the sufferers, in such a way that, if the latter be not very ill, they know well enough that it is an illusion; but if the illness is more severe they actually move according to the appearances. The cause of these occurrences is that the faculty in virtue of which the controlling sense judges is not identical with that in virtue of which presentations come before the mind. A proof of this is, that the sun presents itself as only a foot in diameter, though often something else gainsays the presentation. Again, when the fingers are crossed, the one object [placed between them] is felt [by the touch] as two; but yet we deny that it is two; for sight is more authoritative than touch. Yet, if touch stood alone, we should actually have pronounced the one object to be two. The ground of such false judgments is that any appearances whatever present themselves, not only when its object stimulates a sense, but also when the sense by itself alone is stimulated, provided only it be stimulated in the same manner as it is by the object. For example, to persons sailing past the land seems to move, when it is really the eye that is being moved by something else [the moving ship].

PROPHESYING BY DREAMS

. . . The most skilful interpreter of dreams is he who has the faculty of observing resemblances. Any one may interpret dreams which are vivid and plain. But, speaking of "resemblances," I mean that dream presentations are analogous to the forms reflected in water, as indeed we have already stated. In the latter case, if the motion in the water be great, the reflexion has no resemblance to its original, nor do the forms resemble the real objects. Skilful, indeed, would he be in interpreting such reflexions who could rapidly discern, and at a glance comprehend, the scattered and distorted fragments of such forms, so as to perceive that one of them represents a man, or a horse, or anything whatever.

Historia Animalium

If now this something that constitutes the form of the living being be the soul, or part of the soul, or something that without the soul cannot exist; as would seem to be the case, seeing at any rate that when the soul departs, what is left is no longer a living animal, and that none of the parts remain what they were before, excepting in mere configuration, like the animals that in the fable are turned into stone; if, I say, this be so, then it will come within the province of the natural philosopher to inform himself concerning the soul, and to treat of it, either in its entirety, or, at any rate, of that part of it which constitutes the essential character of an animal; and it will be his duty to say what his soul or this part of a soul is; and to discuss the attributes that attach to this essential character, especially as nature is spoken of in two senses, and the nature of a thing is either its matter or its essence; nature as essence including both the motor cause and the final cause. Now it is in the latter of these two senses that either the whole soul or some part of it constitutes the nature of an animal; and inasmuch as it is the presence of the soul that enables matter to constitute the animal nature, much more than it is the presence of matter which so enables the soul, the inquirer into nature is bound on every ground to treat of the soul rather than of the matter. For though the wood of which they are made constitutes the couch and the tripod, it only does so because it is capable of receiving such and such a form.

What has been said suggests the question, whether it is the whole soul or only some part of it, the consideration of which comes within the province of natural science. Now if it be of the whole soul that this should treat, then there is no place for any other philosophy beside it. For as it belongs in all cases to one and the same science to deal with correlated subjects—one and the same science, for instance, deals with sensation and with objects of sense—and as therefore the intelligent soul and the objects of intellect, being correlated, must belong to one and the same science, it follows that natural science will have to include the whole universe in its province. But perhaps it is not the whole soul, nor all its parts collectively, that constitutes the source of motion; but there may be one part, identical with that in plants, which is the source of growth, another, namely the sensory part, which is the source of change of quality, while still another, and this not the intellectual part, is the source of locomotion. I say not the intellectual part; for other animals than man have the power of locomotion, but in none but him is there intellect.

Editors' Note:

After the stupendous heights reached by Socrates, Plato, and Aristotle, it may well seem that there is no place to go but down. Another way of looking at the matter is to note that the social, intellectual, and moral structure which gave rise to Athenian philosophy was rapidly disintegrating. The Peloponnesian Wars had wracked the great Greek city-states, and the remaining fragile structure had been overrun by Philip of Macedon and his son, Alexander the Great. Greek civilization continued, indeed it may be said to have continued until the fall of Constantinople in 1453, but the light had begun to go out of its eyes. It suffered, as Gilbert Murray said, a "failure of nerve." Relativism rather than confidence, and comfort rather than aspiration, were needed by men clinging to hope in the face of emptiness or despair.

It is natural, as Gilbert Murray points out,* that the great philosophical systems should take the form of an effort at rigor, self-control, aspiration for the eternal verities, as incorporated in the Stoic philosophy of loyalty and obedience to nature, or the doctrine

* *Five Stages of Greek Religion,* 3rd ed. (New York: Doubleday, 1955).

of Epicurus, that man might well make the best of this sad life and create a philosophy as free of fear and as rich in immediate well-being as possible. Epicurus, building his philosophy upon the simple materialism of Democritus, and shrewdly following the pleasure-pain theory as espoused by so many of his predecessors, believed that a life free of despair and free of the fear induced by religion, with its threats of punishment after death, may create a good—because simple and not extravagant—set of claims upon this life. The moral aspiration of the Epicureans in terms of simplicity and self-control was as great as that of the Stoics. The Stoics often had the advantage, since it was not difficult to make men believe that the simple doctrine of pleasure in this life, as advocated by the Epicureans, must mean an irresponsible cultivation of the moment's pleasures regardless of consequences—a view directly contrary to that which Epicurus himself taught. The Stoics had also the advantage of creating a complex and subtle psychology of perception and memory which, though it is evidently not very original, offered actual content to the study of the mind. Note, for example, in Diogenes Laertius' description of the Stoic psychology: "All our thoughts are formed either by indirect perception, or by similarity, or by analogy, or transposition, or combination, or opposition." But it is mainly in their simple and stalwart ethical injunctions that they are known to succeeding generations of men; in fact, so deep a hold does Stoicism have upon mankind that we still use the term "take it philosophically" to mean *stoically*, that is, without protest against what nature brings, rather than using the word *philosophically* to refer to a dozen other possible life principles.

THE STOICS AND THE EPICUREANS: THE WAY TO LIVE by *Richard P. McKeon*

The Stoics and the Epicureans—and in general the philosophers and scientists of the Hellenistic Age, the period after the death of Alexander the Great—sought foundations for their inquiries in preliminary determination of the "criteria" or "standards" by which truth and probability are ascertained and certified. The world of the mind therefore took precedence over the world of cosmology, of metaphysics, and of science in their ingenious and detailed investigations of the relative reliability of sensation, imagination, judgment, understanding, and reason of verifiable statements and generalizations. Epicurus and his followers argued that sensation is the only ultimate test of truth. Zeno and many of the later Stoics found the criterion in "presentation" or "impression," a more general concept, since the other powers of the mind as well as the senses place objects before it for scrutiny (indeed, the meaning of the term they employed, *phantasia,* moves from "presentation" to "imagination" to "fancy"), and they argued that among the presentations of the mind, one variety, the "apprehending presentation" (*phantasia kataleptikē*), presents real objects. The choice of criterion is reflected in the theories of logic and of scientific method developed in the philosophical speculations of the period. According to the Epicureans, the soul is composed of atoms and finds the test of its information concerning the world of atoms about it in sense impressions; the method which they constructed on that foundation in opposition to verbal dialectics and logics is their "canonic." According to the Stoics also, the universal is corporeal, but it is ordered by soul and mind, and the apprehensions of the human soul reproduce structures in things; their logic of signs, significates, and denotations relates structures of symbols and meanings to the presented structures of things.

Philosophic inquiry into the grounds on which organizations of knowledge are built led to inquiry into the problems of cognition along new lines, and philosophic inquiry into problems of morals and ethics led to a reorientation and expansion of inquiries into the nature of the passions and emotions. The Stoic conception of the functions of the mind made the passions "perturbations" and the study of the nature of these perturbations was a necessary adjunct of a moral system in which the influence of the perturbations of the mind is controlled or eliminated by reason and duty. Descartes boasted, when he wrote his *Treatise on the Passions* in the seventeenth century, that he was the first to apply the scientific method to the passions, yet his basic distinctions are derived from medieval elaborations of Stoic schematisms for the classification and enumeration of the passions. The Epicureans were convinced that virtue consists in acting in accordance with one's nature. This objective can be attained if fear and ignorance—particularly fear of death and of the gods, and ignorance of the nature of the world—were reduced or eliminated, since man would then act in response to natural forces rather than to the inhibitions and suppression of anxiety and superstition. The object of this endeavor and the criterion of success in it is pleasure.

Zeno and Chrysippus were reputed to have been among the most prolific of Greek philosophers. Only fragments of their writings and of the writings of the other Greek Stoics survive. We do have the writings of the Roman Stoics—Seneca, Marcus Aurelius, and Epictetus—in which the widely influential moral doctrine, which has become the primary meaning of "Stoicism," is elaborated from the theories of the Greek Stoics and, in the writings of Seneca, physical and psychological positions are set forth. The writings of Epicurus were even more voluminous, and we do have a few passages from his works somewhat longer than "fragments"—three letters concerning his doctrines and a collection of Maxims. On the other hand, the great Latin poem in which Lucretius expounds the Epicurean philosophy is intact. There are therefore attractive reasons for turning to the Roman Stoics and Epicureans for an exposition of the positions of these schools, but the analysis of the criteria of knowledge and of the operation of the passions is more concise and better organized in Diogenes Laertius' account of Zeno and in remains of Epicurus. The Stoic and Epicurean positions attributed to Zeno and Epicurus are therefore presented in the following selection.*

A presentation [or mental impression, *phantasia*] is an imprint on the soul: the name having been appropriately borrowed from the imprint made by a seal upon the wax. There are two species of presentation, the

* From Diogenes Laertius, *Lives of the Philosophers* VII, 45–156, trans. by R. D. Hicks, Loeb Classical Library (Cambridge, Mass., Harvard University Press). Reprinted by permission of the publishers.

one apprehending [*kataleptikē*] a real object, the other not. The former, which they take to be the test of reality, is defined as that which proceeds from a real object, agrees with that object itself, and has been imprinted seal-fashion and stamped upon the mind: the latter, or non-apprehending, that which does not proceed from any real object, or if it does, fails to agree with the reality itself, not being clear and distinct.

. . .

"The Stoics agree to put in the forefront the doctrine of presentation and sensation, inasmuch as the standard by which the truth of things is tested is generically a presentation, and again the theory of assent and that of apprehension and thought, which precedes all the rest, cannot be stated apart from presentation. For presentation comes first; then thought, which is capable of expressing itself, puts into the form of a proposition that which the subject receives from a presentation."

There is a difference between the process and the outcome of presentation. The latter is a semblance in the mind such as may occur in sleep, while the former is the act of imprinting something on the soul, that is a process of change, as is set forth by Chrysippus in the second book of his treatise *De Anima*. For, says he, we must not take "impression" in the literal sense of the stamp of a seal, because it is impossible to suppose that a number of such impressions should be in one and the same spot at one and the same time. The presentation meant is that which comes from a real object, agrees with that object, and has been stamped, imprinted, and pressed seal-fashion on the soul, as would not be the case if it came from an unreal object.

According to them some presentations are data of sense and others are not: the former are the impressions conveyed through one or more sense-organs; while the latter, which are not data of sense, are those received through the mind itself, as is the case with incorporeal things and all the other presentations which are received by reason. Of sensuous impressions some are from real objects and are accompanied by yielding and assent on our part. But there are also presentations that are appearances and no more, purporting, as it were, to come from real objects.

Another division of presentations is into rational and irrational, the former being those of rational creatures, the latter those of the irrational. Those which are rational are processes of thought, while those which are irrational have no name. Again, some of our impressions are scientific, others unscientific: at all events a statue is viewed in a totally different way by the trained eye of a sculptor and by an ordinary man.

The Stoics apply the term sense or sensation (*aisthēsis*) to three things: (1) the current passing from the principal part of the soul to the senses, (2) apprehension by means of the senses, (3) the apparatus of the sense-organs, in which some persons are deficient. Moreover, the activity of the sense-organs is itself also called sensation. According to them it is by sense that we apprehend black and white, rough and smooth, whereas it is by reason that we apprehend the conclusions of demonstration, for instance the existence of gods and their providence. General notions, indeed, are gained in the following ways: some by direct contact, some by resemblance, some by analogy, some by transposition, some by composition, and some by contrariety.

By incidence or direct contact have come our notions of sensible things; by resemblance notions whose origin is something before us, as the notion of Socrates which we get from his bust; while under notions derived from analogy come those which we get (1) by way of enlargement like that of Tityos or the Cyclops, or (2) by way of diminution, like that of the Pygmy. And thus, too, the centre of the earth was originally conceived on the analogy of smaller spheres. Of notions obtained by transposition creatures with eyes on the chest would be an instance, while the centaur exemplifies those reached by composition, and death those due to contrariety. Furthermore, there are notions which imply a sort of transition to the realm of the imperceptible: such are those of space and of the meaning of terms. The notions of justice and goodness come by nature. Again, privation originates notions; for instance, that of the man without hands. Such are their tenets concerning presentation, sensation, and thought.

The standard of truth they declare to be the apprehending presentation, i.e. that which comes from a real object—according to Chrysippus in the twelfth book of his *Physics* and to Antipater and Apollodorus. Boëthius, on the other hand, admits a plurality of standards, namely intelligence, sense-perception, appetency, and knowledge; while Chrysippus in the first book of his *Exposition of Doctrine* contradicts himself and declares that sensation and preconception are the only standards, preconception being a general notion which comes by the gift of nature (an innate conception of universals or general concepts). Again, certain others of the older Stoics make Right Reason the standard; so also does Posidonius in his treatise *On the Standard*. . . .

. . .

The ethical branch of philosophy they divide as follows: (1) the topic of impulse; (2) the topic of things good and evil; (3) that of the passions; (4) that of virtue; (5) that of the end; (6) that of primary value and of actions; (7) that of duties or the befitting; and (8) of inducements to act or refrain from acting. The foregoing is the subdivision adopted by Chrysippus, Archedemus, Zeno of Tarsus, Apollodorus, Diogenes, Antipater, and Posidonius, and their disciples. Zeno of Citium and Cleanthes treated the subject somewhat less elaborately, as might be expected in an older generation. They, however, did subdivide Logic and Physics as well as Ethics.

An animal's first impulse, say the Stoics, is to self-preservation, because nature from the outset endears it to itself, as Chrysippus affirms in the first book of his work *On Ends:* his words are, "The dearest thing to every animal is its own constitution and its consciousness thereof"; for it was not likely that nature should estrange the living thing from itself or that she should leave the creature she has made without either estrangement from or affection for its own constitution. We are forced then to conclude that nature in constituting the animal made it near and dear to itself; for so it comes to repel all that is injurious and give free access to all that is serviceable or akin to it.

As for the assertion made by some people that pleasure is the object to which the first impulse of animals is directed, it is shown by the Stoics to be false. For pleasure, if it is really felt, they declare to be a by-product, which never comes until nature by itself has sought and found the means suitable to the animal's existence or constitution; it is an aftermath comparable to the condition of animals thriving and plants in full bloom. And nature, they say, made no difference originally between plants and animals, for she regulates the life of plants too, in their case without impulse and sensation, just as also certain processes go on of a vegetative kind in us. But when in the case of animals impulse has been superadded, whereby they are enabled to go in quest of their proper aliment, for them, say the Stoics, nature's rule is to follow the direction of impulse. But when reason by way of a more perfect leadership has been bestowed on the beings we call rational, for them life according to reason rightly becomes the natural life. For reason supervenes to shape impulse scientifically.

This is why Zeno was the first (in his treatise *On the Nature of Man*) to designate as the end "life in agreement with nature" (or living agreeably to nature), which is the same as a virtuous life, virtue being the goal towards which nature guides us. So too Cleanthes in his treatise *On Pleasure,* as also Posidonius, and Hecato in his work *On Ends.* Again, living virtuously is equivalent to living in accordance with experience of the actual course of nature, as Chrysippus says in the first book of his *De Finibus;* for our individual natures are parts of the nature of the whole universe. And this is why the end may be defined as live in accordance with nature, or, in other words, in accordance with our own human nature as well as that of the universe, a life in which we refrain from every action forbidden by the law common to all things, that is to say, the right reason which pervades all things, and is identical with this Zeus, lord and ruler of all that is. And this very thing constitutes the virtue of the happy man and the smooth current of life, when all actions promote the harmony of the spirit dwelling in the individual man with the will of him who orders the universe. Diogenes then expressly declares the end to be to act with good reason in the selection of what is natural. Archedemus says the end is to live in the performance of all befitting actions.

By the nature with which our life ought to be in accord, Chrysippus understands both universal nature and more particularly the nature of man, whereas Cleanthes takes the nature of the universe alone as that which should be followed, without adding the nature of the individual.

And virtue, he holds, is a harmonious disposition, choice-worthy for its own sake and not from hope or fear of any external motive. Moreover, it is in virtue that happiness consists; for virtue is the state of mind which tends to make the whole of life harmonious. When a rational being is perverted, this is due to the deceptiveness of external pursuits or sometimes to the influence of associates. For the starting-points of nature are never perverse.

. . .

According to the Stoics there is an eight-fold division of the soul: the five senses, the faculty of speech, the intellectual faculty, which is the mind itself, and the generative faculty, being all parts of the soul. Now from falsehood there results perversion, which extends to the mind; and from this perversion arise many passions or emotions, which are causes of instability. Passion, or emotion, is defined by Zeno as an irrational and unnatural movement in the soul, or again as impulse in excess.

The main, or most universal, emotions, according to Hecato in his treatise *On the Passions,* book ii., and Zeno in his treatise with the same title, constitute four great classes, grief, fear, desire or craving, pleasure. They hold the emotions to be judgements, as is stated by Chrysippus in his treatise *On the Passions:* avarice being a supposition that money is a good, while the case is similar with drunkenness and profligacy and all the other emotions.

And grief or pain they hold to be an irrational mental contraction. Its species are pity, envy, jealousy, rivalry, heaviness, annoyance, distress, anguish, distraction. Pity is grief felt at undeserved suffering; envy, grief at others' prosperity; jealousy, grief at the possession by another of that which one desires for oneself; rivalry, pain at the possession by another of what one has oneself. Heaviness or vexation is grief which weighs us down, annoyance that which coops us up and straitens us for want of room, distress a pain brought on by anxious thought that lasts and increases, anguish painful grief, distraction irrational grief, rasping and hindering us from viewing the situation as a whole.

Fear is an expectation of evil. Under fear are ranged the following emotions: terror, nervous shrinking, shame, consternation, panic, mental agony. Terror is a fear which produces fright; shame is fear of disgrace; nervous shrinking is a fear that one will have to act; consternation is fear due to a presentation of some unusual occurrence; panic is fear with pressure exercised by sound; mental agony is fear felt when some issue is still in suspense.

Desire or craving is irrational appetency, and under it are ranged the following states: want, hatred, contentiousness, anger, love, wrath, resentment. Want, then, is a craving when it is baulked and, as it were, cut off from its object, but kept at full stretch and attracted towards it in vain. Hatred is a growing and lasting desire or craving that it should go ill with somebody. Contentiousness is a craving or desire connected with partisanship; anger a craving or desire to punish one who is thought to have done you an undeserved injury. The passion of love is a craving from which good men are free; for it is an effort to win affection due to the visible presence of beauty. Wrath is anger which has long rankled and has become malicious, waiting for its opportunity, as is illustrated by the lines:

> Even though for the one day he swallow his anger, yet doth he still keep his displeasure thereafter in his heart, till he accomplish it.

Resentment is anger in an early stage.

Pleasure is an irrational elation at the accruing of what seems to be choiceworthy; and under it are ranged ravishment, malevolent joy, delight, transport. Ravishment is pleasure which charms the ear. Malevolent joy is pleasure at another's ills. Delight is the mind's propulsion to weakness, its name in Greek (*terpsis*) being akin to *trepsis* or turning. To be in transports of delight is the melting away of virtue.

And as there are said to be certain infirmities in the body, as for instance gout and arthritic disorders, so too there is in the soul love of fame, love of pleasure, and the like. By infirmity is meant disease accompanied by weakness; and by disease is meant a fond imagining of something that seems desirable. And as in the body there are tendencies to certain maladies such as colds and diarrhoea, so it is with the soul, there are tendencies like enviousness, pitifulness, quarrelsomeness, and the like.

Also they say that there are three emotional states which are good, namely, joy, caution, and wishing. Joy, the counterpart of pleasure, is rational elation; caution, the counterpart of fear, rational avoidance; for though the wise man will never feel fear, he will yet use caution. And they make wishing the counterpart of desire (or craving), inasmuch as it is rational appetency. And accordingly, as under the primary passions are classed certain others subordinate to them, so too is it with the primary eupathies or good emotional states. Thus under wishing they bring well-wishing or benevolence, friendliness, respect, affection; under caution, reverence and modesty; under joy, delight, mirth, cheerfulness.

. . .

The world, in their view, is ordered by reason and providence: so says Chrysippus in the fifth book of his treatise *On Providence* and Posidonius in his work *On the Gods,* book iii.—inasmuch as reason pervades every part of it, just as does the soul in us. Only there is a difference of degree; in some parts there is more of it, in others less. For through some parts it passes as a "hold" or containing force, as is the case with our bones and sinews; while through others it passes as intelligence, as in the ruling part of the soul. Thus, then, the whole world is a living being, endowed with soul and reason.

. . .

The doctrine that the world is a living being, rational, animate and intelligent, is laid down by Chrysippus in the first book of his treatise *On Providence,* by Appolodorus in his *Physics,* and by Posidonius. It is a living thing in the sense of an animate substance endowed with sensation; for animal is better than non-animal, and nothing is better than the world, *ergo* the world is a living being. And it is endowed with soul, as if clear from our several souls being each a fragment of it.

. . .

Nature in their view is an artistically working fire, going on its way to create; which is equivalent to a fiery, creative, or fashioning breath. And the soul is a nature capable of perception. And they regard it as the breath of life, congenital with us; from which they infer first that it is a body and secondly that it survives death. Yet it is perishable, though the soul of the universe, of which the individual souls of animals are parts, is indestructible. . . .

MARCUS AURELIUS

The Enchiridion, or Manual *

I

Of things some are in our power, and others are not. In our power are opinion (*hypolēpsis*), movement towards a thing (*hormē*), desire, aversion (*enklisis,* turning from a thing); and in a word, whatever are our own acts: not in our power are the body, property, reputation, offices (magisterial power), and in a word, whatever are not our own acts. And the things in our power are by nature free, not subject to restraint nor hindrance: but the things not in our power are weak, slavish, subject to restraint, in the power of others. Remember then that if you think the things which are by nature slavish to be free, and the things which are in the power of others to be your own, you will be hindered, you will lament, you will be disturbed, you will blame both gods and men: but if you think that only which is your own to be your own, and if you think that what is another's, as it really is, belongs to another, no man will ever compel you, no man will hinder you, you will never blame any man, you will accuse no man, you will do nothing involuntarily (against your will), no man will harm you, you will have no enemy, for you will not suffer any harm.

If then you desire (aim at) such great things, remember that you must not (attempt to) lay hold of them with small effort; but you must leave alone some things entirely, and postpone others for the present. But if you wish for these things also (such great things), and power (office) and wealth, perhaps you will not gain even these very things (power and wealth) because you aim also at those former things (such great things): certainly you will fail in those things through which alone happiness and freedom are secured. Straightway then practice saying to every harsh appearance, You are an appearance, and in no manner what you appear to be. Then examine it by the rules which you possess, and by this first and chiefly, whether it relates to the things which are in our power or to things which are not in our power: and if it relates to any thing which is not in our power, be ready to say that it does not concern you.

II

Remember that desire contains in it the profession (hope) of obtaining that which you desire; and the profession (hope) in aversion (turn-

* From *The Meditations of Marcus Aurelius and Epictetus* (Chicago: Henry Regnery Company, 1956), pp. 169–174.

ing from a thing) is that you will not fall into that which you attempt to avoid: and he who falls in his desire is unfortunate; and he who falls into that which he would avoid, is unhappy. If then you attempt to avoid only the things contrary to nature which are within your power, you will not be involved in any of the things which you would avoid. But if you attempt to avoid disease or death or poverty, you will be unhappy. Take away then aversion from all things which are not in our power, and transfer it to the things contrary to nature which are in our power. But destroy desire completely for the present. For if you desire anything which is not in our power, you must be unfortunate: but of the things in our power, and which it would be good to desire, nothing yet is before you. But employ only the power of moving towards an object and retiring from it; and these powers indeed only slightly and with exceptions and with remission.

III

In every thing which pleases the soul, or supplies a want, or is loved, remember to add this to the (description, notion); what is the nature of each thing, beginning from the smallest? If you love an earthen vessel, say it is an earthen vessel which you love; for when it has been broken, you will not be disturbed. If you are kissing your child or wife, say that it is a human being whom you are kissing, for when the wife or child dies, you will not be disturbed.

IV

When you are going to take in hand any act, remind yourself what kind of an act it is. If you are going to bathe, place before yourself what happens in the bath; some splashing the water, others pushing against one another, others abusing one another, and some stealing: and thus with more safety you will undertake the matter, if you say to yourself, I now intend to bathe, and to maintain my will in a manner comfortable to nature. And so you will do in every act: for thus if any hindrance to bathing shall happen, let this thought be ready: it was not this only that I intended, but I intended also to maintain my will in a way conformable to nature; but I shall not maintain it so if I am vexed at what happens.

V

Men are disturbed not by the things which happen, but by the opinions about the things: for example, death is nothing terrible, for if it were, it would have seemed so to Socrates; for the opinion about death, that it is terrible, is the terrible thing. When then we are impeded or disturbed or grieved, let us never blame others, but ourselves, that is, our opinions. It is the act of an ill-instructed man to blame others for his own bad condition; it is the act of one who has begun to be instructed, to lay the blame on himself; and of one whose instruction is completed, neither to blame another, nor himself.

. . .

VIII

Seek not that the things which happen should happen as you wish; but wish the things which happen to be as they are, and you will have a tranquil flow of life.

EPICURUS AND HIS SCHOOL *

They reject dialectic as superfluous; holding that in their inquiries the physicists should be content to employ the ordinary terms for things. Now in *The Canon* Epicurus affirms that our sensations and preconceptions and our feelings are the standards of truth; the Epicureans generally make perceptions of mental presentations to be also standards. His own statements are also to be found in the *Summary* addressed to Herodotus and in the *Sovran Maxims.* Every sensation, he says, is devoid of reason and incapable of memory; for neither is it self-caused nor, regarded as having an external cause, can it add anything thereto or take anything therefrom. Nor is there anything which can refute sensations or convict them of error: one sensation cannot convict another and kindred sensation, for they are equally valid; nor can one sensation refute another which is not kindred but heterogeneous, for the objects which the two senses judge are not the same; nor again can reason refute them, for reason is wholly dependent on sensation; nor can one sense refute another, since we pay equal heed to all. And the reality of separate perceptions guarantees the truth of our senses. But seeing and hearing are just as real as feeling pain. Hence it is from plain facts that we must start when we draw inferences about the unknown. For all our notions are derived from perceptions, either by actual contact or by analogy, or resemblance, or composition, with some slight aid from reasoning. And the objects presented to madmen and to people in dreams are true, for they produce effects—i.e. movements in the mind—which that which is unreal never does.

* From Diogenes Laertius, *Lives of the Philosophers* X, 31–66, trans. by R. D. Hicks, Loeb Classical Library (Cambridge, Mass., Harvard University Press). Reprinted by permission of the publishers.

By preconception they mean a sort of apprehension or a right opinion or notion, or universal idea stored in the mind; that is, a recollection of an external object often presented, e.g. Such and such a thing is a man: for no sooner is the word "man" uttered than we think of his shape by an act of preconception, in which the senses take the lead. Thus the object primarily denoted by every term is then plain and clear. And we should never have started an investigation, unless we had known what it was that we were in search of. For example: The object standing yonder is a horse or a cow. Before making this judgement, we must at some time or other have known by preconception the shape of a horse or a cow. We should not have given anything a name, if we had not first learnt its form by way of preconception. It follows, then, that preconceptions are clear. The object of a judgement is derived from something previously clear, by reference to which we frame the proposition, e.g. "How do we know that this is a man?" Opinion they also call conception or assumption, and declare it to be true and false; for it is true if it is subsequently confirmed or if it is not contradicted by evidence, and false if it is not subsequently confirmed or is contradicted by evidence. Hence the introduction of the phrase, "that which awaits" confirmation, e.g. to wait and get close to the tower and then learn what it looks like at close quarters.

They affirm that there are two states of feeling, pleasure and pain, which arise in every animate being, and that the one is favourable and the other hostile to that being, and by their means choice and avoidance are determined; and that there are two kinds of inquiry, the one concerned with things, the other with nothing but words. So much, then, for his division and criterion in their main outline.

. . .

"Again, there are outlines or films, which are of the same shape as solid bodies, but of a thinness far exceeding that of any object that we see. For it is not impossible that there should be found in the surrounding air combinations of this kind, materials adapted for expressing the hollowness and thinness of surfaces, and effluxes preserving the same relative position and motion which they had in the solid objects from which they come. To these films we give the name of 'images' or 'idols.' Furthermore, so long as nothing comes in the way to offer resistance, motion through the void accomplishes any imaginable distance in an inconceivably short time. For resistance encountered is the equivalent of slowness, its absence the equivalent of speed.

"Not that, if we consider the minute times perceptible by reason alone, the moving body itself arrives at more than one place simultaneously (for this too is inconceivable), although in time perceptible to sense it does arrive simultaneously, however different the point of departure from that conceived by us. For if it changed its direction, that would be equivalent to its meeting with resistance, even if up to that point we allow nothing to impede the rate of its flight. This is an elementary fact which in itself is well worth bearing in mind. In the next place the exceeding thinness of the images is contradicted by none of the facts under our observation. Hence also their velocities are enormous, since they always find a void passage to fit them. Besides, their incessant effluence meets with no resistance, or very little, although many atoms, not to say an unlimited number, do at once encounter resistance.

"Besides this, remember that the production of the images is as quick as thought. For particles are continually streaming off from the surface of bodies, though no diminution of the bodies is observed, because other particles take their place. And those given off for a long time retain the position and arrangement which their atoms had when they formed part of the solid bodies, although occasionally they are thrown into confusion. Sometimes such films are formed very rapidly in the air, because they need not have any solid content; and there are other modes in which they may be formed. For there is nothing in all this which is contradicted by sensation, if we in some sort look at the clear evidence of sense, to which we should also refer the continuity of particles in the objects external to ourselves.

"We must also consider that it is by the entrance of something coming from external objects that we see their shapes and think of them. For external things would not stamp on us their own nature of colour and form through the medium of the air which is between them and us, or by means of rays of light or currents of any sort going from us to them, so well as by the entrance into our eyes or minds, to whichever their size is suitable, of certain films coming from the things themselves, these films or outlines being of the same colour and shape as the external things themselves. They move with rapid motion; and this again explains why they present the appearance of the single continuous object, and retain the mutual interconnexion which they had in the object, when they impinge upon the sense, such impact being due to the oscillation of the atoms in the interior of the solid object from which they come. And whatever presentation we derive by direct contact, whether it be with the mind or with the sense-organs, be it shape that is presented or other properties, this shape as presented is the shape of the solid thing, and it is due either to a close coherence of the image as a whole or to a mere remnant of its parts. Falsehood and error always depend upon the intrusion of opinion <when a fact awaits> confirmation or the absence of contradiction, which fact is afterwards frequently not confirmed <or

even contradicted> [*following a certain movement in ourselves connected with, but distinct from, the mental picture presented—which is the cause of error*].

"For the presentations which, e.g., are received in a picture or arise in dreams, or from any other form of apprehension by the mind or by the other criteria of truth, would never have resembled what we call the real and true things, had it not been for certain actual things of the kind with which we come in contact. Error would not have occurred, if we had not experienced some other movement in ourselves, conjoined with, but distinct from, the perception of what is presented. And from this movement, if it be not confirmed or be contradicted, falsehood results; while, if it be confirmed or not contradicted, truth results.

"And to this view we must closely adhere, if we are not to repudiate the criteria founded on the clear evidence of sense, nor again to throw all these things into confusion by maintaining falsehood as if it were truth.

"Again, hearing takes place when a current passes from the object, whether person or thing, which emits voice or sound or noise, or produces the sensation of hearing in any way whatever. This current is broken up into homogeneous particles, which at the same time preserve a certain mutual connexion and a distinctive unity extending to the object which emitted them, and thus, for the most part, cause the perception in that case or, if not, merely indicate the presence of the external object. For without the transmission from the object of a certain interconnexion of the parts no such sensation could arise. Therefore we must not suppose that the air itself is moulded into shape by the voice emitted or something similar; for it is very far from being the case that the air is acted upon by it in this way. The blow which is struck in us when we utter a sound causes such a displacement of the particles as serves to produce a current resembling breath, and this displacement gives rise to the sensation of hearing.

"Again, we must believe that smelling, like hearing, would produce no sensation, were there not particles conveyed from the object which are of the proper sort of exciting the organ of smelling, some of one sort, some of another, some exciting it confusedly and strangely, others quietly and agreeably.

"Moreover, we must hold that the atoms in fact possess none of the qualities belonging to things which come under our observation, except shape, weight, and size, and the properties necessarily conjoined with shape. For every quality changes but the atoms do not change, since, when the composite bodies are dissolved, there must needs be a permanent something, solid and indissoluble, left behind, which makes change possible: not changes into or from the non-existent, but often through differences of arrangement, and sometimes through additions and subtractions of the atoms. Hence these somethings capable of being diversely arranged must be indestructible, exempt from change, but possessed each of its own distinctive mass and configuration. This must remain."

. . .

"Next, keeping in view our perceptions and feelings (for so shall we have the surest grounds for belief), we must recognize generally that the soul is a corporeal thing, composed of fine particles, dispersed all over the frame, most nearly resembling wind with an admixture of heat, in some respects like wind, in others like heat. But, again, there is the third part which exceeds the other two in the fineness of its particles and thereby keeps in closer touch with the rest of the frame. And this is shown by the mental faculties and feelings, by the ease with which the mind moves, and by thoughts, and by all those things the loss of which causes death. Further, we must keep in mind that soul has the greatest share in causing sensation. Still, it would not have had sensation, had it not been somehow confined within the rest of the frame. But the rest of the frame, though it provides this indispensable condition for the soul, itself also has a share, derived from the soul, of the said quality; and yet does not possess all the qualities of soul. Hence on the departure of the soul it loses sentience. For it had not this power in itself; but something else, congenital with the body, supplied it to body: which other thing, through the potentiality actualized in it by means of motion, at once acquired for itself a quality of sentience, and, in virtue of the neighbourhood and interconnexion between them, imparted it (as I said) to the body also.

"Hence, so long as the soul is in the body, it never loses sentience through the removal of some other part. The containing sheath may be dislocated in whole or in part, and portions of the soul may thereby be lost; yet in spite of this the soul, if it manage to survive, will have sentience. But the rest of the frame, whether the whole of it survives or only a part, no longer has sensation, when once those atoms have departed, which, however few in number, are required to constitute the nature of soul. Moreover, when the whole frame is broken up, the soul is scattered and has no longer the same powers as before, nor the same motions; hence it does not possess sentience either.

"For we cannot think of it as sentient, except it be in this composite whole and moving with these movements; nor can we so think of it when the sheaths which enclose and surround it are not the same as those in which the soul is now located and in which it performs these movements. [*He says elsewhere that the soul is composed of the smoothest and roundest of atoms, far superior in both respects to those of fire; that part of it is irrational, this being scattered over the rest of the frame, while the rational part resides in the chest, as is manifest from our fears and our joy; that sleep occurs when the parts of the soul which have been scattered all over the composite organism are held fast in it or dispersed, and afterwards collide with one another by their impacts. The semen is derived from the whole of the body.*]"

We offer Epicureanism also in the words of the philosopher-poet, Lucretius, whose book *On the Nature of Things* is one of the great classics of the later Greco-Roman period; one of the great glimpses of a naturalistic and evolutionary scheme of the universe and of the origins and development of life; and one of the great moral declarations in which the goodness of mankind is held to be capable of achievement through the use of man's own moral sensitivities and efforts. [GM and LBM.]

LUCRETIUS *

. . . Then be it ours with steady mind to clasp
The purport of the skies—the law behind
The wandering courses of the sun and moon;
To scan the powers that speed all life below;
But most to see with reasonable eyes
Of what the mind, of what the soul is made,
And what it is so terrible that breaks
On us asleep, or waking in disease,
Until we seem to mark and hear at hand
Dead men whose bones earth bosomed long ago.

SUBSTANCE IS ETERNAL

This terror, then, this darkness of the mind,
Not sunrise with its flaring spokes of light,
Nor glittering arrows of morning can disperse,

* From Lucretius, *On the Nature of Things,* trans. by William Ellery Leonard, Everyman's Library Edition (New York: E. P. Dutton & Co., 1950), pp. 7–9, 11, 13–14, 96–100, 103–105, 110, 136–138, 144–145, 148.

But only Nature's aspect and her law,
Which, teaching us, hath this exordium:
Nothing from nothing ever yet was born.
Fear holds dominion over mortality
Only because, seeing in land and sky
So much the cause whereof no wise they know,
Men think Divinities are working there.
Meantime, when once we know from nothing still
Nothing can be created, we shall divine
More clearly what we seek: those elements
From which alone all things created are,
And how accomplished by no tool of Gods.
Suppose all sprang from all things: any kind
Might take its origin from any thing,
No fixed seed required. Men from the sea
Might rise, and from the land the scaly breed,
And, fowl full fledged come bursting from the sky;
The hornèd cattle, the herds and all the wild
Would haunt with varying offspring tilth and waste;
Nor would the same fruits keep their olden trees,
But each might grow from any stock or limb
By chance and change. Indeed, and were there not
For each its procreant atoms, could things have
Each its unalterable mother old?
But, since produced from fixèd seeds are all,
Each birth goes forth upon the shores of light
From its own stuff, from its own primal bodies.
And all from all cannot become, because
In each resides a secret power its own.
Again, why see we lavished o'er the lands
At spring the rose, at summer heat the corn,
The vines that mellow when the autumn lures,
If not because the fixèd seeds of things
At their own season must together stream,
And new creations only be revealed
When the due times arrive and pregnant earth
Safely may give unto the shores of light
Her tender progenies?

. . .

And, too, the selfsame power might end alike
All things, were they not still together held

By matter eternal, shackled through its parts,
Now more, now less. A touch might be enough
To cause destruction. For the slightest force
Would loose the weft of things wherein no part
Were of imperishable stock. But now
Because the fastenings of primordial parts
Are put together diversly and stuff
Is everlasting, things abide the same
Unhurt and sure, until some power comes on
Strong to destroy the warp and woof of each:
Nothing returns to naught; but all return
At their collapse to primal forms of stuff.

. . .

The rock-paved highways worn by many feet;
And at the gates the brazen statues show
Their right hands leaner from the frequent touch
Of wayfarers innumerable who greet.
We see how wearing-down hath minished these,
But just what motes depart at any time,
The envious nature of vision bars our sight.
Lastly whatever days and nature add
Little by little, constraining things to grow
In due proportion, no gaze however keen
Of these our eyes hath watched and known. No more
Can we observe what's lost at any time,
When things wax old with eld and foul decay,
Or when salt seas eat under beetling crags.
Thus nature ever by unseen bodies works.

. . .

NATURE AND COMPOSITION OF THE MIND

First, then, I say, the mind which oft we call
The intellect, wherein is seated life's
Counsel and regimen, is part no less
Of man than hand and foot and eyes are parts
Of one whole breathing creature. [But some hold]
That sense of mind is in no fixed part seated,
But is of body some one vital state,—
Named "harmony" by Greeks, because thereby
We live with sense, though intellect be not

In any part: as oft the body is said
To have good health (when health, however, 's not
One part of him who has it), so they place
The sense of mind in no fixed part of man.

Mightily, diversly, meseems they err.
Often the body palpable and seen
Sickens, while yet in some invisible part
We feel a pleasure; oft the other way,
A miserable in mind feels pleasure still
Throughout his body—quite the same as when
A foot may pain without a pain in head.
Besides, when these our limbs are given o'er
To gentle sleep and lies the burdened frame
At random void of sense, a something else
Is yet within us, which upon that time
Bestirs itself in many a wise, receiving
All motions of joy and phantom cares of heart.
Now, for to see that in man's members dwells
Also the soul, and body ne'er is wont
To feel sensation by a "harmony,"
Take this in chief: the fact that life remains
Oft in our limbs, when much of body's gone;
Yet that same life, when particles of heat,
Though few, have scattered been, and through the mouth
Air has been given forth abroad, forthwith
Forever deserts the veins, and leaves the bones.
Thus mayst thou know that not all particles
Perform like parts, nor in like manner all
Are props of weal and safety: rather those—
The seeds of wind and exhalations warm—
Take care that in our members life remains.
Therefore a vital heat and wind there is
Within the very body, which at death
Deserts our frames.

. . .

And this same argument establisheth
That nature of mind and soul corporeal is:
For when 'tis seen to drive the members on,
To snatch from sleep the body, and to change
The countenance, and the whole state of man
To rule and turn,—what yet could never be

Sans contact, and sans body contact fails—
Must we not grant that mind and soul consist
Of a corporeal nature?—And besides
Thou markst that likewise with this body of ours
Suffers the mind and with our body feels.

. . .

Now, then,
Since nature of mind is movable so much,
Consist it must of seeds exceeding small
And smooth and round. Which fact once known to thee,
Good friend, will serve thee opportune in else.
This also shows the nature of the same,
How nice its texture, in how small a space
'Twould go, if once compacted as a pellet:
When death's unvexed repose gets hold on man
And mind and soul retire, thou markest there
From the whole body nothing ta'en in form,
Nothing in weight. Death grants ye everything,
But vital sense and exhalation hot.
Thus soul entire must be of smallmost seeds,
Twined through the veins, the vitals, and the thews,
Seeing that, when 'tis from whole body gone,
The outward figuration of the limbs
Is unimpaired and weight fails not a whit.
Just so, when vanished the bouquet of wine,
Or when an unguent's perfume delicate
Into the winds away departs, or when
From any body savour's gone, yet still
The thing itself seems minished naught to eyes,
Thereby, nor aught abstracted from its weight—
No marvel, because seeds many and minute
Produce the savours and the redolence
In the whole body of the things. And so,
Again, again, nature of mind and soul
'Tis thine to know created is of seeds
The tiniest ever, since at flying-forth
It beareth nothing of the weight away.

. . .

Nor may we suppose
Evil can e'er be rooted up so far
That one man's not more given to fits of wrath,

Another's not more quickly touched by fear,
A third not more long-suffering than he should.
And needs must differ in many things besides
The varied natures and resulting habits
Of humankind—of which not now can I
Expound the hidden causes, nor find names
Enough for all the divers shapes of those
Primordials whence this variation springs.
But this meseems I'm able to declare:
Those vestiges of natures left behind
Which reason cannot quite expel from us
Are still so slight that naught prevents a man
From living a life even worthy of the gods.

So then this soul is kept by all the body,
Itself the body's guard, and source of weal;
For they with common roots cleave each to each,
Nor can be torn asunder without death.
Not easy 'tis from lumps of frankincense
To tear their fragrance forth, without its nature
Perishing likewise: so, not easy 'tis
From all the body nature of mind and soul
To draw away, without the whole dissolved.
With seeds so intertwinèd even from birth,
They're dowered conjointly with a partner-life;
No energy of body or mind, apart,
Each of itself without the other's power,
Can have sensation; but our sense, enkindled
Along the vitals, to flame is blown by both
With mutual motions. Besides the body alone
Is nor begot nor grows, nor after death
Seen to endure. For not as water at times
Gives off the alien heat, nor is thereby
Itself destroyed, but unimpaired remains—
Not thus, I say, can the deserted frame
Bear the dissevering of its joinèd soul,
But, rent and ruined, moulders all away.
Thus the joint contact of the body and soul
Learn from their earliest age the vital motions,
Even when still buried in the mother's womb;
So no dissevering can hap to them,
Without their bane and ill. And thence mayst see

That, as conjoinèd is their source of weal,
Conjoinèd also must their nature be.

. . .

Herein in these affairs nowise take up
What honoured sage, Democritus, lays down—
That proposition, that primordials
Of body and mind, each super-posed on each,
Vary alternately and interweave
The fabric of our members. For not only
Are the soul-elements smaller far than those
Which this our body and inward parts compose,

. . .

Thus, since within the body itself of man
The mind and soul are by such great diseases
Shaken, so miserably in labour distraught,
Why, then, believe that in the open air,
Without a body, they can pass their life,
Immortal, battling with the master winds?

. . .

Now will I undertake an argument—
One for these matters of supreme concern—
That there exist those somewhats which we call
The images of things: these, like to films
Scaled off the utmost outside of the things,
Flit hither and thither through the atmosphere,
And the same terrify our intellects,
Coming upon us waking or in sleep,
When oft we peer at wonderful strange shapes
And images of people lorn of light,
Which oft have horribly roused us when we lay
In slumber—that haply nevermore may we
Suppose that souls get loose from Acheron,
Or shades go floating in among the living,
Or aught of us is left behind at death,
When body and mind, destroyed together, each
Back to its own primordials goes away.

And thus I say that effigies of things,
And tenuous shapes from off the things are sent,

From off the utmost outside of the things,
Which are like films or may be named a rind,
Because the image bears like look and form
With whatso body has shed it fluttering forth—
A fact thou mayst, however dull thy wits,
Well learn from this: mainly, because we see
Even 'mongst visible objects many be
That send forth bodies, loosely some diffused—
Like smoke from oaken logs and heat from fires—
And some more interwoven and condensed—
As when the locusts in the summertime
Put off their glossy tunics, or when calves
At birth drop membranes from their body's surface,
Or when, again, the slippery serpent doffs
Its vestments 'mongst the thorns—for oft we see
The breres augmented with their flying spoils:
Since such takes place, 'tis likewise certain too
That tenuous images from things are sent,
From off the utmost outside of the things.
For why those kinds should drop and part from things,
Rather than others tenuous and thin,
No power has man to open mouth to tell;
Especially, since on outsides of things
Are bodies many and minute which could,
In the same order which they had before,
And with the figure of their form preserved,
Be thrown abroad, and much more swiftly too,
Being less subject to impediments,
As few in number and placed along the front.
For truly many things we see discharge
Their stuff at large, not only from their cores
Deep-set within, as we have said above,
But from their surfaces at times no less—
Their very colours too. And commonly
The awnings, saffron, red and dusky blue,
Stretched overhead in mighty theatres,
Upon their poles and cross-beams fluttering,
Have such an action quite; for there they dye
And make to undulate with their every hue
The circled throng below, and all the stage,
And rich attire in the patrician seats.

And ever the more the theatre's dark walls
Around them shut, the more all things within
Laugh in the bright suffusion of strange glints,
The daylight being withdrawn. And therefore, since
The canvas hangings thus discharge their dye
From off their surface, things in general must
Likewise their tenuous effigies discharge,
Because in either case they are off-thrown
From off the surface. So there are indeed
Such certain prints and vestiges of forms
Which flit around, of subtlest texture made,
Invisible, when separate, each and one.
Again, all odour, smoke, and heat, and such
Streams out of things diffusèdly, because,
Whilst coming from the deeps of body forth
And rising out, along their bending path
They're torn asunder, nor have gateways straight
Wherethrough to mass themselves and struggle abroad.
But contrariwise, when such a tenuous film
Of outside colour is thrown off, there's naught
Can rend it, since 'tis placed along the front
Ready to hand. Lastly those images
Which to our eyes in mirrors do appear,
In water, or in any shining surface,
Must be, since furnished with like look of things,
Fashioned from images of things sent out.

. . .

Nor over-marvellous must this be deemed
In these affairs that, though the films which strike
Upon the eyes cannot be singly seen,
The things themselves may be perceived. For thus
When the wind beats upon us stroke by stroke
And when the sharp cold streams, 'tis not our wont
To feel each private particle of wind
Or of that cold, but rather all at once;
And so we see how blows affect our body,
As if one thing were beating on the same
And giving us the feel of its own body
Outside of us. Again, whene'er we thump
With finger-tip upon a stone, we touch

But the rock's surface and the outer hue,
Nor feel that hue by contact—rather feel
The very hardness deep within the rock.

. . .

And when from far away we do behold
The squarèd towers of a city, oft
Rounded they seem,—on this account because
Each distant angle is perceived obtuse,
Or rather it is not perceived at all;
And perishes its blow nor to our gaze
Arrives its stroke, since through such length of air
Are borne along the idols that the air
Makes blunt the idol of the angle's point
By numerous collidings. When thuswise
The angles of the tower each and all
Have quite escaped the sense, the stones appear
As rubbed and rounded on a turner's wheel—
Yet not like objects near and truly round,
But with a semblance to them, shadowily.

Editors' Note

We like the use of Lucretius made by Dr. John D. Benjamin:*

"Lucretius, poet, philosopher, and intuitive scientist, wrote,† 'Though education may apply a similar polish to various individuals, it still leaves fundamental traces of their several temperaments. It must not be supposed that innate vices can be completely eradicated: one man will still incline more readily to outbursts of rage; another will give way a little sooner to fear; a third will accept some contingencies too impassively. And in a host of other ways men must differ one from another in temperament and so also in the resultant behavior. To unfold here the secret causes of these differences is beyond my power. I cannot even find names for the multi-

* Taken from "The Innate and the Experiential in Development," by John D. Benjamin, M.D., from the Department of Psychiatry and the Child Research Council, University of Colorado School of Medicine. Read at the Pittsburgh Bicentennial Conference, April, 1959. In H. W. Brosin (ed.), *Lectures in Experimental Psychiatry* (Pittsburgh: University of Pittsburgh Press, 1961), pp. 19–42.

† *De Rerum Natura.* Translated as *The Nature of the Universe* by R. E. Latham (Harmonsworth: Penguin Books, 1951), pp. 105–106.

plicity of atomic shapes that give rise to this variety of types. But I am clear that there is one relevant fact I can affirm: the lingering traces of inborn temperament that cannot be eliminated by philosophy are so slight that there is nothing to prevent men from leading a life worthy of the gods.' Of course, we must remember that there have been some few mutations since the time of Lucretius."

Two

FROM THE CLASSICAL TO THE MEDIEVAL

INTRODUCTION

Following upon a great psychological era in the centuries just before the birth of Christ, exemplified in the philosophical and psychological developments in India, in China, and in Greece, there gradually supervened a period of declining insights and more and more mechanical repetition. After the brilliant flashes of Lao-tzu and Chuang-tzu, Chinese philosophy became more or less standardized; Indian philosophy continued creative for several centuries longer, but by the seventh or eighth century of the Christian era was plainly becoming stagnant. Indeed, the civilization as a whole was apparently deteriorating, as Nehru has pointed out.* Greek philosophy, and the Greek civilization as a whole, underwent a decline.

It is often said that the decline of the Western philosophies and psychologies was owing to the invasion of the Barbarians. This will not suffice as an explanation of the fact that the Eastern Empire, anchored at Byzantium (Constantinople), resisted attack from all quarters for more than a thousand years after the time of Constantine (from A.D. 325 to A.D. 1453), yet during this thousand years produced no revival of great philosophy. In the Western Empire, anchored at Rome, there was, indeed, wave after wave of Barbarian invasion to be resisted—less and less effectively—but there were many other factors of which economists have spoken, such as failure of the soil and a poorly contrived land ownership system; and, of course, the advent of new religious faith in a society physically deteriorating might often draw more thoughtful people into religious rather than into secular philosophy. This is just by way of

* Jawaharlal Nehru, *The Discovery of India,* ed. by Robert I. Crane (New York: Doubleday & Co., Anchor Books, 1960).

saying that for a variety of reasons psychology declined for a period of over a thousand years. While some vigorous and original thinking continued to appear in the Greco-Roman world, even during the period of the Barbarian invasions, philosophical and scientific originality appears on the whole to be waning, with Stoicism and Epicureanism fighting a rearguard action against the slow death of the great Greco-Roman system.

During these same centuries the Christian message, and that elaboration of its thought which George Santayana calls "The Christian Epic," took root all about the Mediterranean. Greco-Roman philosophy became colored by Christian questions and answers. Just as Hebrew ways of thinking had become colored by Greek thought, so Roman thought had absorbed much from Greek, and now the Greco-Roman system began to absorb the mixture of Hebrew and other ideas from the Middle East. There came a new conceptualization of the relation of God and man, the process of creation, the nature of sin and man's fall, and through it all, the conception of the will, in which inhered the possibility of following, or of defying, the Deity's plan for human life.

The conception of the Savior, the incarnate God who had died for the liberation and eternal joyful fulfillment of man's spiritual life, offered in itself basic problems of psychology which had received relatively little attention either in Hebrew or in Greek thought. The conception of sin, and indeed the fundamental conception of evil in the universe, had been developed by the fifth century B.C. in the religious system of Zoroaster, just as a place for sin had developed in the Hindu and Buddhist systems. For the Jews there had been no well-worked-out conception of freedom of choice through which sin and the salvation from sinfulness could be defined. Yet it was among the Jews that the conception of man's unworthiness and the conception of moral default had been developed through the years of the prophets, and through the later Greco-Hebraic interaction, which we call Hellenism. Christianity was full of the message of sin and redemption. The following are the extraordinary words by St. Paul regarding the sense of helplessness in the face of one's own sinfulness; the problem of the aching and unresolved will toward the good, dragged back by something within us which craves the evil; and through it all the conception of a divine mercy which can under certain conditions restore health to the soul. The will becomes central as never before in a psychological system.

THE NEW TESTAMENT

Romans viii, 14–25

For we know that the law is spiritual: but I am carnal, sold under sin.

For that which I do I allow not: for what I would, that do I not; but what I hate, that do I.

If then I do that which I would not, I consent unto the law that it is good.

Now then it is no more I that do it, but sin that dwelleth in me.

For I know that in me (that is, in my flesh) dwelleth no good thing: for to will is present with me; but how to perform that which is good I find not.

For the good that I would I do not: but the evil which I would not, that I do.

Now if I do that I would not, it is no more I that do it, but sin that dwelleth in me.

I find then a law, that, when I would do good, evil is present with me.

For I delight in the law of God after the inward man:

But I see another law in my members, warring against the law of my mind, and bringing me into captivity to the law of sin which is in my members.

O wretched man that I am! who shall deliver me from the body of this death?

I thank God through Jesus Christ our Lord. So then with the mind I myself serve the law of God; but with the flesh the law of sin.

But it is not only the will and its relation to sin, but also the fulfillment of man through divine love which stands out in the Christian message. Love had been given a central position at times in Hebrew thought, notably the love of God for man and man's love of God. It remains, however, to make love absolutely central, superior to faith and even to duty, and ultimately superior even to the principle of the will. The infinitely radiant message, as familiar to us as anything in the Western tradition, is reflected in these verses from St. Paul's First Letter to the Corinthians.

I Corinthians xiii, 1–13

Though I speak with the tongues of men and of angels, and have not charity, I am become *as* sounding brass, or a tinkling cymbal.

And though I have *the gift of* prophecy, and understand all mysteries, and all knowledge; and though I have all faith, so that I could remove mountains, and have not charity, I am nothing.

And though I bestow all my goods to feed *the poor,* and though I give my body to be burned, and have not charity, it profiteth me nothing.

Charity suffereth long, *and* is kind; charity envieth not; charity vaunteth not itself, is not puffed up,

Doth not behave itself unseemly, seeketh not her own, is not easily provoked, thinketh no evil;

Rejoiceth not in iniquity, but rejoiceth in the truth;

Beareth all things, believeth all things, hopeth all things, endureth all things.

Charity never faileth: but whether *there be* prophecies, they shall fail; whether *there be* tongues, they shall cease; whether *there be* knowledge, it shall vanish away.

For we know in part, and we prophesy in part.

But when that which is perfect is come, then that which is in part shall be done away.

When I was a child, I spake as a child, I understood as a child, I thought as a child: but when I became a man, I put away childish things.

For now we see through a glass, darkly; but then face to face: now I know in part; but then shall I know even as also I am known.

And now abideth faith, hope, charity, these three; but the greatest of these *is* charity.

Through the opening centuries of the Christian era, these problems of sin, of obligation to God, of the means of salvation, and of the relation of spontaneous love to the firm call of duty constantly reappear in the message of the Christian theologians, the Church Fathers, concerned as they are to understand the nature of man in such a way as to give fulfillment of man's destiny within the new Christian system. By general agreement, St. Augustine gives expression to fourth-century conceptions of the abject need of man for God's salvation, the reality of sin and redemption, yet recognizing spontaneous love and also finding a prominent place for a genuine freedom of the will by which man may accept or reject the plan which God has made for his salvation. This preoccupation with the will becomes, even more than was the case with Paul, a psychological challenge. This question may be placed side by side with the Pauline messages quoted above. We shall emphasize St. Augustine's discussion of the will. With the aid of our consultant, Professor Richard McKeon, we shall also look into the thought of St. Augustine regarding love, and into the writings of other philosophers resonant to the Christian message.

ST. AUGUSTINE *

All natures, then, are good simply because they exist and, therefore, have each its own measure of being, its own beauty, even, in a way, its own peace. And when each is in the place assigned by the order of nature, it best preserves the full measure of being that was given to it. Beings not made for eternal life, changing for better or for worse according as they promote the good and improvement of things to which, by the law of the Creator, they serve as means, follow the direction of Divine Providence and tend toward the particular end which forms a part of the general plan for governing the universe. This means that the dissolution which brings mutable and mortal things to their death is not so much a process of annihilation as a progress toward something they were designed to become.

• • •

If one seeks for the efficient cause of their evil will, none is to be found. For, what can make the will bad when it is the will itself which makes an action bad? Thus, an evil will is the efficient cause of a bad action, but there is no efficient cause of an evil will. If there is such a

* From St. Augustine, *The City of God,* trans. by Gerald G. Walsh, S.J., Demetrius B. Zema, S.J., Grace Monahan, O.S.U., and Daniel J. Honan, ed. by Vernon J. Burke (New York: Doubleday & Co., Image Books, 1958), pp. 250–252, 295. Copyright 1950, 1952, 1954, 1958 by Fathers of the Church, Inc.

cause, it either has or has not a will. If it has, then that will is either good or bad. If good, one would have to be foolish enough to conclude that a good will makes a bad will. In that case, a good will becomes the cause of sin—which is utterly absurd. On the other hand, if the hypothetical cause of a bad will has itself a bad will, I would have to ask what made this will bad, and, to put an end to the inquiry: What made the first bad will bad? Now, the fact is that there was no first bad will that was made bad by any other bad will—it was made bad by itself. For, if it were preceded by a cause that made it evil, that cause came first. But, if I am told that nothing made the will evil but that it always was so, then I ask whether or not it existed in some nature.

If this evil will existed in no nature, then it did not exist at all. If it existed in some nature, then it vitiated, corrupted, injured that nature and, therefore, deprived it of some good. An evil will could not exist in an evil nature but only in a good one, mutable enough to suffer harm from this deprivation. For, if no harm were done, then there was no deprivation and, consequently, no right to call the will evil. But, if harm was done, it was done by destroying or diminishing what was good. Thus, an evil will could not have existed from all eternity in a nature in which a previously existing good had to be eliminated before the evil will could harm the nature. But, if it did not exist from all eternity, who, then, caused this evil will?

The only remaining suggestion is that the cause of the evil will was something which had no will. My next question is whether this "something" was superior, inferior, or equal to the will. If superior, then it was better. So, then, how can it have had no will and not rather a good will? If equal, the case is the same: for, as long as two wills are equally good, one cannot produce an evil will in the other. The supposition remains, then, that it was an inferior thing without a will which produced the evil will of the angelic nature which first sinned.

But that thing itself, whatever it was, even though it was low to the lowest point of earthliness, was, without doubt, good since it was a nature and a being having its own character and species in its own genus and order. How, then, can a good thing be the efficient cause of an evil will? How, I ask, can good be the cause of evil? For, when the will, abandoning what is above it, turns itself to something lower, it becomes evil because the very turning itself and not the thing to which it turns is evil. Therefore, an inferior being does not make the will evil but the will itself, because it is a created will, wickedly and inordinately seeks the inferior being.

• • •

I have already said, in previous Books, that God had two purposes in deriving all men from one man. His first purpose was to give unity to the human race by the likeness of nature. His second purpose was to bind mankind by the bond of peace, through blood relationship, into one harmonious whole. I have said further that no member of this race would ever have died had not the first two—one created from nothing and the second from the first—merited this death by disobedience. The sin which they committed was so great that it impaired all human nature—in this sense, that the nature has been transmitted to posterity with a propensity to sin and a necessity to die. Moreover, the kingdom of death so dominated men that all would have been hurled, by a just punishment, into a second and endless death had not some been saved from this by the gratuitous grace of God. This is the reason why, for all the difference of the many and very great nations throughout the world in religion and morals, language, weapons, and dress, there exist no more than the two kinds of society, which, according to our Scriptures, we have rightly called the two cities. One city is that of men who live according to the flesh. The other is of men who live according to the spirit. Each of them chooses its own kind of peace and, when they attain what they desire, each lives in the peace of its own choosing.

The authors from whom we have drawn have indicated the enormous impact of Aristotle upon the whole long, great era which followed the Greeks—an impact not so much by way of specific teaching perpetuated, as by way of an endless redefinition of the great problems of psychology—an agreement, so to speak, to see psychology as Aristotle did, and to make its rational core the enduring core of Western psychology.

But all this is particularly true of the one great central figure, St. Thomas Aquinas, of the thirteenth century, who explicitly undertook to integrate Aristotle with Christian theology. Many, of course, had worked on this intellectual tapestry before, but it was Aquinas who, with his lucid comprehension of the Aristotelian doctrines, saw where they coincided with Christian doctrines, where they fell short of the mark, and where a bridge needed to be built between them. Notably, in the great era of Christian psychology, problems of the feeling life, and especially of impulse and of will, had taken a major role, and it was the great task of St. Thomas

Aquinas to show the central importance of these great problems of feeling and will, at the same time maintaining an Aristotelian conception of the rational soul as transcending feeling and impulse in the purely animal senses of such terms. Again, with Professor Richard McKeon's help, we have selected a few passages from St. Thomas Aquinas whom we use now to exemplify the last outpost of Western philosophical psychology before the proto-Renaissance and the Renaissance of the fourteenth century and beyond.

ST. THOMAS AQUINAS *

Question LXXVIII. The Powers of the Soul in Particular

We next treat of the powers of the soul in particular. The theologian, however, has only to inquire specifically concerning the intellectual and appetitive powers, in which the virtues reside. And since the knowledge of these powers depends to a certain extent on the other powers, our consideration of the powers of the soul in particular will be divided into three parts: first, we shall consider those powers which are a preamble to the intellect; secondly, the intellectual powers; thirdly, the appetitive powers.

Under the first head there are four points of inquiry: (1) The powers of the soul considered generally. (2) The species of powers in the vegetative part of the soul. (3) The exterior senses. (4) The interior senses.

FIRST ARTICLE. WHETHER THERE ARE TO BE DISTINGUISHED FIVE GENERA OF POWERS IN THE SOUL?

. . . The Philosopher says: *The powers are the vegetative, the sensitive, the appetitive, the locomotive, and the intellectual.*

I answer that, There are five genera among the powers of the soul, as above numbered. Of these, three are called souls, and four are called modes of living. The reason of this diversity is that the various souls are distinguished according as the operation of the soul transcends the operation of the corporeal nature in various ways; for the whole corporeal nature is subject to the soul, and is related to it as its matter and instrument. There exists, therefore, an operation of the soul which so far

* From the *Summa Theologica*, in *The Basic Writings of St. Thomas Aquinas*, ed. by Anton C. Pegis (New York: Random House, 1945), I, 733–735, 751–753, 768–770. Copyright 1945 by Random House, Inc. Reprinted by permission of the publishers.

exceeds the corporeal nature that it is not even performed by any corporeal organ; and such is the operation of the *rational soul.* Below this, there is another operation of the soul, which is indeed performed through a corporeal organ, but not through a corporeal quality, and this is the operation of the *sensitive soul.* For though hot and cold, wet and dry, and other such corporeal qualities are required for the work of the senses, yet they are not required in such a way that the operation of the senses takes place by the power of such qualities; but only for the proper disposition of the organ. The lowest of the operations of the soul is that which is performed by a corporeal organ and by the power of a corporeal quality. Yet this transcends the operation of the corporeal nature; because the movements of bodies are caused by an extrinsic principle, while these operations are from an intrinsic principle. For this is common to all the operations of the soul, since every animate thing, in some way, moves itself. Such is the operation of the *vegetative soul;* for digestion, and what follows, is caused instrumentally by the action of heat, as the Philosopher says.

Now the powers of the soul are distinguished generically by their objects. For the higher a power is, the more universal is the object to which it extends, as we have said above. But the object of the soul's operation may be considered in a triple order. For in the soul there is a power whose object is only the body that is united to that soul; and the powers of this genus are called *vegetative,* for the vegetative power acts only on the body to which the soul is united. There is another genus in the powers of the soul which regards a more universal object—namely, every sensible body, and not only the body to which the soul is united. And there is yet another genus in the powers of the soul which regards a still more universal object—namely, not only the sensible body, but universally all being. Therefore it is evident that the latter two genera of the soul's powers have an operation in regard not merely to that which is united to them, but also to something extrinsic. Now, since whatever operates must in some way be united to the object in relation to which it operates, it follows of necessity that this something extrinsic, which is the object of the soul's operation, must be related to the soul in a twofold manner. First, inasmuch as this something extrinsic has a natural aptitude to be united to the soul, and to be by its likeness in the soul. In this way there are two kinds of powers—namely, the *sensitive,* in regard to the less common object, the sensible body; and the *intellectual,* in regard to the most common object, universal being. Secondly, inasmuch as the soul itself has an inclination and tendency to the external thing. And in this way there are again two kinds of powers in the soul: one—*the appetitive*—according to which the soul is referred to something extrinsic as to an end, which is first in the intention; the other—the *locomotive* power—according to which the soul is referred to something extrinsic as to the term of its operation and movement; for every animal is moved for the purpose of realizing its desires and intentions.

The modes of living, on the other hand, are distinguished according to the degrees of living things. There are some living things in which there exists only vegetative power, as plants. There are others in which along with the vegetative there exists also the sensitive, but not the locomotive, power; and such are immovable animals, as shellfish. There are others which, besides this, have locomotive powers, as do the perfect animals, which require many things for their life, and consequently need movement to seek necessaries of life from a distance. And there are some living things which along with these have intellectual power—namely, men. But the appetitive power does not constitute a degree of living things; because *wherever there is sense there is also appetite.*

• • •

FOURTH ARTICLE. WHETHER THE AGENT INTELLECT IS SOMETHING IN THE SOUL?

. . . The Philosopher says that *it is necessary for these differences,* namely, the possible and agent intellect, *to be in the soul.*

I answer that, The agent intellect, of which the Philosopher speaks, is something in the soul. In order to make this evident, we must observe that above the intellectual soul of man we must needs suppose a superior intellect, from which the soul acquires the power of understanding. For what is such by participation, and what is movable, and what is imperfect, always requires the pre-existence of something essentially such, immovable and perfect. Now the human soul is called intellectual by reason of a participation in intellectual power, a sign of which is that it is not wholly intellectual but only in part. Moreover it reaches to the understanding of truth by reasoning, with a certain discursiveness and movement. Even more, it has an imperfect understanding, both because it does not understand everything, and because, in those things which it does understand, it passes from potentiality to act. Therefore there must needs be some higher intellect, by which the soul is helped to understand.

Therefore some held that this intellect, substantially separate, is the agent intellect, which by lighting up the phantasms, as it were, makes them to be actually intelligible. But, even supposing the existence of such a separate agent intellect, it would still be necessary to assign to the human soul some power participating in that superior intellect, by which power the human soul makes things to be actually intelligible.

Such is also the case in other perfect natural things, among which, besides the universal active causes, each one is endowed with its proper powers derived from those universal causes: for the sun alone does not generate man, but in man himself there is the power of begetting man; and in like manner with other perfect animals. Now among these sublunary things nothing is more perfect than the human soul. Therefore we must say that in the soul is some power derived from a higher intellect, whereby it is able to illumine the phantasms.

And we know this by experience, since we perceive that we abstract universal forms from their particular conditions; which is to make them actually intelligible. Now no action belongs to anything except through some principle formally inherent therein, as we have said above of the possible intellect. Therefore the power which is the principle of this action must be something in the soul. For this reason Aristotle compared the agent intellect to light, which is something received into the air, while Plato compared the separate intellect, whose light touches the soul, to the sun, as Themistius says in his commentary on *De Anima* iii.

But the separate intellect, according to the teaching of our Faith, is God Himself, Who is the soul's Creator, and only beatitude; as will be shown later on. Therefore the human soul derives its intellectual light from Him, according to *Ps.* iv. 7, *The light of Thy countenance, O Lord, is signed upon us.*

FIFTH ARTICLE. WHETHER THE AGENT INTELLECT IS ONE IN ALL?

. . . The Philosopher says that the agent intellect is as a light. But light is not the same in the various illuminated things. Therefore the same agent intellect is not in various men.

I answer that, The truth about this question depends on what we have already said. For if the agent intellect were not something belonging to the soul, but were some separate substance, there would be one agent intellect for all men. And this is what they mean who hold that there is one agent intellect for all. But if the agent intellect is something belonging to the soul, as one of its powers, we are bound to say that there are as many agent intellects as there are souls, which are multiplied according to the number of men, as we have said above. For it is impossible that one and the same power belong to various substances.

. . .

Question LXXX. The Appetitive Powers in General

Next we consider the appetitive powers, concerning which there are four heads of consideration: first, the appetitive powers in general; second, sensuality; third, the will; fourth, free choice. Under the first there are two points of inquiry. (1) Whether the appetite should be considered a special power of the soul? (2) Whether the appetite is divided into intellectual and sensitive as distinct powers?

FIRST ARTICLE. WHETHER THE APPETITE IS A SPECIAL POWER OF THE SOUL?

. . . *I answer that,* It is necessary to assign an appetitive power to the soul. To make this evident, we must observe that some inclination follows every form: for example, fire, by its form, is inclined to rise, and to generate its like. Now, the form is found to have a more perfect existence in those things which participate in knowledge than in those which lack knowledge. For in those which lack knowledge, the form is found to determine each thing only to its own being—that is, to the being which is natural to each. Now this natural form is followed by a natural inclination, which is called the natural appetite. But in those things which have knowledge, each one is determined to its own natural being by its natural form, but in such a manner that it is nevertheless receptive of the species of other things. For example, sense receives the species of all sensible things, and the intellect, of all intelligible things; so that the soul of man is, in a way, all things by sense and intellect. In this way, those beings that have knowledge approach, in a way, to a likeness to God, *in Whom all things pre-exist,* as Dionysius says.

Therefore, just as in those beings that have knowledge forms exist in a higher manner and above the manner of natural forms, so there must be in them an inclination surpassing the natural inclination, which is called the natural appetite. And this superior inclination belongs to the appetitive power of the soul, through which the animal is able to desire what it apprehends, and not only that to which it is inclined by its natural form. And so it is necessary to assign an appetitive power to the soul.

• • •

SECOND ARTICLE. WHETHER THE SENSITIVE AND INTELLECTUAL APPETITES ARE DISTINCT POWERS?

. . . *I answer that,* We must needs say that the intellectual appetite is a distinct power from the sensitive appetite. For the appetitive power is a passive power, which is naturally moved by the thing apprehended. Therefore *the apprehended appetible is a mover which is not moved, while the appetite is a moved mover,* as the Philosopher says in *De Anima* iii. and in *Metaph.* xii. Now things passive and movable are differentiated according to the distinction of the corresponding active and motive principles, for the motive must be proportionate to the movable, and the active to the passive. Indeed, the passive power itself has its very nature from its relation to its active principle. Therefore, since what is apprehended by the intellect and what is apprehended by sense are generically different, consequently, the intellectual appetite is distinct from the sensitive.

Three

ISLAMIC PSYCHOLOGY

INTRODUCTION

Under Alexander the Great the civilized world of the West was largely a Hellenized world. From Egypt all the way to the Indus River Greek models became known and respected. Greek statuary and architecture, for example, begins to be recognized in the art works of India, and a two-way communication, through trade, through travelers, through military observers, and even through philosophers, can be observed. In this era Greek philosophy became known in lands far indeed from its source, and Aristotle, as the pinnacle and capstone of Greek philosophy, became known throughout this world, specifically through Greek manuscripts, through Greek libraries, through Greek teachers and travelers. After the year A.D. 622, the hegira of the Islamic world, when Mohammed went from Mecca to Medina, a new civilization was built, founded partly upon the world of the desert, the world of the great sand and the open sky, the world of the almighty and tremendous Allah, the central and ideal reality to an intensely religious, very earnest, simple-minded, and direct nomadic believer. This world, however, was not a naïve or preliterate world. It was a world eager to affirm that Mohammed was Allah's prophet, but, at the same time, it was familiar with Jews, with Christians, and at the extreme eastern fringe, with Hindus and with Buddhists. It was a world with serious intellectual aims. When it found large-caliber ideas, it became interested. Before long (that is, even before the end of the eighth century) there was such a thing as a philosophical system growing within this world of Islam, and before long there were several such systems. They were all rooted in Greek thought, and, in particular, they were all rooted in Aristotle.

Finding that this scholarly world needed to be articulated professionally with our Western psychological system, we again called upon Professor Richard McKeon, of the University of Chicago, to prepare for us material on Islamic psychology. After this venture with the Arabic post-Hellenistic world of Islam we shall then pick up the thread again, and deal with the Christian utilization of Greek sources in a new historical adventure.

A COMPARISON OF ANCIENT CONCEPTIONS OF THE MIND

by Richard P. McKeon

Ancient conceptions of mind were developed in a context of the statement of problems which men face—religious formulations of their relations to the gods, historical and literary presentations of human actions, scientific analyses of man's place in nature, and moral and political inquiries into the bases of individual virtues and group associations. During the development of the Roman Empire, the varieties of conceptions of the soul were enumerated in these contexts and set in opposition to each other. Cicero's dialogues present the radically different theories of the schools of philosophy in application to religious, moral, political, and philosophical questions. Cicero's schematization was to have a lasting influence in the development of conceptions of the mind by Christian philosophers. Jewish and Mohammedan philosophers worked on similar interpretations of ancient doctrines, and in all three of the great traditions of monotheistic religion some questioned whether any of the pagan conceptions were consistent with religion and some adapted ancient analyses to new problems of action, thought, and religion. The variety of conceptions of the nature of the soul and of its functions which ancient Greek thought contributed to the discussion of theological problems in the Middle Ages is strikingly similar to the distinctions which Hindu philosophers derived from their ancient literature.

THE ISLAMIC CONCEPTION OF THE NATURE AND FUNCTIONS OF THE SOUL

At the beginning of the Mohammedan era in A.D. 622, the date of Mohammed's hegira from Mecca to Medina, much of the scientific literature of Greece had been translated into Arabic. The development of the Islamic conception of mind is in part a reaction against and in part an adaptation of Greek analyses of the nature and the functions of the mind. The first speculative theologians of Islam, the Mu'tazilites, beginning about A.D. 723, used reason in the interpretation of revelation. Reason is a "natural light," and both religion and the world are rational. Al Ash'ari (873–935) was first a "Mu'tazilite," but later abandoned that position since God's freedom cannot be constrained by prior laws of reason. In the history of the development of the conception of mind, Mohammedan philosophers—Alkindi, Alfarabi, Avicenna, and Averroës—unlike Christian philosophers, were not theologians, while the Ash'arites and the orthodox theologians argued that reason and philosophy were inadequate to disclose the nature of the soul and explain its relations to God. Many of the arguments against the philosophers were borrowed from the Stoics and the Skeptics, without commitment to materialism and with skepticism limited to doubt concerning the use of argument and reason in the interpretation of discourse of revelation or *kalam*. The investigations of the philosophers built on the doctrines of Plato and Aristotle concerning the nature and functions of the soul and laid the foundations of many conceptions which were used in the development of modern psychology. The issues between the two included questions concerning the relation of individual minds and the universal intelligence, concerning whether the "agent intellect" is particular to individual men or is one for all mankind, and therefore concerning whether immortality is personal or a property of universal understanding.

Avicenna (980–1037) worked out a reconciliation of the Platonic conception of the soul as a spiritual substance and the Aristotelian conception of the soul as a form of the body. The soul animates the body, but this is its function, not its nature. Taken in itself the soul is a substance endowed with a plurality of powers, (1) the nutritive and generative power of the vegetative soul, (2) the powers of perception, imagination, and voluntary motion of the animal soul, and (3) the ability to know intelligible objects, to invent arts, to speculate about natural objects, and to distinguish good from evil of the human soul. The human soul has active and speculative powers. In the course of his examination of the powers of the soul Avicenna elaborated the distinction between the external perception of the five external senses and the apperception of the internal senses, the functions of imagination and the other internal senses, and the persisting substance of the "ego," which had first been used in a technical sense by the Stoics.

Algazali (1058–1111) came to the defense of orthodoxy in the *Restoration of Religious Knowledge* with elaborations of Ash'arite arguments, and he attacked the philosophers, Avicenna in particular, in a work whose title was translated into Latin during the Middle Ages as *The Destruction of the Philosophers,* but which is rendered more accurately by *The Incoherence of the Philosophers.* The last section of the *Incoherence* is concerned with the confusions of the philosophers in the natural sciences; one of their incoherences is their inability to show by demonstrative proof that the soul is a spiritual substance. Averroës (1126–1198) was known as the Commentator because of his extensive commentaries on the works of Aristotle. Among his commentaries is one on Aristotle's *De Anima.* His conception of the nature and the functions of the soul differs from that of Avicenna, and in his refutation of Algazali in *The Incoherence of the Incoherence* (or *The Destruction of the Destruction*) he sometimes pauses in his refutation of Algazali to criticize Avicenna.

AVICENNA *

Concerning the Soul

CHAPTER I. THE VEGETATIVE SOUL

When the elements are mixed together in a more harmonious way, i.e. in a more balanced proportion than in the cases previously mentioned, other beings also come into existence out of them due to the powers of the heavenly bodies. The first of these are plants. Now some plants are grown from seed and set aside a part of the body bearing the reproductive faculty, while others grow from spontaneous generation without seeds.

Since plants nourish themselves they have the faculty of nutrition. And because it is of the nature of plants to grow, it follows that they have the faculty of growth. Again, since it is the nature of certain plants to reproduce their like and to be reproduced by their like, they have a reproductive faculty. The reproductive faculty is different from the faculty of nutrition, for unripe fruits possess the nutritive but not the reproductive faculty; just as they possess the faculty of growth, but not that of reproduction. Similarly, the faculty of nutrition differs from that of growth. Do you not see that decrepit animals have the nutritive faculty but lack that of growth?

The nutritive faculty transmits food and replaces what has been dissolved with it; the faculty of growth increases the substance of the main structural organs in length, breadth, and depth, not haphazard but in such a way that they can reach the utmost perfection of growth. The reproductive faculty gives the matter the form of the thing; it separates from the parent body a part in which a faculty derived from its origin inheres and which, when the matter and the place which are prepared to receive its activity are present, performs its functions.

It will be evident from the foregoing that all vegetable, animal, and human functions are due to faculties over and above bodily functions, and even over and above the nature of the mixture itself.

After the plant comes the animal, which emerges from a compound of elements whose organic nature is much nearer to the mean than the previous two and is therefore prepared to receive the animal soul, having passed through the stage of the vegetable soul. And so the nearer it approaches the mean the greater is its capacity for receiving yet another psychical faculty more refined than the previous one.

* From F. Rahman, *Avicenna's Psychology: An English Translation of Kitab-al-Najat* (New York: Oxford University Press, 1952), pp. 24–40. Copyright 1952 by Oxford University Press.

The soul is like a single genus divisible in some way into three parts. The first is the vegetable soul, which is the first entelechy of a natural body possessing organs in so far as it is reproduced, grows, and assimilates nourishment. Food is a body whose function it is to become similar to the nature of the body whose food it is said to be, and adds to that body either in exact proportion or more or less what is dissolved.

The second is the animal soul, which is the first entelechy of a natural body possessing organs in so far as it perceives individuals and moves by volition.

The third is the human soul, which is the first entelechy of a natural body possessing organs in so far as it acts by rational choice and rational deduction, and in so far as it perceives universals.

The vegetable soul has three faculties. First, the nutritive faculty which transforms another body into a body similar to that in which it is itself present, and replaces what has been dissolved. Secondly, the faculty of growth which increases every aspect of the body in which it resides, by length, breadth, and depth in proportion to the quantity necessary to make it attain its perfection in growth. Thirdly, the reproductive faculty which takes from the body in which it resides a part which is potentially similar to it and acts upon it with the help of other similar bodies, generating and mixing them so as to render that part actually similar to the body (to which it had been only potentially similar).

CHAPTER II. THE ANIMAL SOUL

The animal soul, according to the primary division, has two faculties —the motive and the perceptive. The motive faculty again is of two kinds: either it is motive in so far as it gives an impulse, or in so far as it is active. Now the motive faculty, in so far as it provides the impulse, is the faculty of appetence. When a desirable or repugnant image is imprinted on the imagination of which we shall speak before long, it rouses this faculty to movement. It has two subdivisions: one is called the faculty of desire which provokes a movement (of the organs) that brings one near to things imagined to be necessary or useful in the search for pleasure. The second is called the faculty of anger, which impels the subject to a movement of the limbs in order to repulse things imagined to be harmful or destructive, and thus to overcome them. As for the motive faculty in its active capacity, it is a power which is distributed through the nerves and muscles, and its function is to contract the muscles and to pull the tendons and ligaments towards the starting-point of the movement, or to relax them or stretch them so that they move away from the starting-point.

The perceptive faculty can be divided into two parts, the external sense and the internal sense. The external senses are the five or eight senses. One of them is sight, which is a faculty located in the concave nerve; it perceives the image of the forms of coloured bodies imprinted on the vitreous humour. These forms are transmitted through actually transparent media to polished surfaces. The second is the sense of hearing, which is a faculty located in the nerves distributed over the surface of the ear-hole; it perceives the form of what is transmitted to it by the vibration of the air which is compressed between two objects, one striking and the other being struck, the latter offering it resistance so as to set up vibrations in the air which produce the sound. This vibration of the air outside reaches the air which lies motionless and compressed in the cavity of the ear, moving it in a way similar to that in which it is itself moved. Its waves touch that nerve, and so it is heard.

The third sense is that of smell, a faculty located in the two protuberances of the front part of the brain which resemble the two nipples of the breasts. It perceives the odour conveyed to it by inhaled air, which is either mixed with the vapour in the air or is imprinted on it through qualitative change in the air produced by an odorous body.

The fourth sense is that of taste, a faculty located in the nerves distributed over the tongue, which perceives the taste dissolved from bodies touching it and mingling with the saliva it contains, thus producing a qualitative change in the tongue itself.

The fifth sense is that of touch, which is a faculty distributed over the entire skin and flesh of the body. The nerves perceive what touches them and are affected when it is opposed to them in quality, and changes are then wrought in their constitution or structure.

Probably this faculty is not one species but a genus including four faculties which are all distributed throughout the skin. The first of them judges the opposition between hot and cold; the second that between dry and moist; the third that between hard and soft; and the fourth that between rough and smooth. But their coexistence in the same organ gives the false impression that they are essentially one.

The forms of all the sensibles reach the organs of sense and are imprinted on them, and then the faculty of sensation perceives them. This is almost evident in touch, taste, smell, and hearing. But concerning sight, a different view has been maintained, for some people have thought that something issues from the eye, meets the object of sight, takes its form from without—and that this constitutes the act of seeing. They often call the thing which according to them issues from the eye, light.

But true philosophers hold the view that when an actually transparent body, i.e. a body which has no colour, intervenes between the eye and the object of sight, the exterior form of the coloured body on which light is falling is transmitted to the pupil of the eye and so the eye perceives it.

This transmission is similar to the transmission of colours by means of light being refracted from a coloured thing and giving its colour to another body. The resemblance is not complete, however, for the former is more like an image in a mirror.

The absurdity of the view that light issues from the eye is shown by the following consideration. What emanates is either a body or a non-body. If it is not a body it is absurd to attribute motion and change of place to it, except figuratively in that there may be a power in the eye which transforms the air and other things it encounters into some sort of quality, so that it may be said that this quality "came out of the eye." Likewise, it is absurd to hold the view that it is a body, because if so then either—

(1) it will remain intact, issuing from the eye and reaching to the sphere of the fixed stars. In this case there will have emerged from the eye, despite its smallness, a conical body of immense size, which will have compressed the air and repulsed all the heavenly bodies, or it will have traversed an empty space. Both these views are manifestly absurd. Or—

(2) it will be dispersed, diffused and split up. In that case the percipient animal will of necessity feel something being detached from him and then dispersed and diffused; also, he will perceive the spots where that ray falls to the exclusion of the spots where it does not fall, so that he will only partially perceive the body, sensing some points here and there but missing the major part. Or—

(3) this emanating body is united with the air and the heavens and becomes one with them, so that the uniform whole is like one organ of the animal. In this case the uniform whole in its entirety will possess sensation. This is a most peculiar change indeed! It follows necessarily that if many eyes co-operate, it will be more powerful. Thus a man when in the company of others would have keener sight than when alone, for many people can effect a more powerful change than a single person. Again, this emanating body will necessarily be either simple or composite, and its composite nature will also be of a particular kind. Its motion then must be either voluntary or natural. But we know that this movement is not voluntary and by choice, although the opening and closing of the eyelids are voluntary. The only remaining alternative is that the movement is natural. But the simple natural movement will be only in one direction, not in many; and so the composite movement will also

be, according to the dominant element, only in one direction, not in many. But it is not so with this movement according to those who support the theory of the "issuing body."

Again, if the sensed object is seen through the base of the conical emanating body which touches it, and not through the angle, it will necessarily follow that the shape and magnitude of the object perceived at a distance will also be perceptible as well as its colour. This is because the percipient subject comes in contact with it and encompasses it. But if it is perceived through the angle, I mean the section between the vitrium and the hypothetical cone, then the remoter the object the smaller will be the angle and also the common section, and consequently the form imprinted on it will also be smaller and will be so perceived. Sometimes the angle will be so small that the object will fail to be perceived and so the form will not be seen at all.

As for the second part, namely that the emanating something is not a body but an accident or a quality, this "changing" or "being changed" will inevitably be more powerful with the increase of the percipient subjects. In that case the same absurdity which we mentioned before will arise. Again, the air will either be merely a medium of transmission or percipient in itself. If it is only a medium of transmission and not percipient, then, as we maintain, perception takes place *in* the pupil of the eye and not outside it. But if the percipient is the air, then the same absurdity which we have already mentioned will be repeated; and it will necessarily follow that whenever there is commotion or disturbance in the air, sight will be distorted with the renewal of "change" and the renewed action of the percipient in perceiving one thing after another, just as when a man runs in calm air his perception of minute things is confused. All this shows that sight is not duc to somcthing issuing from us towards the sensed object. It must therefore be due to something coming towards us from the sensed object; since this is not the body of the object, it must be its form. If this view were not correct, the creation of the eye with all its strata and humours and their respective shape and structure would be useless.

CHAPTER III. INTERNAL SENSES

There are some faculties of internal perception which perceive the form of the sensed things, and others which perceive the "intention" thereof. Some faculties, again, can both perceive and act while others only perceive and do not act. Some possess primary perception, others secondary perception. The distinction between the perception of the form and that of the intention is that the form is what is perceived both by the inner soul and the external sense; but the external sense perceives it first and then transmits it to the soul, as, for example, when the sheep perceives the form of the wolf, i.e. its shape, form, and colour. This form is certainly perceived by the inner soul of the sheep, but it is first perceived by its external sense. As for the intention, it is a thing which the soul perceives from the sensed object without its previously having been perceived by the external sense, just as the sheep perceives the intention of harm in the wolf, which causes it to fear the wolf and to flee from it, without harm having been perceived at all by the external sense. Now what is first perceived by the sense and then by the internal faculties is the form, while what only the internal faculties perceive without the external sense is the intention.

The distinction between perception accompanied or unaccompanied by action is this: it is the function of certain internal faculties to combine certain perceived forms and intentions with others and to separate some of them from others, so that they perceive and also act on what they have perceived. Perception unaccompanied by action takes place when the form or the intention is merely imprinted on the sense organ without the percipient having any power to act upon it at all.

The distinction between primary and secondary perception is that in the former the percipient faculty somehow directly acquires the form, while in the latter the form is acquired through another agent which transmits it to the percipient faculty.

One of the animal internal faculties of perception is the faculty of fantasy, i.e. *sensus communis,* located in the forepart of the front ventricle of the brain. It receives all the forms which are imprinted on the five senses and transmitted to it from them. Next is the faculty of representation located in the rear part of the front ventricle of the brain, which preserves what the *sensus communis* has received from the individual five senses even in the absence of the sensed objects.

It should be remembered that receptivity and preservation are functions of different faculties. For instance, water has the power of receiving an imprint, but lacks that of retaining it. Next is the faculty which is called "sensitive imagination" in relation to the animal soul, and "rational imagination" in relation to the human soul. This faculty is located in the middle ventricle of the brain near the vermiform process, and its function is to combine certain things with others in the faculty of representation, and to separate some things from others as it chooses. Then there is the estimative faculty located in the far end of the middle ventricle of the brain, which perceives the non-sensible intentions that exist in the individual sensible objects, like the faculty which judges that the wolf is to be avoided and the child is to be loved. Next there is the retentive and recollective faculty located in the rear ventricle of the brain, which retains what the estimative faculty perceives of non-sensible intentions existing in individual sensible objects. The relation of the retentive to the estimative faculty is the same as that of the faculty called representation to the *sensus communis.* And its relation to the intentions is the same as that of representation to sensed forms.

These, then, are the faculties of the animal soul. Some animals possess all five senses, while others only some of them. Taste and touch must necessarily be created in all animals, and every animal must especially have the sense of touch; but there are animals which lack the sense of smell, hearing, or sight.

CHAPTER IV. THE RATIONAL SOUL

The human rational soul is also divisible into a practical and a theoretical faculty, both of which are equivocally called intelligence. The practical faculty is the principle of movement of the human body, which urges it to individual actions characterized by deliberation and in accordance with purposive considerations. This faculty has a certain correspondence with the animal faculties of appetence, imagination, and estimation, and a certain dual character in itself. Its relationship to the animal faculty of appetence is that certain states arise in it peculiar to man by which it is disposed to quick actions and passions such as shame, laughter, weeping, etc. Its relationship to the animal faculty of imagination and estimation is that it uses that faculty to deduce plans concerning transitory things and to deduce human arts. Finally, its own dual character is that with the help of the theoretical intelligence it forms the ordinary and commonly accepted opinions concerning actions, as, for instance, that lies and tyranny are evil and other similar premisses which, in books of logic, have been clearly distinguished from the purely rational ones. This faculty must govern all the other faculties of the body in accordance with the laws of another faculty which we shall mention, so that it should not submit to them but that they should be subordinated to it, lest passive dispositions arising from the body and derived from material things should develop in it. These passive dispositions are called bad morals. But far from being passive and submissive this faculty must govern the other bodily faculties so that it may have excellent morals.

It is also possible to attribute morals to the bodily faculties. But if the latter predominate they are in an active state, while the practical intelligence is in a passive one. Thus the same thing produces morals in both. But if the practical intelligence predominates, it is in an active state while the bodily faculties are in a passive one, and this is morals in the strict sense (even so there would be two dispositions or moral characters); or character is only one with two different relationships. If we examine them more closely the reason why morals are attributed to this faculty is that the human soul, as will be shown later, is a single substance which is related to two planes—the one higher and the other lower than itself. It has special faculties which establish the relationship between itself and each plane: the practical faculty which the human soul possesses in relation to the lower plane, which is the body, and its control and management; and the theoretical faculty in relation to the higher plane, from which it passively receives and acquires intelligibles. It is as if our soul has two faces: one turned towards the body, and it must not be influenced by any requirements of the bodily nature; and the other turned towards the higher principles, and it must always be ready to receive from what is there in the higher plane and to be influenced by it. So much for the practical faculty.

CHAPTER V. THE THEORETICAL FACULTY AND ITS DEGREES

The function of the theoretical faculty is to receive the impressions of the universal forms abstracted from matter. If these forms are already abstract in themselves, it simply receives them; if not, it makes them immaterial by abstraction, so that no trace whatever of material attachments remains in them. We will explain this later.

Now this theoretical faculty has different relations to these forms. This is because a thing whose function is to receive another thing is its recipient either potentially or actually. Potentiality is spoken of in three different senses *per prius et posterius*. This term may imply absolute potentiality in which nothing has yet become actual nor has the instrument of its actualization even been achieved, for instance the capacity of an infant to write. Secondly, it may imply a relative potentiality when nothing more than the instrument of the acquisition of actuality has been achieved. For example, an older child who has learnt the use of the pen and the inkpot and knows the value or meaning of the letters is said to have the capacity of writing. Thirdly, it may imply this capacity when the instrument has been perfected, and when by means of the instrument the capacity has been made complete, so that the agent may exercise it whenever he wishes without having to learn or acquire it. The intention is all that is required, as in the case of the capacity said to be possessed by a scribe who has reached perfection in his art, even when he is not actually writing. In the first instance it is called absolute or material potentiality; in the second, possible potentiality; and in the third, *habitus*. Sometimes the second is termed *habitus* and the third the perfection of potentiality.

Thus the relation of the theoretical faculty to the abstract immaterial forms which we have mentioned is sometimes of the nature of absolute potentiality; this faculty belongs to the soul which has not yet realized any portion of the perfection potentially belonging to it. In this stage it is called the "material intelligence," a faculty that is present in every individual of the human species. It is called "material" in view of its resemblance to primary matter, which in itself does not possess any of the forms but is the substratum of all forms. And sometimes its relation is of the nature of possible potentiality, i.e. when out of its possible perfections only the primary intelligibles which are the source and the instrument of the secondary intelligibles have been acquired by the "material potentiality." By the primary intelligibles I mean the basic premisses to which assent is given, not through any process of learning, nor even with any consciousness on the part of the subject giving assent that it might be just as possible for him sometimes to abstain from doing so, just as we necessarily believe that the whole is greater than the part, and that things which are equal to the same thing are equal to one another. So long as only this amount of actualization has been achieved, it is called *intellectus in habitu;* it may also be called the actual intelligence in relation to the first potentiality, because the latter cannot actually think at all, whereas this one does so (when it begins to reason). Sometimes its relation is of the nature of perfected potentiality, when, after the primary intelligible forms, it has also acquired secondary ones except that it does not actually contemplate them or (return to them); it has, as it were, conserved them, so that it can actually contemplate those forms when it wills and knows that it can do so. It is called *intellectus in actu,* because it is an intelligence which thinks whenever it wills without needing any further process of acquisition, although it could be called potential intelligence in relation to what comes next. Lastly, its relation to those forms may be of the nature of absolute actuality, as when they are present to it and it actually contemplates and thinks them and also knows that it does so. At this point it becomes the *intellectus acquisitus,* since we shall soon see that the potential intelligence becomes actual only through an intelligence which is always actual, and that, when the potential intelligence makes some sort of contact with it, certain forms are actually imprinted on the former from the latter. Such forms are therefore acquired from without.

These then are the degrees of the faculties which are called theoretical intellects. At the stage of the acquired intelligence the animal genus and its human species are perfected, and here human potentiality becomes at one with the first principles of all existence.

CHAPTER VI. HOW THE RATIONAL SOUL ACQUIRES KNOWLEDGE

The acquisition of knowledge, whether from someone else or from within oneself, is of various degrees. Some people who acquire knowledge come very near to immediate perception, since their potential intellect which precedes the capacity we have mentioned is the most powerful. If a person can acquire knowledge from within himself, this strong capacity is called "intuition." It is so strong in certain people that they do not need great effort, or instruction and actualization, in order to make contact with the active intelligence. But the primary capacity of such a person for this is so powerful that he might also be said to possess the second capacity; indeed, it seems as though he knows everything from within himself. This is the highest degree of this capacity. In this state the material intelligence must be called "Divine Spirit." It belongs to the genus of *intellectus in habitu,* but is so lofty that not all people share it. It is not unlikely, indeed, that some of these actions attributed to the "Divine Intelligence" because of their powerful and lofty nature overflow into the imagination which symbolizes them in sense-imagery and words in the way which we have previously indicated.

What proves this is the evident fact that the intelligible truths are acquired only when the middle term of a syllogism is obtained. This may be done in two ways: sometimes through intuition, which is an act of mind by which the mind itself immediately perceives the middle term. This power of intuition is quickness of apprehension. But sometimes the middle term is acquired through instruction, although even the first principles of instruction are obtained through intuition, since all knowledge can be reduced ultimately to certain intuitive principles handed down by those who first accepted them to their students.

It is possible that a man may find the truth within himself, and that the syllogism may be effected in his mind without any teacher. This varies both quantitatively and qualitatively; quantitatively, because some people possess a greater number of middle terms which they have discovered themselves; and qualitatively, because some people find the term more quickly than others. Now since these differences are unlimited and always vary in degrees of intensity, and since their lowest point is reached in men who are wholly without intuition, so their highest point must be reached in people who possess intuition regarding all or most problems, or in people who have intuition in the shortest possible time. Thus there might be a man whose soul has such an intense purity and is so firmly linked to the rational principles that he blazes with intuition, i.e. with the receptivity of inspiration coming from the active intelligence concerning everything. So the forms of all things contained in the active intelligence are imprinted on his soul either all at once or nearly so, not that he accepts them merely on authority but on account of their logical order which encompasses all the middle terms. For beliefs accepted on authority concerning those things which are known only through their causes possess no rational certainty. This is a kind of prophetic inspiration, indeed its highest form and the one most fitted to be called Divine Power; and it is the highest human faculty.

It should be seen how some of these faculties govern others. You will find the acquired intellect to be the governor whom all the rest serve. It is the ultimate goal. The *intellectus in habitu* serves the *intellectus in actu,* and is in turn served by the material intellect with all its capacities. The practical intellect serves them all, for attachment to the body, as will shortly become clear, exists for the sake of the perfection and purification of the theoretical intellect, and the practical intellect governs this relationship. It is served by the faculty of estimation which, in its turn, is served by two faculties: an anterior and a posterior. The posterior conserves what is brought to it by estimation, while the anterior is the totality of animal faculties. The faculty of representation is served by two faculties of different origins: the appetitive faculty serves it by obeying it, for the representative faculty impels the appetitive to movement, and the faculty of imagination serves it by accepting the combination and separation of its images. In their turn those two are the governors of two groups. The faculty of imagination is served by *fantasis* or *sensus communis,* which is itself served by the five senses, while the appetitive faculty is served by desire and anger. These last two are served by the motive faculty distributed through the muscles. Here the animal faculties come to an end.

The animal faculties in their entirety are served by the vegetable faculties, of which the reproductive is the first in rank and the highest one. The faculty of growth serves the reproductive, and the nutritive faculty serves them both. The four "natural" faculties—of digestion, retention, assimilation, and excretion—are subservient to all these. The digestive faculty is served on the one hand by the retentive and the assimilative, and on the other by the excretive. The four physical qualities serve these, with cold subservient to heat, while dryness and moisture serve them both. This is the last degree of the faculties.

CHAPTER VII. THE DIFFERENCE BETWEEN PERCEPTION BY SENSE, IMAGINATION, ESTIMATION, AND REASON

It is probable that all perception is but the abstraction by the percipient subject of the form of the perceived object in some manner. If, then, it is a perception of some material object, it consists in somehow abstracting its form from its matter. But the kinds of abstraction are different and its grades various. This is because, owing to matter, the material form is subject to certain states and conditions which do not belong to it *qua* form. So sometimes the abstraction of the form is effected with all or some of these attachments, and sometimes it is complete in that the form is abstracted not only from matter but also from the accidents it possesses. For example, the form or quiddity of man is a nature in which all the individuals of the species share equally, while in its definition it is a single unit: although it is merely by accident that it happens to exist in this or that individual and is thus multiplied. This multiplicity does not belong to it in so far as it is the nature of man, for, if multiplicity were essential to this nature, then "man" would not be predicated of what is numerically one. Again, if the quiddity of man were present in Zaid merely because it is his own quiddity, it could not be attributed to 'Amr. Consequently, one of the accidents which occur to the human quiddity through matter is multiplicity and divisibility.

Besides these it is also subject to other accidents, namely, when it is present in any matter it possesses to a certain degree quantity, quality, place, and position. All these are accidents foreign to its nature, since if its possession of this particular measure or any other particular measure of quantity, quality, place, and position were due to its being man's nature, all men would equally participate in all these concepts. It follows that the quiddity of man itself does not necessitate any of these accidents, which must therefore be accidents occurring to it on account of their matter. For the matter with which the form is conjoined has already been subject to them and then sense abstracts the form from matter along with these accidents and its relationship with matter. If this relationship is removed, the process of abstraction will be nullified. This is because sensation cannot disentangle form from matter completely divorced from material accidents, nor can it retain that form after the absence of matter. Thus it seems that it cannot effect a complete detachment of form from matter, but needs the presence of matter if the form is to remain present to it.

But the faculty of representation purifies the abstracted form to a higher degree, since it takes it from matter in such a way that it does not need the presence of matter for the presence of form. For, even after the absence or corruption of matter, the form remains in the representative faculty, although even here it is not divested of its material accidents. Sense neither abstracts it completely from matter, nor from the accidents of matter. But representation does so in the first instance but not in the second, since the forms in representation are, in this respect, the same as the sensed forms and they possess a certain quantity, and position. It is impossible for a form in representation to be such as to admit all the individuals of the species to share in it, for a man in representation resembles always a particular man among men, and there might be men really existing as well as represented who are quite different from that particular man in representation.

The faculty of estimation goes a little farther than this in abstraction, for it receives the intentions which in themselves are non-material, although they accidentally happen to be in matter. This is because shape, colour, position, etc., are attributes which cannot be found except in bodily matters, but good and evil, agreeable and disagreeable, etc., are in themselves non-material entities and their presence in matter is accidental. The proof of their being non-material is this: If it were of their essence to be material, then good and evil, agreeable and disagreeable would be inconceivable except as accidents in a physical body. But sometimes they are conceived in themselves apart from matter. It is clear that in themselves they are non-material and their being in matter is entirely by accident. It is such entities which the faculty of estimation perceives; and thus it perceives non-material objects which it abstracts from matter. This abstraction is relatively more perfect and nearer the absolute than in the previous two forms of the process. For all this, however, it does not abstract the form from all accidents of matter, because it apprehends it in its individuality and according to its particular matter and its attachments to sensible images conditioned by material accidents with the cooperation of representation. But the faculty in which the fixed forms are either the forms of existents which are not at all material and do not occur in matter by accident, or the forms of existents which in themselves are not material but happen to be so by accident, or the forms of material existents though purified in all respects from material attachments—such a faculty obviously perceives the forms by taking them as completely abstracted from matter in all respects. This is evident in the case of existents which are in themselves free from matter. As to those existents which are present in matter, either because their existence is material or because they are by accident material, this faculty completely abstracts them both from matter and from their material attachments in every respect and perceives them in pure abstraction. Thus in the case of "man" which is predicated of many, this faculty takes the unitary nature of the many, divests it of all material quantity, quality, place, and position, and abstracts it from all these in such a way that it can be attributed to all men. In this way the knowledge of the various judging faculties—sensation, representation, estimation, and intellect—is distinguished; and throughout the present chapter we have been directing our discourse to this very issue.

AVERROËS *

The Second Discussion

Their impotence to show by demonstrative proof that the human soul is a spiritual substance which exists by itself and does not fill space, is neither body nor impressed on a body, is neither continuous with the body nor separated from the body, just as neither God nor the angels according to them is outside or inside the world

Ghazali says:

The discussion of this question demands the exposition of their theory about the animal and human faculties. The animal faculties are divided according to them into motive and apprehensive, and the apprehensive are of two classes, the external and the internal. The external are the five senses, and these faculties are entities impressed on the bodies. The internal are three in number. The first is the representative faculty in the foremost part of the brain behind the faculty of sight; in it the forms of the things seen remain after the closing of the eye, and in this faculty there is impressed and collected what the five senses bring to it, and it is therefore called the common sense. If it did not exist, a man who saw white honey and perceives its sweetness by taste could not, when he saw it a second time, apprehend its sweetness as long as he had not tasted it as he did the first time, but in the common sense there is something which judges that this white is the sweetness, and there is in it, no doubt, a judging element for which both these things, colour and sweetness, are brought together and which determines then that when the one is present the other must be there too.

The second is the estimative faculty, which is that which apprehends the intentions whereas the first apprehends the forms; and the meaning of "forms" is "that which cannot be without matter, i.e. body," whereas the meaning of "intentions" is "that which does not require a body for its existence, although it can happen that it occurs in a body"—like enmity and concord. The sheep perceives the colour, shape, and appearance of the wolf, which are only found in body, but it perceives also that the wolf is its enemy, and the lamb perceives the shape and colour of its mother and then perceives its love and tenderness, and for this reason it

* From Averroës, *Tahafut Al-Tahafut* (*The Incoherence of the Incoherence*), trans. by Simon van der Bergh (New York: Oxford University Press, 1954), I, 333–336. Copyright 1954 by Oxford University Press.

flees from the wolf while it walks behind the mother. Discord and concord need not be in bodies like colour and shape, but it sometimes happens that they occur in bodies. This faculty differs from the first, and is located in the posterior ventricle of the brain.

The third faculty is called in animals the imaginative and in man the cogitative, and its nature is to combine the sensible forms and to compose the intentions with the forms: it is located in the middle ventricle between the place where the forms are kept and that where the intentions are retained. Because of this man can imagine a horse that flies and a being with the head of a man and the body of a horse, and other combinations, although he has never seen such things. It is more appropriate, as will be shown, to join this faculty with the motive faculties than with the apprehensive. The places where these faculties are located are known only through medicine, for if a lesion occurs to one of these ventricles the faculties become defective.

Further, the philosophers affirm that the faculty on which the forms of sensible things are impressed through the five senses retains these forms so that they do not disappear after their reception, for one thing does not retain another through the faculty by which it receives it, for water receives without retaining, while wax receives through its wetness and retains through its dryness, by contrast with water. Through this consideration that which retains is different from that which receives, and this is called the retentive faculty. And in the same way intentions are impressed on the estimative faculty, and a faculty retains them, which is called the memorative. Through this consideration, these internal perceptions, when the imaginative faculty is joined to them, become five in number, like the external faculties.

The motive faculties form two classes, in so far as they are only stimulating motion or executing motion and acting; the stimulating motive faculty is the impulsive and appetitive faculty; this is the faculty which stimulates the acting motive power to move when, in the representative faculty which we have mentioned, there is inscribed the form of something to be sought or avoided. The stimulating faculty has two branches, one called concupiscent which excites to a movement, through which there is an approach to the things represented as necessary or useful in a search for pleasure, and the irascible which excites to a movement through which the thing represented as injurious or mischievous is removed as one seeks to master it. Through this faculty the complete determination to act is affected, which is called will.

The motive faculty which itself executes movement is a faculty which is diffused in the nerves and muscles and has the function of contracting the muscles and drawing the tendons and ligaments which are in contact with the limbs in the direction where this faculty resides, or of relaxing and extending them so that the ligaments and tendons move in the opposite direction. These are the animal faculties of the soul as described in a summary way, without the details.

And as regards the soul which thinks things and is called the rational or discursive soul by the philosophers (and by "discursive" is meant "rational," because discourse is the most typical external operation of reason and therefore the intellective soul takes its name from it), it has two faculties, a knowing and an acting, and both are called intellect, though equivocally. And the acting faculty is one which is a principle moving man's body towards the well-ordered human arts, whose order derives from the deliberation proper to man. The knowing faculty, which is called the speculative, is one which has the function of perceiving the real natures of the intelligibles in abstraction from matter, place, and position; and these are the universal concepts which the theologians call sometimes conditions and sometimes modes, and which the philosophers call abstract universals.

The soul has therefore two faculties on two sides: the speculative faculty on the side of the angels, since through it it receives from the angels knowledge of realities (and this faculty must always be receptive for the things coming from above); and the practical faculty on the inferior side, which is the side of the body which it directs and whose morals it improves. This faculty must rule over all the other bodily faculties, and all the others must be trained by it and subjected to it. It must not itself be affected or influenced by them, but they must be influenced by it, in such a way that there will not through the bodily attributes occur in the soul subservient dispositions, called vices, but that this faculty may remain predominant and arouse in the soul dispositions called virtues.

This is a summary of the human vital faculties, which they distinguished and about which they spoke at great length, and we have omitted the vegetative faculties, since there is no need to mention them as they are not connected with our subject. Nothing of what we have mentioned need be denied on religious grounds, for all these things are observable facts whose habitual course has been provided by God. We only want now to refute their claim that the soul being an essence subsistent by itself can be known by demonstrative rational proofs, and we do not seek to refute those who say that it is impossible that this knowledge should derive from God's power or who believe that the religious law is opposed to this; for perhaps it will be clear at the dividing on the Day of Judgement that the Holy Law regards it as true. However, we reject their claim that this can be known by mere reason and the religious law is not necessary for its knowledge, and we shall ask them to produce their proofs and indeed they have many.

I say:

All this is nothing but an account of the theory of the philosophers about these faculties and his conception of them; only he followed Avicenna, who distinguished himself from the rest of the philosophers by assuming in the animal another faculty than the imaginative, which he calls the estimative faculty and which replaces the cogitative faculty in man, and he says that the ancients applied the term "imaginative faculty" to the estimative, and when they do this then the imaginative faculty in the animal is a substitute for the cogitative faculty in man and will be located in the middle ventricle of the brain. And when the term "imaginative" is applied to the faculty which apprehends shape, this is said to reside in the foremost part of the brain. There is no contradiction in the fact that the retentive and memorative faculties should both be in the posterior part of the brain, for retaining and memory are two in function, but one in their substratum. And what appears from the theory of the ancients is that the imaginative faculty in the animal is that which determines that the wolf should be an enemy of the sheep and that the sheep should be a friend of the lamb, for the imaginative faculty is a perceptive one and it necessarily possesses judgement, and there is no need to introduce another faculty. What Avicenna says would only be possible if the imaginative faculty were not perceptive; and there is no sense in adding another faculty to the imaginative in the animal, especially in an animal which possesses many arts by nature, for its representations are not derived from the senses and seem to be perceptions intermediary between the intellectual and the sensible forms, and the question of these forms is concisely treated in *De sensu et sensato*, and we shall leave this subject here and return to Ghazali's objections against the philosophers.

Ghazali says:

The first proof is that they say that intellectual cognitions inhere in human souls, and are limited and have units which cannot be divided, and therefore their substratum must also be indivisible and every body is divisible, and this proves that the substratum of the cognitions is something incorporeal. One can put this into a logical form according to the figures of logic, but the easiest way is to say that if the substratum of knowledge is a divisible body, then the knowledge which inheres in it must be divisible too: but the inherent knowledge is not divisible, and therefore the substratum is not a body: and this is a mixed hypothetical syllogism in which the consequent is denied, from which there follows the denial of the antecedent in all cases; and there is no doubt about the validity of this figure of the syllogism, nor again about its premisses, for the major is that everything inherent in something divisible is necessarily divisible, the divisibility of its substratum being assumed, and this is a major about which one cannot have any doubt. The minor is that knowledge as a unity inheres in man and is not divided, for its infinite division is impossible, and if it is limited, then it comprises no doubt units which cannot be divided: and in short, when we know a thing, we cannot assume that a part can cease and a part remain, because it has no parts.

The objection rests on two points. It may be said:

"How will you refute those who say that the substratum of knowledge is an atom in space which cannot be divided, as is known from the theory of the theologians?" And then there remains nothing to be said against it but to question its possibility, and to ask how all that is known can exist in one atom, whereas all the atoms which surround this one are deprived of it although they are near to it. But to question its possibility has no value, as one can also turn it against the doctrine of the philosophers, by asking how the soul can be one single thing which is not in space or outside the body, either continuous with it or separated from it. However, we should not stress this first point, for the discussion of the problem of the atom is lengthy, and the philosophers have geometrical proofs against it whose discussion is intricate, and one of their many arguments is to ask "Does one of the sides of an atom between two atoms touch the identical spot the other side touches or not?" The former is impossible, because its consequence would be that the two sides coincided, whereas a thing that is in contact with another is in contact, and the latter implies the affirmation of a plurality and divisibility, and the solution of this difficulty is long and we need not go deeper into it and will now turn to the other point.

Your affirmation that everything which inheres in a body must be divisible in contradicted by what you say of the estimative faculty of the sheep where the hostility of the wolf is concerned, for in the judgement of one single thing no division can be imagined, since hostility has no part, so that one part of it might be perceived and another neglected.

Four

THE RENAISSANCE AND THE ENLIGHTENMENT

INTRODUCTION

The conception of human nature which had gradually taken shape in more than a thousand years of interaction between the Greco-Roman outlook and the Christian teaching had reached a stable and satisfying form. Just as the cathedrals represented the moral and esthetic aspirations of mankind, so the philosophy of St. Thomas Aquinas represented the rational and orderly systematization of theology and its intimate union with the teachings of Aristotle.

We saw earlier how the Greco-Roman outlook had gradually been shattered by physical, economic, and moral forces that were too great for it. A millennium later the intellectual, esthetic, and moral unity of the thirteenth century had reached a high pitch. There were, however, many forces already evident in the thirteenth century which began to challenge it. The development here and there of new trade routes by land and sea, the use of the mariner's compass, and of gunpowder and other military tools, the progressive rediscovery of the Greek and Roman civilization, ushered in a new social order. By the fifteenth century a rebirth or renaissance had begun to spread rapidly over Europe. This rebirth was in some respects an actual rebirth of the Greco-Roman spirit. Indeed, Greek scholars, fleeing from the falling city of Constantinople in 1453, brought a knowledge and love of things Greek to Italy and to the West. The poet Petrarch and his contemporaries made every inch of Greco-Roman antiquity, every shred of its poetry and sculpture, the basis for the new expression. The commercial expansion of the maritime powers after the voyages of Columbus and Vasco da Gama represented a restless adventuresome quest of new wealth and of new discovery. All this tended to pose a fresh challenge to the philosopher; the old philosophies must, in the spirit of the new times, be challenged, just as everything else was challenged. The Polish monk Copernicus put the sun at the center and the planets at various points, steering their paths around the sun. This, together with a rapid restoration of Greek medicine, and soon the beginning of the dissection of the human body, had direct and tremendous implications for psychology. Man was to be seen now not solely in terms of theological definitions, but in terms of fresh acts of discovery. Just as the adventurers to the new world brought back new conceptions of what human life was like, so the new instruments—mariner's compass, magnet, and, a moment later, Galileo's telescope—expressed the need to examine all first principles regarding man, as regarding everything else.

Just as we found among the early Greek philosophers the need to challenge everything and get to the heart and core of reality, so now we find in the Renaissance a succession of philosophers outdoing one another in the struggle to get back to first principles, to find what can really be known, to get beyond all authorities, and to deduce by the clear light of intellectual inquiry the nature of the world and of the mind itself which conducts the inquiry.

Some have challenged this conception of a "rebirth." Yet on the one hand there was the beginning of the rediscovery of the great classical civilization of the Mediterranean world, as Roman architecture, Roman poetry, and in time Greek poetry, drama, and philosophy flooded the scholar's world; and the "revival of learning" was upon us. At the same time the new attention to Greek mathematics in the work of Galileo and the experimental science which followed made clear that the old world was in fact offering a *new* world; that the new continents and the new scientific and artistic dimensions of our own European life were transforming this world almost within the twinkling of an eye. Here and there, indeed, there was nostalgia for the old, as in Albrecht Dürer's fantasy of "melancholy." Man realized that the safe and good world of medieval spirituality was gone and that something fraught with a strange foreboding was at hand. The same basic doubt appears in the cynicism of Machiavelli, who reminds the prince that fear is more potent than love in controlling the public.

Yet, despite the intense dislocations and sufferings of the Renaissance, the wars, the plagues, the tortures, the persecutions, the primary note to which man returns in the Renaissance is the *spirit of discovery* in the work of Galileo, the spirit of exploration in the work of Columbus, the spirit of beauty as expressed in Leonardo da Vinci; and the conception of a new world heralded everywhere in the West has been a striving for new definitions of the meaning of life. If there is any doubt about this, look for a moment at Germany in the sixteenth century, in contrast to France or Italy, for Germany is only slowly responding to the Renaissance and gets the main effect of it a century or two later; or look at Russia, in which there is but little of the Renaissance to be identified, or at Greece, to whom these magnificent reawakenings were made forever impossible by the conquest of Byzantium by the Turks in 1453. The Renaissance is definitely a matter of Western Europe.

It is, of course, for this reason that our psychological stream, as it begins flowing again, flows through the channels of Italian, French, Dutch, British, and, a little later, German, thought, simultaneously with the medical, scientific, and artistic revivals, and reaches its fullest expression wherever free contemplation, a pure philosophical spirit, or a challenge to observe and to speculate on the economic and political events of the times is offered. As it happened, the two greatest figures in the remaking of psychology were both Aristotelian scholars, who, along with the students of the new physics of the seventeenth century, usher in the new era in psychology. These two are René Descartes and Thomas Hobbes.

Like many other thinkers, ancient and modern, Descartes began with a search for some principle which was safe and solid, which would convince him of the reality of a proposition which was beyond all doubt or conjecture, and which would allow deductive thinking to derive from this central principle a sound system of knowledge about what really exists. The reader will recall that in the age of Socrates and the Sophists, the question whether knowledge is more than "appearance" had been agitated back and forth, as indeed it still is. Descartes convinced himself that since he was aware of his own thought by virtue of the sheer fact that he was doubting and thinking, he could achieve certainty that he himself existed.

RENÉ DESCARTES

Meditations on the First Philosophy *

I. OF THE THINGS OF WHICH WE MAY DOUBT

Several years have now elapsed since I first became aware that I had accepted, even from my youth, many false opinions for true, and that consequently what I afterwards based on such principles was highly doubtful . . .

To-day, then, since I have opportunely freed my mind from all cares, [and am happily disturbed by no passions], and since I am in the secure possession of leisure in a peaceable retirement, I will at length apply myself earnestly and freely to the general overthrow of all my former opinions. But, to this end, it will not be necessary for me to show that the whole of these are false—a point, perhaps, which I shall never reach; but as even now my reason convinces me that I ought not the less carefully to withhold belief from what is not entirely certain and indubitable, than from what is manifestly false, it will be sufficient to justify the rejection of the whole if I shall find in each some ground for doubt. Nor for this purpose will it be necessary even to deal with each belief individually, which would be truly an endless labour; but, as the removal from below of the foundation necessarily involves the downfall of the whole edifice, I will at once approach the criticism of the principles on which all my former beliefs rested.

All that I have, up to this moment, accepted as possessed of the highest truth and certainty, I received either from or through the senses. I observed, however, that these sometimes misled us; and it is the part of prudence not to place absolute confidence in that by which we have even once been deceived. . . .

* From René Descartes, *Meditations on the First Philosophy,* trans. by John Veitch, in Benjamin Rand (ed.), *Modern Classical Philosophers* (2nd ed.; Boston: Houghton Mifflin Company, 1924), pp. 117–118, 122–124, 127. Copyright 1924 by Benjamin Rand.

II. OF THE NATURE OF THE HUMAN MIND; AND THAT IT IS MORE EASILY KNOWN THAN THE BODY

The Meditation of yesterday has filled my mind with so many doubts, that it is no longer in my power to forget them. Nor do I see, meanwhile, any principle on which they can be resolved; and, just as if I had fallen all of a sudden into very deep water, I am so greatly disconcerted as to be unable either to plant my feet firmly on the bottom or sustain myself by swimming on the surface. I will, nevertheless, make an effort, and try anew the same path on which I had entered yesterday, that is, proceed by casting aside all that admits of the slightest doubt, not less than if I had discovered it to be absolutely false; and I will continue always in this track until I shall find something that is certain, or at least, if I can do nothing more, until I shall know with certainty that there is nothing certain. Archimedes, that he might transport the entire globe from the place it occupied to another, demanded only a point that was firm and immoveable; so also, I shall be entitled to entertain the highest expectations, if I am fortunate enough to discover only one thing that is certain and indubitable.

I suppose, accordingly, that all the things which I see are false (fictitious); I believe that none of those objects which my fallacious memory represents ever existed; I suppose that I possess no senses; I believe that body, figure, extension, motion, and place are merely fictions of my mind. What is there, then, that can be esteemed true? Perhaps this only, that there is absolutely nothing certain.

But how do I know that there is not something different altogether from the objects I have now enumerated, of which it is impossible to entertain the slightest doubt? Is there not a God, or some being, by whatever name I may designate him, who causes these thoughts to arise in my mind? But why suppose such a being, for it may be I myself am capable of producing them? Am I, then, at least not something? But I before denied that I possessed senses or a body; I hesitate, however, for what follows from that? Am I so dependent on the body and the senses that without these I cannot exist? But I had the persuasion that there was absolutely nothing in the world, that there was no sky and no earth, neither minds nor bodies; was I not, therefore, at the same time, persuaded that I did not exist? Far from it; I assuredly existed, since I was persuaded. But there is I know not what being, who is possessed at once of the highest power and the deepest cunning, who is constantly employing all his ingenuity in deceiving me. Doubtless, then, I exist, since I am deceived; and, let him deceive me as he may, he can never bring it about that I am nothing, so long as I shall be conscious that I am something. So that it must, in fine, be maintained, all things being maturely and carefully considered, that this proposition (*pronunciatum*) I am, I exist, is necessarily true each time it is expressed by me, or conceived in my mind. . . .

But what, then, am I? A thinking thing, it has been said. But what is a thinking thing? It is a thing that doubts, understands [conceives], affirms, denies, wills, refuses, that imagines also, and perceives. Assuredly it is not little, if all these properties belong to my nature. But why should they not belong to it? Am I not that very being who now doubts of almost everything; who, for all that, understands and conceives certain things; who affirms one alone as true, and denies the others; who desires to know more of them, and does not wish to be deceived; who imagines many things, sometimes even despite his will; and is likewise percipient of many, as if through the medium of the senses. Is there nothing of all this as true as that I am, even although I should be always dreaming, and although he who gave me being employed all his ingenuity to deceive me? Is there also any one of these attributes that can be properly distinguished from my thought, or that can be said to be separate from myself? For it is of itself so evident that it is I who doubt, I who understand, and I who desire, that it is here unnecessary to add anything by way of rendering it more clear. And I am as certainly the same being who imagines; for, although it may be (as I before supposed) that nothing I imagine is true, still the power of imagination does not cease really to exist in me and to form part of my thought. In fine, I am the same being who perceives, that is, who apprehends certain objects as by the organs of sense, since, in truth, I see light, hear a noise, and feel heat. But it will be said that these presentations are false, and that I am dreaming. Let it be so. At all events it is certain that I seem to see light, hear a noise, and feel heat; this cannot be false, and this is what in me is properly called perceiving (*sentire*), which is nothing else than thinking. From this I begin to know what I am with somewhat greater clearness and distinctness than heretofore.

Whatever the modern reader may think of Descartes' certainty about his own existence, he will probably be glad to see the attention given by Descartes to the actual *course of thought* as contrasted with the *rules of thought* that are set up in Aristotle's logic. At the same time, he may wonder whether the fact that thoughts *occur* tells anything about the *conditions* under which thoughts can exist or be observed. Descartes thinks that he has demonstrated the reality of the "I," the first person singular. But are there not thoughts which passed a moment ago and which now have been forgotten, which therefore could not be caught and introspectively described; and indeed may not the course of such thoughts be an expression of *events of which we are wholly unaware?* From this vantage point we may go on to ask whether the existence of these conscious processes which we call thoughts proves anything about an enduring substance, ego, self, first person singular, which remains unchanged. In fact, as William James was to say, in 1890, the existence of a thought does not prove the existence of a thinker. We may be dealing with a stream which is not substantively the same stream that it will be tomorrow; it has some continuity of form, but in substance there is no necessary "first person singular" except by inference. Indeed, if we look closely we find we are still dealing with a philosopher's preference for deductive philosophical method rather than a willingness to observe more closely what the exact tissue and texture of his thought may be.

Descartes' claim to a major position as a *psychologist* is surely warranted by his ingenuity in the application of mathematics and mechanics to psychological processes. Two vast descriptive systems for the apprehension of mathematical reality had existed: the method of geometry as it had descended from Euclid, and the system of algebra as derived from India and from the Arabs. The one method appeals to the "visual imagination" and represents the world in terms of points, lines, surfaces, solids; the other method appeals to a conceptual imagination which is little, if at all, concerned with visual representation. It says that $(A + B)^2 = A^2 + 2AB + B^2$. It remained for Descartes to show in his "Analytical Geometry" that any geometrical proposition has its algebraic expression and that any algebraic expression can be represented in the terms of plane geometry. It is possible, indeed, to mark off by "Cartesian coordinates" a geometric representation of any system of quantitative relationships. We find ourselves here embarking upon a new way of looking at the whole world of those objects which are capable of being measured and the measurements integrated into a mechanics by means of which we can predict eclipses, drive motorcars, and launch projectiles or men at the moon. It was the same Descartes who applied this way of thinking to the human body, and who proudly said that he would treat emotions "after the manner of physics."

We might think that as a mathematical craftsman he would be the first of all the mechanistically minded psychologists. Here, however, we encounter a paradox. He is the great mechanist and the great anti-mechanist. While Descartes went on confidently to show that the bodies of animals are machines and their behavior can be predicted in machine language, he resolutely rejected any such concept in the case of man. He showed, as in the passage about to be quoted, that the *body* of man obeys such laws, but that the soul of man, being an "unextended thing" occupying no space, intervenes in the physical actions of the body, and guides human conduct in a manner which lies utterly beyond the realm of mechanism. While it was relatively easy for LaMettrie, a century later, to write *Man a Machine,* and to hold that the principle of mechanical causation applies fully to man, just as it applies to animals, Descartes clung to the doctrine of "dualism" (see page 12), finding a place for psychological study of rational processes above and beyond the world of physics. Let us let Descartes have his say on the mind-body interaction:

Passions of the Soul *

ARTICLE XVI

How all the limbs can be moved by the objects of the senses and by the spirits without the aid of the soul.

Finally, it is to be observed that the machine of our body is so constructed that all the changes which occur in the motion of the spirits may cause them to open certain pores of the brain rather than others, and, reciprocally, that when any one of these pores is opened in the least degree more or less than is usually by the action of the nerves which

* From René Descartes, *Passions of the Soul,* trans. by Henry A. P. Torrey, in Benjamin Rand (ed.), *The Classical Psychologists* (Boston: Houghton Mifflin Company, 1912), pp. 172–174, 176–178. Copyright 1912 by Benjamin Rand.

serve the senses, this changes somewhat the motion of the spirits, and causes them to be conducted into the muscles which serve to move the body in the way in which it is commonly moved on occasion of such action; so that all the movements which we make without our will contributing thereto (as frequently happens when we breathe, or walk, or eat, and, in fine, perform all those actions which are common to us and the brutes) depend only on the conformation of our limbs and the course which the spirits, excited by the heat of the heart, naturally follow in the brain, in the nerves, and in the muscles, in the same way that the movement of a watch is produced by the force solely of its mainspring and the form of its wheels. . . .

ARTICLE XXX

That the soul is united to all parts of the body conjointly.

But, in order to understand all these things more perfectly, it is necessary to know that the soul is truly joined to the entire body, and that it cannot properly be said to be in any one of its parts to the exclusion of the rest, because the body is one, and in a manner indivisible, on account of the arrangement of its organs, which are so related to one another, that when any one of them is taken away, that makes the whole body defective: and because the soul is of a nature which has no relation to extension, or to dimensions, or other properties of the matter of which the body is composed, but solely to the whole collection of its organs, as appears from the fact that we cannot at all conceive of the half or the third of a soul, nor what space it occupies, and that it does not become any smaller when any part of the body is cut off, but that it separates itself entirely from it when the combination of its organs is broken up.

ARTICLE XXXI

That there is a small gland in the brain in which the soul exercises its functions more particularly than in the other parts.

It is, also, necessary to know that, although the soul is joined to the entire body, there is, nevertheless, a certain part of the body in which it exercises its functions more particularly than in all the rest; and it is commonly thought that this part is the brain, or, perhaps, the heart: the brain, because to it the organs of sense are related; and the heart, because it is as if there the passions are felt. But, after careful examination, it seems to me quite evident that the part of the body in which the soul immediately exercises its functions is neither the heart, nor even the brain as a whole, but solely the most interior part of it, which is a certain very small gland, situated in the middle of its substance, and so suspended above the passage by which the spirits of its anterior cavities communicate with those of the posterior, that the slightest motions in it may greatly affect the course of these spirits, and, reciprocally, that the slightest changes which take place in the course of the spirits may greatly affect the motions of this gland.

ARTICLE XXXII

How this gland is known to be the principal seat of the soul.

The reason which convinces me that the soul cannot have in the whole body any other place than this gland where it exercises its functions immediately, is the consideration that the other parts of our brain are all double, just as also we have two eyes, two hands, two ears, and, in fine, all the organs of our external senses are double; and inasmuch as we have but one single and simple thought of the same thing at the same time, there must necessarily be some place where the two images which by means of the two eyes, or the two other impressions which come from a single object by means of the double organs of the other senses, may unite in one before they reach the mind, in order that they may not present to it two objects in place of one; and it may easily be conceived that these images or other impressions unite in this gland, through the medium of the spirits which fill the cavities of the brain; but there is no other place whatever in the whole body, where they can thus be united, except as they have first been united in this gland.

ARTICLE XXXIV

How the soul and the body act one upon the other.

Let us conceive, then, that the soul has its principal seat in this little gland in the middle of the brain, whence it radiates to all the rest of the body by means of the spirits, the nerves, and even of the blood, which, participating in the impressions of the mind, can carry them by means of the arteries into all the members; and, bearing in mind what has been said above concerning the machine of our body, to wit, that the minute filaments of our nerves are so distributed throughout all its parts that, on occasion of the different motions which are excited there by means of sensible objects, they open in divers manners the pores of the brain, which causes the animal spirits contained in these cavities to enter in various ways into the muscles, by means of which they can move the limbs in all the different ways of which they are capable, and, also, that all the other causes, which in other ways can set the spirits in motion, have the effect to turn them upon various muscles [keeping all this in mind], let us add here that the little gland which is the principal seat of the soul is so suspended between the cavities which contain the spirits, that it can be affected by them in all the different ways that there are sensible differences in objects; but that it can also be variously affected by the soul, which is of such a nature that it receives as many different impressions—that is to say, that it has as many different perceptions—as there occur different motions in this gland; as also, reciprocally, the machine of the body is so composed that from the simple fact that this gland is variously affected by the soul, or by whatever other cause, it impels the spirits which surround it toward the pores of the brain, which discharge them by means of the nerves upon the muscles, whereby it causes them to move the limbs. . . .

ARTICLE XL

The principal effect of the passions.

It is to be noted that the principal effect of all the passions in man is that they incite and dispose the mind to will the things to which they prepare the body, so that the sentiment of fear incites it to will to fly; that of courage, to will to fight; and so of the rest.

ARTICLE XLI

The power of the mind over the body.

But the will is so free in its nature that it can never be constrained; and of the two kinds of thoughts which I have distinguished in the mind —of which one is its actions, that is, its volitions; the other its passions, taking this word in its most general signification, comprehending all sort of perceptions—the first of these are absolutely in its power, and can be changed only indirectly by the body, while, on the contrary, the last depend absolutely on the movements which give rise to them, and they can be affected only indirectly by the mind, except when it is itself the cause of them. And the whole action of the mind consists in this, that by the simple fact of its willing anything it causes the little gland, to which it is closely joined, to produce the result appropriate to the volition.

ARTICLE XLIII

How the mind can imagine, attend, and move the body.

Thus, when it is desired to imagine something which has never been seen, the will has the power to cause the gland to move in the manner requisite to impel the spirits toward the pores of the brain by the opening of which that thing can be represented; so, when one wills to keep his attention fixed for some time upon the same object, this volition keeps the gland inclined during that time in the same direction; so, finally, when one wills to walk or to move his body in any way, this volition causes the gland to impel the spirits toward the muscles which serve that purpose.

❀

Descartes' mind-body dualism began to run into rougher and rougher water as physical and biological science progressed. Just as Harvey's principle of the circulation of the blood (1627) had begun to push mechanical concepts more and more into the problems of physiology, it became harder and harder for the soul to weave its way in and out, so to speak, through the physical agencies studied by physiology. But in historical terms this is selling Descartes short. There was in Descartes' conception of reflex action, as embodied in the reflex behavior of animals, a principle congenial to the newly developing life sciences, and one destined to a long and vigorous career.

The work of Descartes marks a new epoch in philosophy and in psychology. Indeed, many would begin modern psychology with him. For 150 years he was the center and core of French psychology; his two great successors and followers achieve their place in the record by developing and making more vivid some of the more central doctrines of Descartes. Malebranche developed the physiological aspects of Descartes' speculations and suggested that the emotional life as experienced in its inwardness by men who love or fear, or hope or despair, may be a reverberation of the inner physiological responses at the time, while the brilliant materialist LaMettrie asked whether the machine-like behavior of animals might likewise be found in mankind, and whether we might not quite literally call man a machine.

The world of Descartes appears to be the world of mathematics and mechanics. But it is likewise the world of the philosopher's anxiety to be as scientific in the study of his own soul as he is in the study of numbers, lines, and surface. We shall have to conceive him in both these roles, as physicist-mathematician, and as contender for the precious prize of absolute philosophical certainty. Indeed, his psychology partakes of both qualities.

THOMAS HOBBES

The basic forces acting upon Descartes—the new mathematics and physics, the decline of ancient authorities, the resulting conception that man is knowable as he has never been knowable before, and that there are methods by which the inquiry may be pursued—were all acting upon the thoughtful Englishman of the same era. Opinions will differ as to the intellectual stature of the English philosopher-psychologist Thomas Hobbes, who in the same era set English empiricism—that is, the direct derivation of knowledge from experience—upon a new path. Certainly Hobbes, friend of many of the philosophers and public figures of Britain and France, derived a considerable part of his psychology from Aristotle and a considerable part of his mathematics and physics from Descartes (including, of course, the ideas which Descartes himself was deriving from Italy). On the other hand, there can be no doubt that the new empiricism, and the new reliance upon physics, were pushed by Hobbes much further than by anyone else. He saw and boldly pushed forward the ancient conception that material particles in motion could be the explanation both of the physical world and of human life (see pages 78–93), in this manner reviving the doctrines of Democritus and Epicurus, and at the same time paying closer attention to the social conditions of man's psychological life than had ever been attempted since the time of Aristotle. He welded together the physical and the political conception of mankind, in a form intensely meaningful as one watches the whirling new kaleidoscope of economic and political change in that era. As Croome Robertson notes: "He attempted a task which no other adherent of the new mechanical philosophy conceived—nothing less than such a universal construction of human knowledge as would bring society and man . . . within the same principles of scientific explanation as were found applicable to the world of nature." *

Hobbes' chief works took shape before and during the Civil War (1641–1649) of Crown and Parliament. After a sojourn in France he returned, when the political coast was clear enough, to

* *Encyclopaedia Britannica,* 11th ed., Vol. XIII, p. 552.

watch the consequences of civil war, consolidate his theory of individual human response and of the political form of the revolution, and publish his ideas, in 1650.

Hobbes presupposes that the mind is an expression of matter in motion. Motion within the body is the cause of psychological activities (a doctrine highly reminiscent of Democritus). This motion is guided by social circumstances into our loyalties, fears, prides, and hates. The social order—the Leviathan—expresses "humane nature," as in turn human nature determines the structure of the social order.

He attacked whole ranges of psychological problems, from sensation and perception, through memory, association, and fantasy, to the will, offering empirical observations which still charm us: let the reader "consider, if he also find not the same in himself." Rather an extraordinary scope and range of psychological effort for the period, or, indeed, for any period! He is one of the great systematic psychologists. He was not liked by gentle, earnest people, who thought him arrogant and patently anti-religious. But the empiricism of his approach became important in the whole subsequent life of British psychology.

Leviathan * *or the Matter, Form, and Power of a Commonwealth, Ecclesiastical and Civil*

PART I. OF MAN

CHAPTER I. OF SENSE

Concerning the thoughts of man, I will consider them first singly, and afterwards in train, or dependence upon one another. Singly, they are every one a *representation* or *appearance,* of some quality, of other accident of a body without us, which is commonly called an *object.* Which object worketh on the eyes, ears, and other parts of a man's body; and by diversity of working, produceth diversity of appearances.

The original of them all, is that which we call SENSE, for there is no conception in a man's mind, which hath not at first, totally or by parts, been begotten upon the organs of sense. The rest are derived from that original.

* From Thomas Hobbes, *Leviathan,* in Benjamin Rand (ed.), *Modern Classical Philosophers* (2nd ed.; Boston: Houghton Mifflin Company, 1924), pp. 57–62, 64–66. Copyright 1924 by Benjamin Rand.

To know the natural cause of sense is not very necessary to the business now in hand; and I have elsewhere written of the same at large. Nevertheless, to fill each part of my present method, I will briefly deliver the same in this place.

The cause of sense, is the external body, or object, which presseth the organ proper to each sense, either immediately, as in the taste and touch; or mediately, as in seeing, hearing, and smelling; which pressure, by the mediation of the nerves, and other strings and membranes of the body, continued inwards to the brain and heart, causeth there a resistance, or counterpressure or endeavour of the heart to deliver itself, which endeavour, because *outward,* seemeth to be some matter without. And this *seeming,* or *fancy,* is that which men call *sense;* and consisteth, as to the eye, in a *light,* or *colour figured;* to the ear, in a *sound;* to the nostril, in an *odour;* to the tongue and palate, in a *savour;* and to the rest of the body, in *heat, cold, hardness, softness,* and such other qualities as we discern by *feeling.* All which qualities, called *sensible,* are in the object, that causeth them, but so many several motions of the matter, by which it presseth our organs diversely. Neither in us that are pressed, are they anything else, but divers motions; for motion produceth nothing but motion. But their appearance to us is fancy, the same waking, that dreaming. And as pressing, rubbing, or striking the eye, makes us fancy a light; and pressing the ear, produceth a din; so do the bodies also we see, or hear, produce the same by their strong, though unobserved action. For if those colours and sounds were in the bodies, or objects that cause them, they could not be severed from them, as by glasses, and in echoes by reflection, we see they are; where we know the thing we see is in one place, the appearance in another. And though at some certain distance, the real and very object seem invested with the fancy it begets in us; yet still the object is one thing, the image or fancy is another. So that sense, in all cases, is nothing else but original fancy, caused, as I have said, by the pressure, that is, by the motion, of external things upon our eyes, ears, and other organs thereunto ordained.

. . .

CHAPTER II. OF IMAGINATION

That when a thing lies still, unless somewhat else stir it, it will lie still for ever, is a truth that no man doubts of. But that when a thing is in motion, it will eternally be in motion, unless somewhat else stay it, though the reason be the same, namely, that nothing can change itself, is not so easily assented to. For men measure, not only other men, but all other things, by themselves; and because they find themselves subject after motion to pain, and lassitude, think everything else grows weary of motion, and seeks repose of its own accord; little considering, whether it be not some other motion, wherein that desire of rest they find in themselves, consisteth. From hence it is, that the schools say, heavy bodies fall downwards, out of an appetite to rest, and to conserve their nature in that place which is most proper for them; ascribing appetite, and knowledge of what is good for their conservation, which is more than man has, to things inanimate, absurdly.

When a body is once in motion, it moveth, unless something else hinder it, eternally; and whatsoever hindreth it, cannot in an instant, but in time, and by degrees, quite extinguish it; and as we see in the water, though the wind cease, the waves give not over rolling for a long time after: so also it happeneth in that motion, which is made in the internal parts of a man, then, when he sees, dreams, etc. For after the object is removed, or the eye shut, we still retain an image of the thing seen, though more obscure than when we see it. And this is it, the Latins call *imagination,* from the image made in seeing; and apply the same, though improperly, to all the other senses. But the Greeks call it *fancy;* which signifies *appearance,* and is as proper to one sense, as to another. IMAGINATION, therefore, is nothing but *decaying sense;* and is found in men, and many other living creatures, as well sleeping, as waking.

The decay of sense in men waking, is not the decay of the motion made in sense; but an obscuring of it, in such manner as the light of the sun obscureth the light of the stars; which stars do no less exercise their virtue, by which they are visible, in the day than in the night. But because amongst many strokes, which our eyes, ears, and other organs receive from external bodies, the predominant only is sensible; therefore, the light of the sun being predominant, we are not affected with the action of the stars. And any object being removed from our eyes, though the impression it made in us remain, yet other objects more present succeeding, and working on us, the imagination of the past is obscured, and made weak, as the voice of a man is in the noise of the day. From whence it followeth, that the longer the time is, after the sight or sense of any object, the weaker is the imagination. For the continual change of man's body destroys in time the parts which in sense were moved: so that distance of time, and of place, hath one and the same effect in us. For as at a great distance of place, that which we look at appears dim, and without distinction of the smaller parts; and as voices grow weak, and inarticulate; so also, after great distance of time, our imagination of the past is weak; and we lose, for example, of cities we have seen, many particular streets, and of actions, many particular circumstances. This *decaying sense,* when we would express the thing itself, I mean *fancy* itself, we call *imagination,* as I said before: but when we would express the decay, and signify that the sense is fading, old, and past, it is called *memory.* So that imagination and memory are but one thing, which for divers considerations hath divers names.

Much memory, or memory of many things, is called *experience.* Again, imagination being only of those things which have been formerly perceived by sense, either all at once, or by parts at several times, the former, which is the imagining the whole object as it was presented to the sense, is *simple* imagination, as when one imagineth a man, or horse, which he hath seen before. The other is *compounded;* as when, from the sight of a man at one time, and of a horse at another, we conceive in our mind a Centaur. So when a man compoundeth the image of his own person with the image of the actions of another man, as when a man imagines himself a Hercules or an Alexander, which happeneth often to them that are much taken with reading of romances, it is a compound imagination, and properly but a fiction of the mind. There be also other imaginations that rise in men, though waking, from the great impression made in sense: as from gazing upon the sun, the impression leaves an image of the sun before our eyes a long time after; and from being long and vehemently attent upon geometrical figures, a man shall in the dark, though awake, have the images of lines and angles before his eyes; which kind of fancy hath no particular name, as being a thing that doth not commonly fall into men's discourse.

The imaginations of them that sleep are those we call *dreams.* And these also, as also all other imaginations, have been before, either totally or by parcels, in the sense. And because in sense, the brain and nerves, which are the necessary organs of sense, are so benumbed in sleep as not easily to be moved by the action of external objects, there can happen in sleep no imagination, and therefore no dream, but what proceeds from the agitation of the inward parts of man's body; which inward parts, for the connexion they have with the brain, and other organs, when they be distempered, do keep the same in motion; whereby the imaginations there formerly made appear as if a man were waking; saving that the organs of sense being now benumbed, so as there is no new object, which can master and obscure them with a more vigorous impression, a dream must needs be more clear, in this silence of sense, than our waking thoughts. And hence it cometh to pass, that it is a hard matter, and by many thought impossible, to distinguish exactly between sense and dreaming. For my part, when I consider that in dreams I do not often nor constantly think of the same persons, places, objects, and actions, that I do waking; nor remember so long a train of coherent thoughts, dreaming, as at other times; and because waking I often observe the absurdity of dreams, but never dream of the absurdities of my waking thoughts; I am well satisfied, that being awake, I know I dream not, though when I dream I think myself awake.

. . .

CHAPTER III. OF THE CONSEQUENCE OR TRAIN OF IMAGINATIONS

By *Consequence,* or TRAIN of thoughts, I understand that succession of one thought to another which is called, to distinguish it from discourse in words, *mental discourse.*

When a man thinketh on anything whatsoever, his next thought after is not altogether so casual as it seems to be. Not every thought to every thought succeeds indifferently. But as we have no imagination, whereof we have not formerly had sense, in whole, or in parts, so we have no transition from one imagination to another, whereof we never had the like before in our senses. The reason whereof is this. All fancies are motions within us, relics of those made in the sense; and those motions that immediately succeeded one another in the sense continue also together after sense; insomuch as the former coming again to take place and be predominant, the latter followeth, by coherence of the matter moved, in such manner as water upon a plane table is drawn which way any one part of it is guided by the finger. But because in sense, to one and the same thing perceived, sometimes one thing, sometimes another succeedeth, it comes to pass in time, that in the imagining of anything, there is no certainty what we shall imagine next; only this is certain, it shall be something that succeeded the same before, at one time or another.

This train of thoughts, or mental discourse, is of two sorts. The first is *unguided, without design,* and inconstant; wherein there is no passionate thought to govern and direct those that follow, to itself, as the end and scope of some desire, or other passion: in which case the thoughts are said to wander, and seem impertinent one to another, as in a dream. Such are commonly the thoughts of men, that are not only without company, but also without care of anything; though even then their thoughts are as busy as at other times, but without harmony; as the sound which a lute out of tune would yield to any man, or in tune to one that could not play. And yet in this wild ranging of the mind, a man may oft-times perceive the way of it, and the dependence of one thought upon another. For in a discourse of our present civil war, what could seem more impertinent than to ask, as one did, what was the value of a Roman penny? Yet the coherence to me was manifest enough. For the thought of the war, introduced the thought of the delivering up the king to his enemies; the thought of that, brought in the thought of the delivering up of Christ; and that again the thought of the thirty pence, which was the price of that treason; and thence easily followed that malicious question, and all this in a moment of time; for thought is quick.

The second is more constant, as being *regulated* by some desire, and design. For the impression made by such things as we desire, or fear, is strong and permanent, or, if it cease for a time, of quick return: so strong it is sometimes, as to hinder and break our sleep. From desire, ariseth the thought of some means we have seen produce the like of that which we aim at; and from the thought of that, the thought of means to that means; and so continually till we come to some beginning within our own power. And because the end, by the greatness of the impression, comes often to mind, in case our thoughts begin to wander, they are quickly again reduced into the way: which observed by one of the seven wise men, made him give men this precept, which is now worn out, *Respice finem;* that is to say, in all your actions, look often upon what you would have as the thing that directs all your thoughts in the way to attain it.

The train of regulated thoughts is of two kinds: one, when of an effect imagined we seek the causes, or means that produce it; and this is common to man and beast. The other is, when imagining anything whatsoever, we seek all the possible effects that can by it be produced; that is to say, we imagine what we can do with it, when we have it. Of which I have not at any time seen any sign, but in man only; for this is a curiosity hardly incident to the nature of any living creature that has no other passion but sensual, such as are hunger, thirst, lust, and anger. In sum, the discourse of the mind, when it is governed by design, is nothing but *seeking,* or the faculty of invention, which the Latins called *sagacitas,* and *solertia;* a hunting out of the causes of some effect, present or past; or of the effects of some present or past cause. Sometimes a man seeks what he hath lost; and from that place and time wherein he misses it, his mind runs back, from place to place, and time to time, to find where, and when he had it; that is to say, to find some certain and limited time and place, in which to begin a method of seeking. Again, from thence his thoughts run over the same places and times, to find what action or other occasion might make him lose it. This we call *remembrance,* or calling to mind: the Latins call it *reminiscentia,* as it were a *re-conning* of our former actions.

Sometimes a man knows a place determinate, within the compass whereof he is to seek; and then his thoughts run over all the parts thereof, in the same manner as one would sweep a room to find a jewel; or as a spaniel ranges the field till he find a scent: or as a man should run over the alphabet, to start a rhyme.

❁

Hobbes has managed to revive and advertise a mechanism like that of Democritus and to combine it with a mathematical view of nature like that of his contemporary, Galileo. For psychology, this is sure to lead into a renewed interest in mechanistic physiology. But it does much more. It directs attention to the empirical character of psychology; one finds the laws of the mind as one watches one's own thoughts. At the same time it lays the foundation for the psychology of men interacting with society.

JOHN LOCKE

Thus by the middle of the seventeenth century we have in both France and Britain a brilliant new leadership in the direction of a self-confident psychology, utilizing to be sure the great tradition from Aristotle, but pointing to the power of direct observation and of mathematics, and breathing a confidence that more can be known.

We noted that Descartes had shared with the ancients the belief that it is necessary to get down to first principles, namely the things of which one may really make confident assertions, such as one's own thoughts, one's own existence. The same desire to get down to the nature of human experience, the basis for sound observation and reasonable deduction, appears in the celebrated treatise by John Locke, *An Essay Concerning Human Understanding*. To understand the enormous impact of this essay upon Western civilization one must consider the new intellectual world into which the seventeenth century was moving.

Three vast new frontiers were beginning to emerge as a result of geographical discoveries, political discoveries, scientific discoveries. The development of new trade routes, the accumulation of capital, the investment in maritime adventures, the availability of a "surplus" population, led to the spread of a European type of civilization almost all over the coastal or fringe lands of the world, and the rapid penetration inland following decade by decade. Second, partly because this effort was more easily handled by the new merchant and investor groups than by kings and princes, and partly because the sheer rapidity of merchant and maritime strength led to the seizure of power, thoughtful men everywhere began to think more about power and its relation to reason and to take for granted the conception that man's reason rather than his dependence upon authority is his guide toward a good life here and hereafter. The extolling of the power of reason meant everywhere that men were asking just what this inner light of reason really consisted of; it made men believe that they could find the truth for themselves, and that they could devise an educational system based upon encouragement of the mind to move in its own way. Yet these two forces could not in themselves have increased confidence in man's capacity for reason had it not been for the rapid rise of science. Science was a direct demonstration that man could discover the truth by using his mind; moreover, it turned its light back upon the human thought which had given rise to it and showed the thinking mind what its own nature was. It was the nature of science to illuminate the world about man and the inner nature of man's capacities.

One of the greatest events in the history of science, the birth of Sir Isaac Newton, had occurred a few years before the end of Hobbes' long life. Newton, a Cambridge University student during the year of the great plague, stayed home during part of this period and worked through some fundamental laws relating to the movements of bodies in space from which later developed much of the structure of modern physics. He saw, as time went on, that to understand and to apply this description of the world's events in terms of precise definitions of the movements of bodies, he must develop an adequate mathematics, and from this starting point he developed the differential calculus.

During his astronomical and mathematical studies, Newton formulated a universal law of gravitation, a series of simple mathematical definitions of the ways in which bodies act upon one another. (From this flowed, in the eighteenth century, Laplace's *Celestial Mechanics.*) Newton was equally interested, however, in light and optics. By means of a prism he broke white light into the hues of the rainbow. Generations of reverent followers, standing at Newton's window in the suite of rooms which he used in Cambridge, have been able to visualize almost exactly what the young Newton did.

Newton quickly became the center of the new "natural philosophy," organized in terms of mass, gravity, time, space, and number. British thought was soon precipitated into a vast wave of admiration and excitement. Alexander Pope wrote:

> Nature and nature's laws lay hid in night;
> God said, "Let Newton be," and all was light.

The impact upon philosophy and upon psychology was immense. Newton's work showed the vast significance of science, and in particular of quantitative science, upon the understanding of the universe, and ultimately of all bodies, including man's own body. It pointed to physical principles which governed the human body. Specifically, his studies of the mathematics of the pendulum were applied before long to the study of movements within nerves and suggested ways in which such pendular movements could explain the nature of perception, association, and thought (see pages 172–175). It soon suggested a physical basis for specific psychological observations, showing, for example, how an experience—like that of viewing white light—could be traced to components whose physical basis could be studied by methods of physical science. These applications of Newtonian principles were in full swing within a few decades.

John Locke is an expression of the new rationality, the new trust in human reason, which Newton inspired: one may refer to it as the Age of Enlightenment. More than that, he is an expression of the rationality and confidence of the era of the new commercial empire-building. He undertook to increase man's confidence in human powers of analysis, to give a basis upon which a rational educational philosophy could be founded, and to give man that confidence in his own ability to grasp and adapt to the universe, that all might regard themselves as sharing with the Deity in the comprehension and utilization of the eternal principles of order on which Nature and, in particular, human nature are based.

This was of huge social and political importance. In an era in which the spread of education and the spread of the "rights of man" were fundamental ideas dawning in the consciousness of Western Europe, great significance attaches to the democratic spirit which can thrive when men believe in one another's capacity for orderly and intelligible mental processes. It is natural to think of Locke as one of the architects of rationality in religion and education. He has been regarded by European and American educators as one of the great prophets of the possibility of education which will accept and constructively use human nature, instead of railing at it or attempting to box it in.

Our excerpts from Locke will not do justice to his role as philosopher or as a teacher regarding the modalities of democracy and education; they will have to be concerned primarily with the celebrated passages in which Locke observes how ideas get into the mind through the operation of our senses, how they are elaborated, where their limitations and strengths lie, and above all, how an empirical method can directly yield valid psychological laws.

It is not implied that Locke himself saw all the implications of what he was doing. Nor, indeed, is his work entirely clear, self-contained, and logical. It obtained the reputation of being clear and logical partly because this was the direction in which science and Western thought were turning; and partly because Locke pointed the way toward the development of political institutions based upon rationality rather than fear, and an educational system based on giving each generation the chance to expand into the full use of reason and of rational political institutions. How much of all this is psychology it will not be our place to discuss at length. The philosophers and the political scientists have devoted enormous quantities of subtle and illuminating consideration to John Locke's work. Our place here is to consider in terms of psychology just what he did with reference to the doctrine of the perceiving and thinking mind;

to show why he convinced mankind all over again that there is nothing in the mind that did not enter through the senses (an ancient and a medieval doctrine, widely held and many times reasserted long before Locke); and why he created an atmosphere in which the study of perception and of the association of ideas prevailed over the concern with emotion and impulse almost until the time of the evolutionary theory 150 years later.

An Essay Concerning Human Understanding *

INTRODUCTION

1. *An Inquiry into the understanding, pleasant and useful.* Since it is the *understanding* that sets man above the rest of sensible beings, and gives him all the advantage and dominion which he has over them; it is certainly a subject, even for its nobleness, worth our labour to inquire into. The understanding, like the eye, whilst it makes us see and perceive all other things, takes no notice of itself; and it requires art and pains to set it at a distance and make it its own object. But whatever be the difficulties that lie in the way of this inquiry; whatever it be that keeps us so much in the dark to ourselves; sure I am that all the light we can let in upon our minds, all the acquaintance we can make with our own understandings, will not only be very pleasant, but bring us great advantage, in directing our thoughts in the search of other things.

2. *Design.* This, therefore, being my purpose—to inquire into the original, certainty, and extent of *human knowledge,* together with the grounds and degrees of *belief, opinion,* and *assent;*—I shall not at present meddle with the physical consideration of the mind; or trouble myself to examine wherein its essence consists; or by what motions of our spirits or alterations of our bodies we come to have any *sensation* by our organs, or any *ideas* in our understandings; and whether those ideas do in their formation, any or all of them, depend on matter or not. These are speculations which, however curious and entertaining, I shall decline, as lying out of my way in the design I am now upon. It shall suffice to my present purpose, to consider the discerning faculties of a man, as they are employed about the objects which they have to do with. And I shall imagine I have not wholly misemployed myself in the thoughts I shall have on this occasion, if, in this historical, plain method, I can give any account of the ways whereby our understandings

* From John Locke, *An Essay Concerning Human Understanding,* collated and annotated by Alexander Campbell Fraser (Oxford: The Clarendon Press). Reprinted by permission of the publishers.

come to attain those notions of things we have; and can set down any measures of the certainty of our knowledge; or the grounds of those persuasions which are to be found amongst men, so various, different, and wholly contradictory; and yet asserted somewhere or other with such assurance and confidence, that he that shall take a view of the opinions of mankind, observe their opposition, and at the same time consider the fondness and devotion wherewith they are embraced, the resolution and eagerness wherewith they are maintained, may perhaps have reason to suspect, that either there is no such thing as truth at all, or that mankind hath no sufficient means to attain a certain knowledge of it.

3. *Method.* It is therefore worth while to search out the bounds between opinion and knowledge; and examine by what measures, in things whereof we have no certain knowledge, we ought to regulate our assent and moderate our persuasion. In order whereunto I shall pursue this following method:

First, I shall inquire into the original of those *ideas,* notions, or whatever else you please to call them, which a man observes, and is conscious to himself he has in his mind; and the ways whereby the understanding comes to be furnished with them.

Secondly, I shall endeavour to show what *knowledge* the understanding hath by those ideas; and the certainty, evidence, and extent of it.

Thirdly, I shall make some inquiry into the nature and grounds of *faith* or *opinion:* whereby I mean that assent which we give to any proposition as true, of whose truth yet we have no certain knowledge. And here we shall have occasion to examine the reasons and degrees of *assent.*

4. *Useful to know the extent of our comprehension.* If by this inquiry into the nature of the understanding, I can discover the powers thereof; how far they reach; to what things they are in any degree proportionate; and where they fail us, I suppose it may be of use to prevail with the busy mind of man to be more cautious in meddling with things exceeding its comprehension; to stop when it is at the utmost extent of its tether; and to sit down in a quiet ignorance of those things which, upon examination, are found to be beyond the reach of our capacities. We should not then perhaps be so forward, out of an affection of an universal knowledge, to raise questions, and perplex ourselves and others with disputes about things to which our understandings are not suited; and of which we cannot frame in our minds any clear or distinct perceptions, or whereof (as it has perhaps too often happened) we have not any notions at all. If we can find out how far the understanding can extend its view; how far it has faculties to attain certainty; and in what cases it can only

judge and guess, we may learn to content ourselves with what is attainable by us in this state.

• • •

BOOK II. OF IDEAS

2. *All ideas come from sensation or reflection.* Let us then suppose the mind to be, as we say, white paper, void of all characters, without any ideas:—How comes it to be furnished? Whence comes it by that vast store which the busy and boundless fancy of man has painted on it with an almost endless variety? Whence has it all the *materials* of reason and knowledge? To this I answer, in one word, from EXPERIENCE. In that all our knowledge is founded; and from that it ultimately derives itself. Our observation employed either, about external sensible objects, or about the internal operations of our minds perceived and reflected on by ourselves, is that which supplies our understandings with all the *materials* of thinking. These two are the fountains of knowledge, from whence all the ideas we have, or can naturally have, do spring.

3. *The objects of sensation one source of ideas.* First, our Senses, conversant about particular sensible objects, do convey into the mind several distinct perceptions of things, according to those various ways wherein those objects do affect them. And thus we come by those *ideas* we have of *yellow, white, heat, cold, soft, hard, bitter, sweet,* and all those which we call sensible qualities; which when I say the senses convey into the mind, I mean, they from external objects convey into the mind what produces there those perceptions. This great source of most of the ideas we have, depending wholly upon our senses, and derived by them to the understanding, I call SENSATION.

4. *The operations of our minds, the other source of them.* Secondly, the other fountain from which experience furnisheth the understanding with ideas is,—the perception of the operations of our own mind within us, as it is employed about the ideas it has got;—which operations, when the soul comes to reflect on and consider, do furnish the understanding with another set of ideas, which could not be had from things without. And such are *perception, thinking, doubting, believing, reasoning, knowing, willing,* and all the different actings of our own minds;—which we being conscious of, and observing in ourselves, do from these receive into our understandings as distinct ideas as we do from bodies affecting our senses. This source of ideas every man has wholly in himself; and though it be not sense, as having nothing to do with external objects, yet it is very like it, and might properly enough be called *internal sense.* But as I call the other SENSATION, so I call this REFLECTION, the ideas it

affords being such only as the mind gets by reflecting on its own operations within itself. By reflection then, in the following part of this discourse, I would be understood to mean, that notice which the mind takes of its own operations, and the manner of them, by reason whereof there come to be ideas of these operations in the understanding. These two, I say, viz. external material things, as the objects of SENSATION, and the operations of our own minds within, as the objects of REFLECTION, are to me the only originals from whence all our ideas take their beginnings. The term *operations* here I use in a large sense, as comprehending not barely the actions of the mind about its ideas, but some sort of passions arising sometimes from them, such as is the satisfaction or uneasiness arising from any thought.

5. *All our ideas are of the one or the other of these.* The understanding seems to me not to have the least glimmering of any ideas which it doth not receive from one of these two. *External objects* furnish the mind with the ideas of sensible qualities, which are all those different perceptions they produce in us; and *the mind* furnishes the understanding with ideas of its own operations.

These, when we have taken a full survey of them, and their several modes, combinations, and relations, we shall find to contain all our whole stock of ideas; and that we have nothing in our minds which did not come in one of these two ways. Let any one examine his own thoughts, and thoroughly search into his understanding; and then let him tell me, whether all the original ideas he has there, are any other than of the objects of his senses, or of the operations of his mind, considered as objects of his reflection. And how great a mass of knowledge soever he imagines to be lodged there, he will, upon taking a strict view, see that he has not any idea in his mind but what one of these two have imprinted;—though perhaps, with infinite variety compounded and enlarged by the understanding, as we shall see hereafter.

6. *Observable in children.* He that attentively considers the state of a child, at his first coming into the world, will have little reason to think him stored with plenty of ideas, that are to be the matter of his future knowledge. It is *by degrees* he comes to be furnished with them. And though the ideas of obvious and familiar qualities imprint themselves before the memory begins to keep a register of time or order, yet it is often so late before some unusual qualities come in the way, that there are few men that cannot recollect the beginning of their acquaintance with them. And if it were worth while, no doubt a child might be so ordered as to have but a very few, even of the ordinary ideas, till he were grown up to a man. But for all that are born into the world, being surrounded with bodies that perpetually and diversely affect them, a vari-

ety of ideas, whether care be taken of it or not, are imprinted on the minds of children. Light and colours are busy at hand everywhere, when the eye is but open; sounds and some tangible qualities fail not to solicit their proper senses, and force an entrance to the mind;—but yet, I think, it will be granted easily, that if a child were kept in a place where he never saw any other but black and white till he were a man, he would have no more ideas of scarlet or green, than he that from his childhood never tasted an oyster, or a pine-apple, has of those particular relishes.

. . .

8. *Ideas of reflection later, because they need attention.* And hence we see the reason why it is pretty late before most children get ideas of the operations of their own minds; and some have not any very clear or perfect ideas of the greatest part of them all their lives. Because, though they pass there continually, yet, like floating visions, they make not deep impressions enough to leave in their mind clear, distinct, lasting ideas, till the understanding turns inward upon itself, reflects on its own operations, and makes them the objects of its own contemplation. Children when they come first into it, are surrounded with a world of new things, which, by a constant solicitation of their senses, draw the mind constantly to them; forward to take notice of new, and apt to be delighted with the variety of changing objects. Thus the first years are usually employed and diverted in looking abroad. Men's business in them is to acquaint themselves with what is to be found without; and so growing up in a constant attention to outward sensations, seldom make any considerable reflection on what passes within them, till they come to be of riper years; and some scarce ever at all.

❀

Almost everyone of note in British psychology after Locke is in some sense his follower. We cannot do justice to the manifold currents of Lockean psychology that are to be found at work remaking the image of man and the mind of man through the Age of the Enlightenment, the eighteenth century, and the Romantic period at the beginning of the nineteenth. We shall, however, allow ourselves one simple and, we believe, crystal-clear example of what happens when Locke's ideas are taken with utter seriousness, among them the conception that ideas have a dynamic of their own, that we need consider no living organism, no soul, no self, no person, but just *ideas*—ideas arriving, as Locke said, from sensations, and remaining while new sensations are added. It is the Frenchman Etienne Bonnot de Condillac to whom we refer, who charmingly suggested that we need only endow a statue with the sense of smell; and if we note what the use of this sensory function actually means, we shall soon have a complete psychology of the perceptual and reasoning capacities.

CONDILLAC

Treatise on the Sensations *

II. HOW THE UNDERSTANDING WORKS IN A MAN LIMITED TO THE SENSE OF SMELL

And How the Different Degrees of Pleasure and Pain Are the Principle of Its Cognitions

1. *The statue capable of attention.* At the first smell our statue's capacity of feeling is entirely due to the impression which is made upon its sense organ. This is what I call attention.

2. *Of enjoying and suffering.* From this moment it begins to enjoy or to suffer. For if the capacity of feeling is confined to a pleasant smell, there is enjoyment; and if it is confined to an unpleasant smell, there is suffering.

. . .

6. *Dawn of memory.* The smell is not wholly forgotten when the odoriferous substance which caused it has ceased to act on the sense organ, for the attention retains it, and an impression remains stronger or weaker according as the attention has been more or less vivid. This is memory.

7. *Division of the capacity of feeling between smell and memory.* When our statue is a new smell, it has still present that which it had been the moment before. Its capacity of feeling is divided between the memory and the smell. The first of these faculties is attentive to the past sensation, whilst the second is attentive to the present sensation.

8. *Memory only a mode of feeling.* There are then in the statue two

* From Etienne Bonnot de Condillac, *Treatise on the Sensations,* trans. by Geraldine Carr (Los Angeles: University of Southern California School of Philosophy, 1930), pp. 4, 6–7, 9, 43–44.

ways of feeling. They differ only in one being related to a present sensation and the other to a sensation which no longer exists but of which the impression still remains. Ignorant of any objects acting upon it, ignorant even of its own sense organ, it usually distinguishes the memory of a sensation from a present sensation only insofar as it feels the one feebly, the other vividly.

9. *The feeling of it can be more vivid than the sensation.* I say *usually* because memory is not always a feeble feeling, nor is sensation always a vivid feeling. For whenever the memory is recalling the past forcibly and the sense organ, on the contrary, is receiving only slight impressions, then the feeling of a present sensation is much less vivid than the memory of a sensation which no longer exists.

10. *The statue distinguishes in itself a succession.* Thus, whenever an odoriferous substance is making an impression on the sense organ itself, there is another smell present to the memory, because the impression of another odoriferous substance subsists in the brain, to which the sense organ has already transmitted it. By passing as it were through these two states the statue feels that it is no longer what it was. The knowledge of this change makes it relate the first smell to a different moment from that in which it is experiencing the second, and this makes it perceive a difference between existing in one state and remembering having existed in another.

. . .

14. *It compares.* If after having repeatedly smelled rose and pink the statue then smells rose, the passive attention which is caused by the smell is entirely the present smell of rose, and the active attention which is caused by the memory is divided between the recollection which remains of the smells of rose and pink. Now modes of being can only divide the capacity of feeling insofar as they are compared; for comparing is nothing else but giving attention to two ideas at the same time.

. . .

VI. THE SELF OR PERSONALITY OF A MAN LIMITED TO THE SENSE OF SMELL

1. *Of the personality of the statue.* Our statue being capable of memory, there is no smell which does not recall to it that it was once another smell. Herein lies its personality. If it is able to say "I" it can say it in all the states of its duration; and at each time its "I" will embrace all the moments of which it might have preserved recollection.

2. *It cannot say "I" at the first moment of its existence.* I admit that it could not say "I" at the first smell. What we understand by this word "I" seems to be only possible in a being who notices that in the present moment he is no longer what he has been. So long as there is no change, he exists without any reflexion upon himself; but as soon as he changes, he judges that he is the same as he formerly was in another state, and he says "I."

This observation makes it clear that at the first moment of his existence the statue is not able to form desires, for before being able to say *I desire*, it must have said "I" or "me."

3. *The "I" is at one and the same time the consciousness of what it is, and the remembrance of what it has been.* Smells of which the statue has no recollection, do not enter into the idea which it has of its personality. They are then for it, as though it had never smelled them. They are as much strangers to its "I" as the colours and sounds of which it has as yet no knowledge. Its "I" is only the collection of the sensations which it experiences, and those which memory recalls to it. In a word it is immediate knowledge of what it is for itself, and remembrance of what it has been.

• • •

18. *Surprise gives increasing activity to the operations of the soul.* Surprise makes it feel more strongly the difference of its modes. The sharper the passage of the one to the other the greater the surprise, and the more striking will be the contrasts of the pleasures and the pains which accompany the changes. Its attention, determined by the pleasures and pains it feels, is now applied with greatest liveliness to the succeeding sensations. It then compares them with more attention, and can judge their relations better. Consequently surprise increases the activity of the operations of its soul. But since it only increases it by making it notice a sharper contrast between pleasant and unpleasant feelings, pleasure and pain are always the prime mover of the faculties.

Condillac thus earns the title of "arch-sensationist" of all time. Follow your nose, with *all* its powers, and you will smell out reality.

But to return to the English-speaking world: The principle of the "association of ideas" was picked up quickly by the Scottish skeptic

David Hume and by a thoughtful young bishop, George Berkeley, who developed various aspects of the new association theory. Hume showed the *limitations* which the principle of association places upon our capacity really to know anything; Berkeley uses the principle of association to show how we can take in with our eyes the solid three-dimensional objects about us.

If Condillac is Locke's most literal disciple, David Hume is the most hostile. While seeming to accept Locke's association of ideas, he goes on to show that there is really no empirical ground for believing in any such prototype of clear rationality as Locke had suggested. We cannot really hope to know anything but the stream of our associations. We are essentially cast back into the maelstrom of the Sophists. It is only when "making merry with our friends" that our doubts about reality and the capacity of our own minds are momentarily put to rest.

With these and with other British and French philosophers of the first half of the eighteenth century, we shall not try to deal. Rather, our attention will be given to one profound addition to Locke's conception of the association of ideas, namely the idea that this association depends upon physiological properties of the brain. Locke had himself expressly said that he would not "meddle with the physical considerations of the mind." Exactly the opposite was the concern of the physician David Hartley, who, by offering an ingeniously conceived brain physiology as the basis for the association of ideas, gave the psychological school of "Associationism" a substance and a name, founding and launching what is undoubtedly the longest and richest stream of psychological doctrine through all of modern times.

DAVID HARTLEY

Hartley's medical interests on the one hand, and his religious beliefs on the other hand, led him to find something very precious in the principle of the association of ideas. Just how he got hold of these ideas we do not know, but Lockean ideas had spread far in the first half of the eighteenth century, and an obscure "Reverend Mr. Gay" had written, in 1746, a little essay (long since lost) on the principle of "association" as the guide to the understanding of the human mind. Three years later Hartley systematically develops, with due acknowledgment, this idea from the Reverend Mr. Gay, and gives us his own extraordinary book, *Observations of Man, His Frame, His Duty, and His Expectations.* Taking over from Newton the theory of the pendulum swinging according to a definite rhythm which can be mathematically stated, Hartley undertook to show that the nerves as they function give rise in the brain, specifically in the "white medullary substance of the brain," to the rhythmic or pendulum-like vibrations which in a certain order give rise respectively to the rhythms of sensory experience; and when a second time the nerves are thrown into the same vibration they give rise a second time to the same experiences. The memory images, in other words, are simply reverberations of the original sensory experiences. Aristotle—and Hobbes, too—had said, "imagination is decaying sense." But now Hartley puts memory on a physiological basis (Spinoza had offered the same principle nearly 100 years before) and undertakes to show us that the "trains of association and thought" run off into certain pathways rather than others because we have been stimulated, our senses aroused, by experiences forced upon us in a certain order. There is no place here for active attention; there is even less concern with activity, in fact, than there is in Hobbes. But there is the grand conception of the human body as being so constructed by the Deity that it can, in its due rhythms, engender the rhythms of sensory experience and of memory. This puts an end to any Cartesian principle of dualism as fully as was the case with Hobbes. But whereas Hobbes had been unclear as to how the motions in the brain could give rise to perception and feeling, Hartley mobilizes the Newtonian pendulum movements to serve as substrate. He is, moreover, so specific in his description of the associative processes that he convinces a long line of followers that here at last is the basis for a scientific psychology.

Observations on Man, His Frame, His Duty, and His Expectations *

INTRODUCTION

Man consists of two parts, body and mind.

The first is subjected to our senses and inquiries, in the same manner as the other parts of the external material world.

The last is that substance, agent, principle, etc. to which we refer the sensations, ideas, pleasures, pains, and voluntary motions.

Sensations are those internal feelings of the mind, which arise from the impressions made by external objects upon the several parts of our bodies.

All our other internal feelings may be called *ideas.* Some of these appear to spring up in the mind of themselves, some are suggested by words, others arise in other ways. Many writers comprehend *sensations* under *ideas;* but I everywhere use these words in the senses here ascribed to them.

CHAPTER I. THE DOCTRINES OF VIBRATIONS AND ASSOCIATION IN GENERAL

My chief design in the following chapter is briefly to explain, establish, and apply the doctrines of *vibrations* and *association.* The first of these doctrines is taken from the hints concerning the performance of sensation and motion, which Sir Isaac Newton has given at the end of his Principia, and in the Questions annexed to his Optics; the last, from what Mr. Locke, and other ingenious persons since his time, have delivered concerning the influence of *association* over our opinions and affections, and its use in explaining those things in an accurate and precise way, which are commonly referred to the power of habit and custom, is a general and indeterminate one.

The doctrine of *vibrations* may appear at first sight to have no connexion with that of *association;* however, if these doctrines be found in fact to contain the laws of the bodily and mental powers respectively, they must be related to each other, since the body and mind are. One may expect, that *vibrations* should infer *association* as their effect, and *association* point to *vibrations* as its cause. I will endeavour, in the present chapter, to trace out this mutual relation.

* From David Hartley, *Observations on Man, His Frame, His Duty, and His Expectations,* in Benjamin Rand (ed.), *The Classical Psychologists* (Boston: Houghton Mifflin Company, 1912), pp. 313, 315–319, 322–325.

The proper method of philosophizing seems to be, to discover and establish the general laws of action, affecting the subject under consideration, from certain select, well-defined, and well-attested phænomena, and then to explain and predict the other phænomena by these laws. This is the method of analysis and synthesis recommended and followed by Sir Isaac Newton.

I shall not be able to execute, with any accuracy, what the reader might expect of this kind, in respect of the doctrines of *vibrations* and *association,* and their general laws, on account of the great intricacy, extensiveness, and novelty of the subject. However, I will attempt a sketch in the best manner I can, for the service of future inquirers.

Section I. The Doctrine of Vibrations, and its Use for explaining the Sensations

PROP. I—*The white medullary Substance of the Brain, spinal Marrow, and the Nerves proceeding from them, is the immediate Instrument of Sensation and Motion.*

Under the word *brain,* in these observations, I comprehend all that lies within the cavity of the skull, i.e. the *cerebrum,* or *brain* properly so called, the *cerebellum,* and the *medulla oblongata.*

This proposition seems to be sufficiently proved in the writings of physicians and anatomists; from the structure and functions of the several organs of the human body; from experiments on living animals; from the symptoms of diseases, and from dissections of morbid bodies. Sensibility, and the power of motion, seem to be conveyed to all the parts, in their natural state, from the brain and spinal marrow, along the nerves. These arise from the medullary, not the cortical part, every where, and are themselves of a white medullary substance. When the nerves of any part are cut, tied, or compressed in any considerable degree, the functions of that part are either entirely destroyed, or much impaired. When the spinal marrow is compressed by a dislocation of the *vertebræ* of the back, all the parts, whose nerves arise below the place of dislocation, become paralytic. When any considerable injury is done to the medullary substance of the brain, sensation, voluntary motion, memory, and intellect, are either entirely lost, or much impaired; and if the injury be very great, this extends immediately to the vital motions also, viz. to those of the heart, and organs of respiration, so as to occasion death. But this does not hold equally in respect of the cortical substance of the brain; perhaps not at all, unless as far as injuries done to it extend themselves to the medullary substance. In dissections after apoplexies, palsies, epilepsies, and other distempers affecting the sensations and motions, it is usual to find some great disorder in the brain, from preternatural tumours, from blood, matter, or serum, lying upon the brain, or in its ventricles, etc. This may suffice as general evidence for the present. The particular reasons of some of these phænomena, with more definite evidences, will offer themselves in the course of these observations.

PROP. II.—*The white medullary Substance of the Brain is also the immediate Instrument, by which Ideas are presented to the Mind: or, in other words, whatever Changes are made in this Substance, corresponding Changes are made in our Ideas; and vice versa.*

The evidence for this proposition is also to be taken from the writings of physicians and anatomists; but especially from those parts of these writings which treat of the faculties of memory, attention, imagination, etc. and of mental disorders. It is sufficiently manifest from hence, that the perfection of our mental faculties depends upon the perfection of this substance; that all injuries done to it affect the trains of ideas proportionably; and that these cannot be restored to their natural course till such injuries be repaired. Poisons, spirituous liquors, opiates, fevers, blows upon the head, etc. all plainly affect the mind, by first disordering the medullary substance. And evacuations, rest, medicines, time, as plainly restore the mind to its former state, by reversing the foregoing steps. But there will be more and more definite evidence offered in the course of these observations.

PROP. III.—*The Sensations remain in the Mind for a short time after the sensible Objects are removed.*

This is very evident in the sensations impressed on the eye. Thus, to use Sir Isaac Newton's words, "If a burning coal be nimbly moved round in a circle, with gyrations continually repeated, the whole circle will appear like fire; the reason of which is, that the sensation of the coal, in the several places of that circle, remains impressed on the *sensorium* until the coal return again to the same place. And so in a quick consecution of the colours" (viz. red, yellow, green, blue, and purple, mentioned in the experiment, whence this passage is taken) "the impression of every colour remains on the *sensorium* until a revolution of all the colours be completed, and that first colour return again. The impressions therefore of all the successive colours are at once in the *sensorium*—and beget a sensation of white."

Thus also, when a person has had a candle, a window, or any other lucid and well-defined object, before his eyes for a considerable time, he may perceive a very clear and precise image thereof to be left in the *sensorium,* fancy, or mind (for these I consider as equivalent expressions in our entrance upon these disquisitions) for some time after he has closed his eyes. At least this will happen frequently to persons who are attentive to these things in a gentle way; for, as this appearance escapes the notice of those who are entirely inattentive, so too earnest a desire and attention prevents it, by introducing another state of mind or fancy. . . .

PROP. IV.—*External Objects impressed upon the Senses occasion, first in the Nerves on which they are impressed, and then in the Brain, Vibrations of the small, and as one may say, infinitesimal, medullary Particles.*

These vibrations are motions backwards and forwards of the small particles; of the same kind with the oscillations of pendulums, and the tremblings of the particles of sounding bodies. They must be conceived to be exceedingly short and small, so as not to have the least efficacy to disturb or move the whole bodies of the nerves or brain. For that the nerves themselves should vibrate like musical strings, is highly absurd; nor was it ever asserted by Sir Isaac Newton, or any of those who have embraced his notion of the performance of sensation and motion, by means of *vibrations*.

In like manner we are to suppose the particles which vibrate, to be of the inferior orders, and not those biggest particles, on which the operations in chemistry, and the colours of natural bodies, depend, according to the opinion of Sir Isaac Newton.

PROP. IX.—*Sensory Vibrations, by being often repeated, beget, in the medullary Substance of the Brain, a Disposition to diminutive Vibrations, which may also be called Vibratiuncles, and Miniatures, corresponding to themselves respectively.*

This correspondence of the diminutive vibrations to the original sensory ones, consists in this, that they agree in kind, place, and line of direction; and differ only in being more feeble, i.e. in degree.

This proposition follows from the foregoing. For since sensations, by being often repeated, beget ideas, it cannot but be that those vibrations, which accompany sensations, should beget something which may accompany ideas in like manner; and this can be nothing but feebler vibrations, agreeing with the sensory generating vibrations in kind, place, and line of direction.

Or thus: By the first proposition it appears, that some motion must be excited in the medullary substance, during each sensation; by the fourth, this motion is determined to be a vibratory one: since therefore some motion must also, by the second, be excited in the medullary substance during the presence of each idea, this motion cannot be any other than a vibratory one: else how should it proceed from the original vibration attending the sensation, in the same manner as the idea does from the sensation itself? It must also agree in kind, place, and line of direction, with the generating vibration. A vibratory motion, which recurs *t* times in a second, cannot beget a diminutive one that recurs ½ *t,* or 2*t* times; nor one originally impressed on the region of the brain corresponding to the auditory nerves, beget diminutive vibrations in the region corresponding to the optic nerves; and so of the rest. The line of direction must likewise be the same in the original and derivative vibrations. It remains, therefore, that each simple idea of sensation be attended by diminutive vibrations of the same kind, place, and line of direction, with the original vibrations attending the sensation itself: or, in the words of the proposition, that sensory vibrations, by being frequently repeated, beget a disposition to diminutive vibrations corresponding to themselves respectively. We may add, that the vibratory nature of the motion which attends ideas, may be inferred from the continuance of some ideas, visible ones for instance, in the fancy for a few moments.

. . .

PROP. X.— *Any Sensations* A, B, C, *etc. by being associated with one another a sufficient Number of Times, get such a Power over the corresponding Ideas* a, b, c, *etc. that any one of the Sensations* A, *when impressed alone, shall be able to excite in the Mind,* b, c, *etc. the Ideas of the rest.*

Sensations may be said to be associated together, when their impressions are either made precisely at the same instant of time, or in the contiguous successive instants. We may therefore distinguish association into two sorts, the synchronous, and the successive.

The influence of association over our ideas, opinions, and affections, is so great and obvious, as scarcely to have escaped the notice of any writer who has treated of these, though the word *association,* in the particular sense here affixed to it, was first brought into use by Mr. Locke. But all that has been delivered by the ancients and moderns, concerning the power of habit, custom, example, education, authority, party-prejudice, the manner of learning the manual and liberal arts, etc. goes upon this doctrine as its foundation, and may be considered as the detail of it, in various circumstances. I here begin with the simplest case, and shall proceed to more and more complex ones continually, till I have exhausted what has occurred to me upon this subject. . . .

. . . It is to be observed, that, in successive associations, the power of raising the ideas is only exerted according to the order in which the association is made. Thus, if the impressions *A, B, C,* be always made in the order of the alphabet, *B* impressed alone will not raise *a,* but *c* only. Agreeably to which it is easy to repeat familiar sentences in the order in which they always occur, but impossible to do it readily in an inverted one. The reason of this is, that the compound idea, *c, b, a,* corresponds to the compound sensation *C, B, A;* and therefore require the impression of *C, B, A,* in the same manner as *a, b, c,* does that of *A, B, C.* This will, however, be more evident, when we come to consider the associations of vibratory motions, in the next proposition.

It is also to be observed, that the power of association grows feebler, as the number either of synchronous or successive impressions is increased, and does not extend, with due force, to more than a small one, in the first and simplest cases. But, in complex cases, or the associations of associations, of which the memory, in its full extent, consists, the powers of the mind, deducible from this source, will be found much greater than any person, upon his first entrance on these inquiries, could well imagine.

Hartley has thus revived the ancient springs of associationism as represented in Aristotle and in the Stoics; he has made much more clear the structure of John Locke's "Association of Ideas" ; and he has provided a physiological basis and a very intriguing one, too, for the processes of memory, free association, and fantasy. He has by implication suggested that the feeling tones of pleasantness and unpleasantness can likewise be associated with ideas, that pleasant ideas lead to certain consequences which unpleasant ideas could not produce. This, if developed into a psychology of action and of purpose, would involve our saying that it is the conjunction of pleasantness with an idea which leads to our pursuing it, and the conjunction of unpleasantness which leads to our avoiding it. This would be very much like the classical hedonism which we encountered among the Greeks.

It is very important, indeed, for a budding associationism to be explicit about this principle. Without it Hartley's ideas, like Locke's, might seem to mean that action follows from the sheer association of ideas with one another, or with acts, and that the pleasantness or unpleasantness of the consequences in the past or anticipated in the future would be irrelevant. A serious psychology of action must not take this irresponsible step. It must provide for the fact that men are influenced by the weal or woe which follows from their acts. We set up educational and political systems, systems of trade and systems of punishment, based upon the pleasantness or the unpleasantness of the outcome of our acts.

JEREMY BENTHAM

It was Jeremy Bentham who first saw this principle in all its coherence and all its force. As an economist, he had to see it because at the end of the eighteenth century men were concerned with the loss of the old landmarks of economic and social reality. In the new industrial society men were made or broken through failure to foresee or to act in consequence of the good and bad outcomes of previous acts; the political and economic system was plainly based upon the constant development of new systems of reward and punishment following from new investments, inventions, economic policies. Bentham happened to be especially interested in the psychology of delinquency and crime, in deterrent punishment, in the need to develop a legal and penal system which would prevent crime and channel human activities into paths which brought satisfaction to the doer as well as to those upon whom his acts brought their effects.

Bentham's *Principles of Morals and Legislation* is thus a necessary dynamic adjunct to the associationism of Locke and Hartley. More than that, it is a timely psychological treatise in the midst of the rapidly developing Industrial Revolution, where men were being driven from their farms and were seeking a pittance in the labor market of the cities in which the newly established factory system offered all the livelihood there was.

Bentham works his way a step at a time, simply and clearly, as did Locke, to a rational interpretation of man's plight. The individual man must, of course, act so as to bring himself the maximum of pleasure and the minimum of pain, and all men in society in their interaction must bring about "the greatest good of the greatest number" leading into the "sum total of human happiness." The economic order must be so constructed that each man's private quest of gains and satisfactions, and avoidance of pains and retributions, guarantees maximal satisfactions and minimum frustrations to others. This "laissez-faire" doctrine, akin to the French economic outlook of the period, is not only a kind of economics; it is also a psychology, indeed, also a philosophy of social behavior. Because of its emphasis upon utility, it came to be known as *utilitarianism,* reaching a more adequate expression in an essay by that name of John Stuart Mill, who at the same time developed the association psychology as it came through Hartley and Bentham, and justified the definition of goals and ends in terms of pleasures and pains. As had happened earlier with Epicurus, the doctrine did not look good to those who demanded something with a vivid and ringing appeal to the more beautiful and complex sentiments of mankind. For Thomas Carlyle it became the "profit and loss philosophy" and was commonly held not to be the morally enlightening principle for which it was offered, but a debasement of human moral aspirations. However the morals of the matter may lie, there is no doubt that this reactivation of hedonism, this redefinition of associationism, so that it became a doctrine of human motives, played a considerable part in the practical psychology of practical people during the nineteenth century. It became the substance of the "political economy" of the new industrial order, and seemed to its followers to be the essence of clarity, simplicity, and convincingness. The only reason why it did not finally take hold upon nineteenth-century man as *the* one rational outlook upon a changing society was the advent of the evolutionary principle in the hands of Charles Darwin. To get the feeling of the eighteenth-century union of *associationism* and *hedonism,* one needs but a few pages of Jeremy Bentham.

The Principles of Morals and Legislation *

CHAPTER I. OF THE PRINCIPLE OF UTILITY

I. Nature has placed mankind under the governance of two sovereign masters, *pain* and *pleasure.* It is for them alone to point out what we ought to do, as well as to determine what we shall do. On the one hand

* From Jeremy Bentham, *The Principles of Morals and Legislation* (New York: Hafner Publishing Company, The Hafner Library of Classics, 1948), pp. 1–3, 33–42, 55–57.

the standard of right and wrong, on the other the chain of causes and effects, are fastened to their throne. They govern us in all we do, in all we say, in all we think: every effort we can make to throw off our subjection, will serve but to demonstrate and confirm it. In words a man may pretend to abjure their empire: but in reality he will remain subject to it all the while. The *principle of utility* recognises this subjection, and assumes it for the foundation of that system, the object of which is to rear the fabric of felicity by the hands of reason and of law. . . .

II. . . . By the principle of utility is meant that principle which approves or disapproves of every action whatsoever, according to the tendency which it appears to have to augment or diminish the happiness of the party whose interest is in question: or, what is the same thing in other words, to promote or to oppose that happiness. I say of every action whatsoever; and therefore not only of every action of a private individual, but of every measure of government.

III. By utility is meant that property in any object, whereby it tends to produce benefit, advantage, pleasure, good, or happiness (all this in the present case comes to the same thing) or (what comes again to the same thing) to prevent the happening of mischief, pain, evil, or unhappiness to the party whose interest is considered: if that party be the community in general, then the happiness of the community: if a particular individual, then the happiness of that individual.

IV. The interest of the community is one of the most general expressions that can occur in the phraseology of morals: no wonder that the meaning of it is often lost. When it has a meaning, it is this. The community is a fictitious *body,* composed of the individual persons who are considered as constituting as it were its *members.* The interest of the community then is, what?—the sum of the interests of the several members who compose it.

. . .

CHAPTER V. PLEASURES AND PAINS, THEIR KINDS

I. Having represented what belongs to all sorts of pleasures and pains alike, we come now to exhibit, each by itself, the several sorts of pains and pleasures. Pains and pleasures may be called by one general word, interesting perceptions. Interesting perceptions are either simple or complex. The simple ones are those which cannot any one of them be resolved into more: complex are those which are resolvable into divers simple ones. A complex interesting perception may accordingly be composed either, 1. Of pleasures alone: 2. Of pains alone: or, 3. Of a pleasure or pleasures, and a pain or pains together. What determines a lot of pleasure, for example, to be regarded as one complex pleasure, rather than as divers simple ones, is the nature of the exciting cause. Whatever pleasures are excited all at once by the action of the same cause, are apt to be looked upon as constituting all together but one pleasure.

II. The several simple pleasures of which human nature is susceptible, seem to be as follows: 1. The pleasures of sense. 2. The pleasures of wealth. 3. The pleasures of skill. 4. The pleasures of amity. 5. The pleasures of a good name. 6. The pleasures of power. 7. The pleasures of piety, 8. The pleasures of benevolence. 9. The pleasures of malevolence. 10. The pleasures of memory. 11. The pleasures of imagination. 12. The pleasures of expectation. 13. The pleasures dependent on association. 14. The pleasures of relief.

III. The several simple pains seem to be as follows: 1. The pains of privation. 2. The pains of the senses. 3. The pains of awkwardness. 4. The pains of enmity. 5. The pains of an ill name. 6. The pains of piety. 7. The pains of benevolence. 8. The pains of malevolence. 9. The pains of the memory. 10. The pains of the imagination. 11. The pains of expectation. 12. The pains dependent on association.

IV. 1. The pleasures of sense seem to be as follows: 1. The pleasures of the taste or palate; including whatever pleasures are experienced in satisfying the appetites of hunger and thirst. 2. The pleasure of intoxication. 3. The pleasures of the organ of smelling. 4. The pleasures of the touch. 5. The simple pleasures of the ear; independent of association. 6. The simple pleasures of the eye; independent of association. 7. The pleasure of the sexual sense. 8. The pleasure of health: or, the internal pleasureable feeling or flow of spirits (as it is called) which accompanies a state of full health and vigour; especially at times of moderate bodily exertion. 9. The pleasures of novelty: or, the pleasures derived from the gratification of the appetite of curiosity, by the application of new objects to any of the senses.

V. 2. By the pleasures of wealth may be meant those pleasures which a man is apt to derive from the consciousness of possessing any article or articles which stand in the list of instruments of enjoyment or security, and more particularly at the time of his first acquiring them; at which time the pleasure may be styled a pleasure of gain or a pleasure of acquisition: at other times a pleasure of possession.

3. The pleasures of skill, as exercised upon particular objects, are those which accompany the application of such particular instruments of enjoyment to their uses, as cannot be so applied without a greater or less share of difficulty or exertion.

VI. 4. The pleasures of amity, or self-recommendation, are the pleasures that may accompany the persuasion of a man's being in the acquisition or the possession of the good-will of such or such assignable person or persons in particular: or, as the phrase is, of being upon good terms with him or them: and as a fruit of it, of his being in a way to have the benefit of their spontaneous and gratuitous services.

VII. 5. The pleasures of a good name are the pleasures that accompany the persuasion of a man's being in the acquisition or the possession of the good-will of the world about him; that is, of such members of society as he is likely to have concerns with; and as a means of it, either their love or their esteem, or both: and as a fruit of it, of his being in the way to have the benefit of their spontaneous and gratuitous services. These may likewise be called the pleasures of good repute, the pleasures of honour, or the pleasures of the moral sanction.

VIII. 6. The pleasures of power are the pleasures that accompany the persuasion of a man's being in a condition to dispose people, by means of their hopes and fears, to give him the benefit of their services: that is, by the hope of some service, or by the fear of some disservice, that he may be in the way to render them.

IX. 7. The pleasures of piety are the pleasures that accompany the belief of a man's being in the acquisition or in possession of the good-will or favour of the Supreme Being: and as a fruit of it, of his being in a way of enjoying pleasures to be received by God's special appointment, either in this life, or in a life to come. These may also be called the pleasures of religion, the pleasures of a religious disposition, or the pleasures of the religious sanction.

X. 8. The pleasures of benevolence are the pleasures resulting from the view of any pleasures supposed to be possessed by the beings who may be the objects of benevolence; to wit, the sensitive beings we are acquainted with; under which are commonly included, 1. The Supreme Being. 2. Human beings. 3. Other animals. These may also be called the pleasures of good-will, the pleasures of sympathy, or the pleasures of the benevolent or social affections.

XI. 9. The pleasures of malevolence are the pleasures resulting from the view of any pain supposed to be suffered by the beings who may become the objects of malevolence: to wit, 1. Human beings. 2. Other animals. These may also be styled the pleasures of ill-will, the pleasures of the irascible appetite, the pleasures of antipathy, or the pleasures of the malevolent or dissocial affections.

XII. 10. The pleasures of the memory are the pleasures which, after having enjoyed such and such pleasures, or even in some cases after having suffered such and such pains, a man will now and then experience, at recollecting them exactly in the order and in the circumstances in which they were actually enjoyed or suffered. These derivative pleasures may of course be distinguished into as many species as there are of original perceptions, from whence they may be copied. They may also be styled pleasures of simple recollection.

XIII. 11. The pleasures of the imagination are the pleasures which may be derived from the contemplation of any such pleasures as may happen to be suggested by the memory, but in a different order, and accompanied by different groups of circumstances. These may accordingly be referred to any one of the three cardinal points of time, present, past, or future. It is evident they may admit of as many distinctions as those of the former class.

XIV. 12. The pleasures of expectation are the pleasures that result from the contemplation of any sort of pleasure, referred to time *future,* and accompanied with the sentiment of *belief.* These also may admit of the same distinctions.

XV. 13. The pleasures of association are the pleasures which certain objects or incidents may happen to afford, not of themselves, but merely in virtue of some association they have contracted in the mind with certain objects or incidents which are in themselves pleasurable. Such is the case, for instance, with the pleasure of skill, when afforded by such a set of incidents as compose a game of chess. This derives its pleasurable quality from its association partly with the pleasures of skill, as exercised in the production of incidents pleasurable of themselves: partly from its association with the pleasures of power. Such is the case also with the pleasure of good luck, when afforded by such incidents as compose the game of hazard, or any other game of chance, when played at for nothing. This derives its pleasurable quality from its association with one of the pleasures of wealth; to wit, with the pleasure of acquiring it.

XVI. 14. Farther on we shall see pains grounded upon pleasures; in like manner may we now see pleasures grounded upon pains. To the catalogue of pleasures may accordingly be added the pleasures of *relief:* or, the pleasures which a man experiences when, after he has been enduring a pain of any kind for a certain time, it comes to cease, or to abate. These may of course be distinguished into as many species as there are of pains: and may give rise to so many pleasures of memory, of imagination, and of expectation.

XVII. 1. Pains of privation are the pains that may result from the thought of not possessing in the time present any of the several kinds of pleasures. Pains of privation may accordingly be resolved into as many kinds as there are of pleasures to which they may correspond, and from the absence whereof they may be derived.

XVIII. There are three sorts of pains which are only so many modifications of the several pains of privation. When the enjoyment of any particular pleasure happens to be particularly desired, but without any expectation approaching to assurance, the pain of privation which thereupon results takes a particular name, and is called the pain of *desire,* or of unsatisfied desire.

XIX. Where the enjoyment happens to have been looked for with a degree of expectation approaching to assurance, and that expectation is made suddenly to cease, it is called a pain of disappointment.

XX. A pain of privation takes the name of a pain of regret in two cases: 1. Where it is grounded on the memory of a pleasure, which having been once enjoyed, appears not likely to be enjoyed again: 2. Where it is grounded on the idea of a pleasure, which was never actually enjoyed, nor perhaps so much as expected, but which might have been enjoyed (it is supposed) had such or such a contingency happened, which, in fact, did not happen.

XXI. 2. The several pains of the senses seem to be as follows: 1. The pains of hunger and thirst: or the disagreeable sensations produced by the want of suitable substances which need at times to be applied to the alimentary canal. 2. The pains of the taste: or the disagreeable sensations produced by the application of various substances to the palate, and other superior parts of the same canal. 3. The pains of the organ of smell: or the disagreeable sensations produced by the effluvia of various substances when applied to that organ. 4. The pains of the touch: or the disagreeable sensations produced by the application of various substances to the skin. 5. The simple pains of the hearing: or the disagreeable sensations excited in the organ of that sense by various kinds of sounds: independently (as before) of association. 6. The simple pains of the sight: or the disagreeable sensations if any such there be, that may be excited in the organ of that sense by visible images, independent of the principle of association. 7. The pains resulting from excessive heat or cold, unless these be referable to the touch. 8. The pains of disease: or the acute and uneasy sensations resulting from the several diseases and indispositions to which human nature is liable. 9. The pain of exertion, whether bodily or mental: or the uneasy sensation which is apt to accompany any intense effort, whether of mind or body.

XXII. 3. The pains of awkwardness are the pains which sometimes result from the unsuccessful endeavour to apply any particular instruments of enjoyment or security to their uses, or from the difficulty a man experiences in applying them.

XXIII. 4. The pains of enmity are the pains that may accompany the persuasion of a man's being obnoxious to the ill-will of such or such an assignable person or persons in particular: or, as the phrase is, of being upon ill terms with him or them: and, in consequence, of being obnoxious to certain pains of some sort or other, of which he may be the cause.

XXIV. 5. The pains of an ill-name, are the pains that accompany the persuasion of a man's being obnoxious, or in a way to be obnoxious to the ill-will of the world about him. These may likewise be called the pains of ill-repute, the pains of dishonour, or the pains of the moral sanction.

XXV. 6. The pains of piety are the pains that accompany the belief of a man's being obnoxious to the displeasure of the Supreme Being: and in consequence to certain pains to be inflicted by his especial appointment, either in this life or in a life to come. These may also be called the pains of religion; the pains of a religious disposition; or the pains of the religious sanction. When the belief is looked upon as well-grounded, these pains are commonly called religious terrors; when looked upon as ill-grounded, superstitious terrors.

XXVI. 7. The pains of benevolence are the pains resulting from the view of any pains supposed to be endured by other beings. These may also be called the pains of good-will, of sympathy, or the pains of the benevolent or social affections.

XXVII. 8. The pains of malevolence are the pains resulting from the view of any pleasures supposed to be enjoyed by any beings who happen to be the objects of a man's displeasure. These may also be styled the pains of ill-will, of antipathy, or the pains of the malevolent or dissocial affections.

XXVIII. 9. The pains of the memory may be grounded on every one of the above kinds, as well of pains of privation as of positive pains. These correspond exactly to the pleasures of the memory.

XXIX. 10. The pains of the imagination may also be grounded on any one of the above kinds, as well of pains of privation as of positive pains: in other respects they correspond exactly to the pleasures of the imagination.

XXX. 11. The pains of expectation may be grounded on each one of the above kinds, as well of pains of privation as of positive pains. These may be also termed pains of apprehension.

XXXI. 12. The pains of association correspond exactly to the pleasures of association.

XXXII. Of the above list there are certain pleasures and pains which suppose the existence of some pleasure or pain of some other person, to which the pleasure or pain of the person in question has regard: such pleasures and pains may be termed *extra-regarding*. Others do not suppose any such thing: these may be termed *self-regarding.* The only pleasures and pains of the extra-regarding class are those of benevolence and those of malevolence: all the rest are self-regarding.

XXXIII. Of all these several sorts of pleasures and pains, there is scarce any one which is not liable, on more accounts than one, to come under the consideration of the law. Is an offence committed? It is the tendency which it has to destroy, in such or such persons, some of these pleasures, or to produce some of these pains, that constitutes the mischief of it, and the ground for punishing it. It is the prospect of some of these pleasures, or of security from some of these pains, that constitutes the motive or temptation, it is the attainment of them that constitutes the profit of the offence. Is the offender to be punished? It can be only by the production of one or more of these pains, that the punishment can be inflicted.

. . . But besides these supervening incidents, there are other circumstances relative to a man, that may have their influence, and which are co-eval to his birth. In the first place, it seems to be universally agreed, that in the original frame or texture of every man's body, there is a something which, independently of all subsequently intervening circumstances, renders him liable to be affected by causes producing bodily pleasure or pain, in a manner different from that in which another man would be affected by the same causes. To the catalogue of circumstances influencing a man's sensibility, we may therefore add his original or radical frame, texture, constitution, or temperament of body.

XXIX. 24. In the next place, it seems to be pretty well agreed, that there is something also in the original frame or texture of every man's mind, which, independently of all exterior and subsequently intervening circumstances, and even of his radical frame of body, makes him liable to be differently affected by the same exciting causes, from what another man would be. To the catalogue of circumstances influencing a man's sensibility, we may therefore further add his original or radical frame, texture, constitution or temperament of mind.

XXX. It seems pretty certain, all this while, that a man's sensibility to causes producing pleasure or pain, even of mind, may depend in a considerable degree upon his original and acquired frame of body. But we have no reason to think that it can depend altogether upon that frame: since, on the one hand, we see persons whose frame of body is as much alike as can be conceived, differing very considerably in respect of their mental frame: and, on the other hand, persons whose frame of mind is as much alike as can be conceived, differing very conspicuously in regard to their bodily frame.

XXXI. It seems indisputable also, that the different sets of external occurrences that may befall a man in the course of his life, will make great differences in the subsequent texture of his mind at any given period: yet still those differences are not solely to be attributed to such occurrences. Equally far from the truth seems that opinion to be (if any such be maintained) which attributes all to nature, and that which attributes all to education. The two circumstances will therefore still remain distinct, as well from one another, as from all others.

XXXII. Distinct however as they are, it is manifest, that at no period in the active part of a man's life can they either of them make their appearance by themselves. All they do is to constitute the latent groundwork which the other supervening circumstances have to work upon: and whatever influence those original principles may have, is so changed and modified, and covered over, as it were, by those other circumstances, as never to be separately discernible. The effects of the one influence are indistinguishably blended with those of the other.

JOHN STUART MILL

Bentham, both rationalist and lover of mankind, strives to find an orderly way of understanding and controlling human behavior which will put an end to the destructiveness of the Industrial Revolution, which was crowding men into factories and blackening England with the "dark Satanic mills" of which William Blake wrote. He defined the nature of economic activity in such a way that each man's simple self-interest, his association of pleasure with certain acts and of pain with other acts, could be so orchestrated in society that it would contribute to the welfare of the whole. To do this he had to assume a simple association psychology, an association established in experience between certain acts and respectively good or bad consequences empirically known; he had to assume elementary hedonism, such as that developed by some of the Greeks, and he had to show the unerring infallibility of the principle of association. He was one of the great founders of criminology and penology because in this way he could show the irrationality of punishment through sheer retribution or a naïve belief that a law aiming at deterrence would inevitably deter sadism, and the possibility of founding correctional principles upon a simple association base. As a psychologist we cannot allow him more space here. We shall turn immediately, then, to James Mill, Jeremy Bentham's disciple and friend, who among his many activities as historian, literary man, editor of one of the leading reviews, found it possible to formulate a remarkably lucid and systematic association psychology; and to his remarkable son, John Stuart Mill.

Father-and-son combinations in psychology are not numerous, and this is the first we encounter. Ardent associationist that he was, James Mill assumed that his first-born son, arriving in this world in 1806, could be made into just about anything his father wanted him to be. The little boy began his classical education in the nursery, and during the years of what would have been school, he sat on one side of the table while his father sat on the other. In this manner he studied and received the necessary coaching in the classics, in history, and in logic. He began long walks with his father at the age of thirteen, in which they discussed political economy, and was soon readying himself for the three great fields in which he made his adult contribution: logic, economics, and psychology.

Before he was twenty, he awoke to discover that all of his aims and values in life had been established in him by his father by the simple process of association—that is, by approval and disapproval of ideas and values. This was a melancholy discovery. It was only in reading a story full of sympathy that feeling returned to him, and he decided there was something for him in life sounder than arbitrary associations. He never repudiated the main substance, however, of his father's teaching. In his own work he reconstructed the work of Bentham to give a larger degree of creativeness and spontaneity to the life of the mind. And in how beautiful and orderly a way he developed Bentham's principle of the greatest good of the greatest number, in the form of the philosophy known as utilitarianism, can be judged below (page 195).

To catch and hold the force of associationism—the dominant psychology in Britain for 200 years and still broadly influential—there is no better way than to read John Stuart Mill's account of his own associationist education at the hands of his devoted—and brilliant, and authoritarian—father.

Autobiography *

My father, the son of a petty tradesman and (I believe) small farmer, at Northwater Bridge, in the county of Angus, was, when a boy, recommended by his abilities to the notice of Sir John Stuart, of Fettercairn, one of the Barons of the Exchequer in Scotland, and was, in consequence, sent to the University of Edinburgh at the expense of a fund established by Lady Jane Stuart (the wife of Sir John Stuart) and some other ladies for educating young men for the Scottish Church. He there went through the usual course of study, and was licensed as a Preacher, but never followed the profession; having satisfied himself that he could not believe the doctrines of that or any other Church. . . .

. . . a considerable part of almost every day was employed in the instruction of his children: in the case of one of whom, myself, he exerted an amount of labour, care, and perseverance rarely, if ever, employed for a similar purpose, in endeavouring to give, according to his own conception, the highest order of intellectual education.

A man who, in his own practice, so vigorously acted up to the principle of losing no time, was likely to adhere to the same rule in the instruction of his pupil. I have no remembrance of the time when I began to learn Greek. I have been told that it was when I was three years old. My earliest recollection on the subject, is that of committing to memory what my father termed Vocables, being lists of common Greek words, with their signification in English, which he wrote out for me on cards. . . .

What he was himself willing to undergo for the sake of my instruction, may be judged from the fact, that I went through the whole process of preparing my Greek lessons in the same room and at the same table at which he was writing: and as in those days Greek and English lexicons were not, and I could make no more use of a Greek and Latin lexicon than could be made without having yet begun to learn Latin, I was forced to have recourse to him for the meaning of every word which I did not know. This incessant interruption, he, one of the most impatient of men, submitted to, and wrote under that interruption several volumes of his History and all else that he had to write during those years.

The only thing besides Greek, that I learnt as a lesson in this part of

* From John Stuart Mill, *Autobiography* (New York: The Liberal Arts Press, 1957), pp. 4–9, 13–15, 19, 86–92, 94–96. © 1957 by the Liberal Arts Press, Inc. Reprinted by permission of the Liberal Arts Press Division of the Bobbs-Merrill Company.

my childhood, was arithmetic: this also my father taught me: it was the task of the evenings, and I well remember its disagreeableness. But the lessons were only a part of the daily instruction I received. Much of it consisted in the books I read by myself, and my father's discourses to me, chiefly during our walks. From 1810 to the end of 1813 we were living in Newington Green, then an almost rustic neighbourhood. My father's health required considerable and constant exercise, and he walked habitually before breakfast, generally in the green lanes towards Hornsey. In these walks I always accompanied him, and with my earliest recollections of green fields and wild flowers, is mingled that of the account I gave him daily of what I had read the day before. To the best of my remembrance, this was a voluntary rather than a prescribed exercise. I made notes on slips of paper while reading, and from these, in the morning walks, I told the story to him; for the books were chiefly histories, of which I read in this manner a great number: Robertson's histories, Hume, Gibbon; but my greatest delight, then and for long afterwards, was Watson's Philip the Second and Third. The heroic defence of the Knights of Malta against the Turks, and of the revolted provinces of the Netherlands against Spain, excited in me an intense and lasting interest. . . .

. . . but when I came to the American war, I took my part, like a child as I was (until set right by my father) on the wrong side, because it was called the English side. In these frequent talks about the books I read, he used, as opportunity offered, to give me explanations and ideas respecting civilization, government, morality, mental cultivation, which he required me afterwards to restate to him in my own words. . . .

Aristotle's Rhetoric, which, as the first expressly scientific treatise on any moral or psychological subject which I had read, and containing many of the best observations of the ancients on human nature and life, my father made me study with peculiar care, and throw the matter of it into synoptic tables. . . .

From about the age of twelve, I entered into another and more advanced stage in my course of instruction; in which the main object was no longer the aids and appliances of thought, but the thoughts themselves. This commenced with Logic, in which I began at once with the Organon, and read it to the Analytics inclusive, but profited little by the Posterior Analytics, which belong to a branch of speculation I was not yet ripe for. Contemporaneously with the Organon, my father made me read the whole or parts of several of the Latin treatises on the scholastic logic; giving each day to him, in our walks, a minute account of what I had read, and answering his numerous and searching questions. After this, I went in a similar manner, through the "Computatio sive Logica" of Hobbes, a work of a much higher order of thought than the books of the school logicians, and which he estimated very highly. . . .

I know nothing, in my education, to which I think myself more indebted for whatever capacity of thinking I have attained. The first intellectual operation in which I arrived at any proficiency, was dissecting a bad argument, and finding in what part the fallacy lay: and though whatever capacity of this sort I attained was due to the fact that it was an intellectual exercise in which I was most perseveringly drilled by my father, yet it is also true that the school logic, and the mental habits acquired in studying it, were among the principal instruments of this drilling. I am persuaded that nothing, in modern education, tends so much, when properly used, to form exact thinkers, who attach a precise meaning to words and propositions, and are not imposed on by vague, loose, or ambiguous terms. The boasted influence of mathematical studies is nothing to it; for in mathematical processes, none of the real difficulties of correct ratiocination occur. It is also a study peculiarly adapted to an early stage in the education of philosophical students, since it does not presuppose the slow process of acquiring, by experience and reflection, valuable thoughts of their own. They may become capable of disentangling the intricacies of confused and self-contradictory thought, before their own thinking faculties are much advanced; a power which, for want of some such discipline, many otherwise able men altogether lack; and when they have to answer opponents, only endeavour, by such arguments as they can command, to support the opposite conclusion, scarcely even attempting to confute the reasonings of their antagonists; and, therefore, at the utmost, leaving the question, as far as it depends on argument, a balanced one. . . .

This new employment of his time caused no relaxation in his attention to my education. It was in this same year, 1819, that he took me through a complete course of political economy. His loved and intimate friend, Ricardo, had shortly before published the book which formed so great an epoch in political economy; a book which never would have been published or written, but for the entreaty and strong encouragement of my father; for Ricardo, the most modest of men, though firmly convinced of the truth of his doctrines, deemed himself so little capable of doing them justice in exposition and expression, that he shrank from the idea of publicity. . . .

A CRISIS IN MY MENTAL HISTORY. ONE STAGE ONWARD

For some years after this I wrote very little, and nothing regularly, for publication: and great were the advantages which I derived from the intermission. It was of no common importance to me, at this period, to be able to digest and mature my thoughts for my own mind only, without any immediate call for giving them out in print. . . .

From the winter of 1821, when I first read Bentham, and especially from the commencement of the Westminster Review, I had what might truly be called an object in life; to be a reformer of the world. My conception of my own happiness was entirely identified with this object. The personal sympathies I wished for were those of fellow labourers in this enterprise. I endeavoured to pick up as many flowers as I could by the way; but as a serious and permanent personal satisfaction to rest upon, my whole reliance was placed on this; and I was accustomed to felicitate myself on the certainty of a happy life which I enjoyed, through placing my happiness in something durable and distant, in which some progress might be always making, while it could never be exhausted by complete attainment. This did very well for several years, during which the general improvement going on in the world and the idea of myself as engaged with others in struggling to promote it, seemed enough to fill up an interesting and animated existence. But the time came when I awakened from this as from a dream. It was in the autumn of 1826. I was in a dull state of nerves, such as everybody is occasionally liable to; unsusceptible to enjoyment or pleasurable excitement; one of those moods when what is pleasure at other times, becomes insipid or indifferent; the state, I should think, in which converts to Methodism usually are, when smitten by their first "conviction of sin." In this frame of mind it occurred to me to put the question directly to myself: "Suppose that all your objects in life were realized; that all the changes in institutions and opinions which you are looking forward to, could be completely effected at this very instant: would this be a great joy and happiness to you?" And an irrepressible self-consciousness distinctly answered, "No!" At this my heart sank within me: the whole foundation on which my life was constructed fell down. All my happiness was to have been found in the continual pursuit of this end. The end had ceased to charm, and how could there ever again be any interest in the means? I seemed to have nothing left to live for.

At first I hoped that the cloud would pass away of itself; but it did not. A night's sleep, the sovereign remedy for the smaller vexations of life, had no effect on it. I awoke to a renewed consciousness of the woful fact. I carried it with me into all companies, into all occupations. Hardly anything had power to cause me even a few minutes oblivion of it. For some months the cloud seemed to grow thicker and thicker. The lines in Coleridge's "dejection"—I was not then acquainted with them—exactly describe my case:

A grief without a pang, void, dark and drear,
A drowsy, stifled, unimpassioned grief,
Which finds no natural outlet or relief
In word, or sigh, or tear.

In vain I sought relief from my favourite books; those memorials of past nobleness and greatness from which I had always hitherto drawn strength and animation. I read them now without feeling, or with the accustomed feeling *minus* all its charm; and I became persuaded, that my love of mankind, and of excellence for its own sake, had worn itself out. I sought no comfort by speaking to others of what I felt. If I had loved any one sufficiently to make confiding my griefs a necessity, I should not have been in the condition I was. I felt, too, that mine was not an interesting, or in any way respectable distress. There was nothing in it to attract sympathy. Advice, if I had known where to seek it, would have been most precious. The words of Macbeth to the physician often occurred to my thoughts. But there was no one on whom I could build the faintest hope of such assistance. My father, to whom it would have been natural to me to have recourse in any practical difficulties, was the last person to whom, in such a case as this, I looked for help. Everything convinced me that he had no knowledge of any such mental state as I was suffering from, and that even if he could be made to understand it, he was not the physician who could heal it. My education, which was wholly his work, had been conducted without any regard to the possibility of its ending in this result; and I saw no use in giving him the pain of thinking that his plans had failed, when the failure was probably irremediable, and, at all events, beyond the power of *his* remedies. Of other friends, I had at that time none to whom I had any hope of making my condition intelligible. It was however abundantly intelligible to myself; and the more I dwelt upon it, the more hopeless it appeared.

My course of study had led me to believe, that all mental and moral feelings and qualities, whether of a good or of a bad kind, were the results of association; that we love one thing, and hate another, take pleasure in one sort of action or contemplation, and pain in another sort, through the clinging of pleasurable or painful ideas to those things, from the effect of education or of experience. As a corollary from this, I had always heard it maintained by my father, and was myself convinced, that the object of education should be to form the strongest possible associations of the salutary class; associations of pleasure with all things beneficial to the great whole, and of pain with all things hurtful to it. This doctrine appeared inexpugnable; but it now seemed to me, on retrospect, that my teachers had occupied themselves but superficially with the means of forming and keeping up these salutary associations. They seemed to have trusted altogether to the old familiar instruments, praise and blame, reward and punishment. Now, I did not doubt that by these means, begun early, and applied unremittingly, intense associations of pain and pleasure, especially of pain, might be created, and might produce desires and aversions capable of lasting undiminished to the end of life. But there must always be something artificial and casual in associations thus produced. The pains and pleasures thus forcibly associated with things, are not connected with them by any natural tie; and it is therefore, I thought, essential to the durability of these associations, that they should have become so intense and inveterate as to be practically indissoluble, before the habitual exercise of the power of analysis had commenced. For I now saw, or thought I saw, what I had always before received with incredulity—that the habit of analysis has a tendency to wear away the feelings: as indeed it has, when no other mental habit is cultivated, and the analysing spirit remains without its natural complements and correctives. The very excellence of analysis (I argued) is that it tends to weaken and undermine whatever is the result of prejudice; that it enables us mentally to separate ideas which have only casually clung together: and no associations whatever could ultimately resist this dissolving force, were it not that we owe to analysis our clearest knowledge of the permanent sequences in nature; the real connexions between Things, not dependent on our will and feelings; natural laws, by virtue of which, in many cases, one thing is inseparable from another in fact; which laws, in proportion as they are clearly perceived and imaginatively realized, cause our ideas of things which are always joined together in Nature, to cohere more and more closely in our thoughts. Analytic habits may thus even strengthen the associations between causes and effects, means and ends, but tend altogether to weaken those which are, to speak familiarly, a *mere* matter of feeling. They are therefore (I thought) favourable to prudence and clear-sightedness, but a perpetual worm at the root both of the passions and of the virtues; and, above all, fearfully undermine all desires, and all pleasures, which are the effects of association, that is, according to the theory I held, all except the purely physical and organic; of the entire insufficiency of which to make life desirable, no one had a stronger conviction than I had. These were the laws of human nature, by which, as it seemed to me, I had been brought to my present state. All those to whom I looked up, were of opinion that the pleasure of sympathy with human beings, and the feelings which made the good of others, and especially of mankind on a large scale, the object of existence, were the greatest and surest sources of happiness. Of the truth of this I was convinced, but to know that a feeling would make me happy if I had it, did not give me the feeling. My education, I thought, had failed to create these feelings in sufficient strength to resist the dissolving influence of analysis, while the whole course of my intellectual cultivation had made precocious and premature analysis the inveterate habit of my mind. I was thus, as I said to myself, left stranded at the commencement of my voyage, with a well-equipped ship and a rudder, but no sail; without any real desire for the ends which I had been so carefully fitted out to work for: no delight in virtue, or the general good, but also just as little in anything else. The fountains of vanity and ambition seemed to have dried up within me, as completely as those of benevolence. I had had (as I reflected) some gratification of vanity at too early an age: I had obtained some distinction, and felt myself of some importance, before the desire of distinction and of importance had grown into a passion: and little as it was which I had attained, yet having been attained too early, like all pleasures enjoyed too soon, it had made me *blasé* and indifferent to the pursuit. Thus neither selfish nor unselfish pleasures were pleasures to me. And there seemed no power in nature sufficient to begin the formation of my character anew, and create in a mind now irretrievably analytic, fresh associations of pleasure with any of the objects of human desire.

These were the thoughts which mingled with the dry heavy dejection of the melancholy winter of 1826–7. During this time I was not incapable of my usual occupations. I went on with them mechanically, by the mere force of habit. I had been so drilled in a certain sort of mental exercise, that I could still carry it on when all the spirit had gone out of it. I even composed and spoke several speeches at the debating society, how, or with what degree of success, I know not. Of four years continual speaking at that society, this is the only year of which I remember next to nothing. Two lines of Coleridge, in whom alone of all writers I have found a true description of what I felt, were often in my thoughts, not at this time (for I had never read them), but in a later period of the same mental malady:

> Work without hope draws nectar in a sieve,
> And hope without an object cannot live.

In all probability my case was by no means so peculiar as I fancied it, and I doubt not that many others have passed through a similar state; but the idiosyncrasies of my education had given to the general phenomenon a special character, which made it seem the natural effect of causes that it was hardly possible for time to remove. I frequently asked myself, if I could, or if I was bound to go on living, when life must be passed in this manner. I generally answered to myself, that I did not think I could possibly bear it beyond a year. When, however, not more than half that duration of time had elapsed, a small ray of light broke in upon my gloom. I was reading, accidentally, Marmontel's "Mémoires," and came to the passage which relates his father's death, the distressed position of the family, and the sudden inspiration by which he, then a mere boy, felt and made them feel that he would be everything to them—would supply the place of all that they had lost. A vivid conception of the scene and its feelings came over me, and I was moved to tears. From this moment my burthen grew lighter. The oppression of the thought that all feeling was dead within me, was gone. I was no longer hopeless: I was not a stick or a stone. I had still, it seemed, some of the material out of which all worth of character, and all capacity for happiness, are made. Relieved from my ever present sense of irremediable wretchedness, I gradually found that the ordinary incidents of life could again give me some pleasure; that I could again find enjoyment, not intense, but sufficient for cheerfulness, in sunshine and sky, in books, in conversation, in public affairs; and that there was, once more, excitement, though of a moderate kind, in exerting myself for my opinions, and for the public good. Thus the cloud gradually drew off, and I again enjoyed life: and though I had several relapses, some of which lasted many months, I never again was as miserable as I had been. . . .

This state of my thoughts and feelings made the fact of my reading Wordsworth for the first time (in the autumn of 1828), an important event in my life. I took up the collection of his poems from curiosity, with no expectation of mental relief from it, though I had before resorted to poetry with that hope. . . .

I had looked into the Excursion two or three years before, and found little in it; and I should probably have found as little, had I read it at this time. But the miscellaneous poems, in the two-volume edition of 1815 (to which little of value was added in the latter part of the author's life), proved to be the precise thing for my mental wants at that particular juncture.

In the first place, these poems addressed themselves powerfully to one of the strongest of my pleasurable susceptibilities, the love of rural objects and natural scenery; to which I had been indebted not only for much of the pleasure of my life, but quite recently for relief from one of my longest relapses into depression. In this power of rural beauty over me, there was a foundation laid for taking pleasure in Wordsworth's poetry; the more so, as his scenery lies mostly among mountains, which, owing to my early Pyrenean excursion, were my ideal of natural beauty. But Wordsworth would never have had any great effect on me, if he had merely placed before me beautiful pictures of natural scenery. Scott does this still better than Wordsworth, and a very second-rate landscape does it more effectually than any poet. What made Wordsworth's poems a medicine for my state of mind, was that they expressed, not mere outward beauty, but states of feeling, and of thought coloured by feeling, under the excitement of beauty. They seemed to be the very culture of the feelings, which I was in quest of. In them I seemed to draw from a source of inward joy, of sympathetic and imaginative pleasure, which could be shared in by all human beings; which had no connexion with struggle or imperfection, but would be made richer by every improvement in the physical or social condition of mankind. From them I seemed to learn what would be the perennial sources of happiness, when all the greater evils of life shall have been removed. And I felt myself at once better and happier as I came under their influence.

This is British associationism at its mature consummation. But there was still one more task to be carried forward to make Hartley's associationism an adequate psychological system. This was to put some flesh on the bare bones of abstract laws of association, and suggest why, as living individuals, we think of the *specific* things we do think of. Thomas Brown was the first great engineer of this process of individual vitalization. This helped in the task of showing how the life of *feeling* and impulse gets into the associationist principle.

THOMAS BROWN

The Secondary Laws of Learning *

The *first* circumstance which presents itself, as modifying the influence of the primary laws, in inducing one associate conception rather than another, is the length of time during which the original feelings from which they flowed, continued, when they co-existed, or succeeded each other. Every one must be conscious, that innumerable objects pass

* From Thomas Brown, "The Secondary Laws of Learning," in Wayne Dennis (ed.), *Readings in the History of Psychology* (New York: Appleton-Century-Crofts, 1948), pp. 125–128.

before him, which are slightly observed at the time, but which form no permanent associations in the mind. The longer we dwell on objects, the more fully do we rely on our future remembrance of them.

In the *second* place, the parts of a train appear to be more closely and firmly associated, as the original feelings have been more lively. We remember brilliant objects, more than those which are faint and obscure. We remember for our whole life-time, the occasions of great joy or sorrow; we forget the occasions of innumerable slight pleasures or pains, which occur to us every hour. That strong feeling of interest and curiosity, which we call attention, not only leads us to dwell longer on the consideration of certain objects, but also gives more vivacity to the objects on which we dwell,—and in both these ways tend, as we have seen, to fix them more strongly in the mind.

In the *third* place, the parts of any train are more readily suggested, in proportion as they have been more *frequently renewed*. It is thus, we remember, after reading them three of four times over, the verses which we could not repeat when we had read them only once.

In the *fourth* place, the feelings are connected more strongly in proportion as they are *more* or *less recent*. Immediately after reading any single line of poetry, we are able to repeat it, though we may have paid no particular attention to it;—in a very few minutes, unless when we have paid particular attention to it, we are no longer able to repeat it accurately—and in a very short time we forget it altogether. There is, indeed, one very striking exception to this law, in the case of old age: for events, which happened in youth, are then remembered, when events of the year preceding are forgotten. Yet, even in the case of extreme age,—when the time is not extended so far back,—the general law still holds; and events, which happened a few hours before, are remembered, when there is total forgetfulness of what happened a few days before.

In the *fifth* place, our successive feelings are associated more closely, as *each has co-existed less with other feelings*. The song, which we have never heard but from one person, can scarcely be heard again by us, without recalling that person to our memory; but there is obviously much less chance of this particular suggestion, if we have heard the same air and words frequently sung by others.

In the *sixth* place, the influence of the primary laws of suggestion is greatly modified by *original constitutional differences,* whether these are to be referred to the mind itself, or to varieties of bodily temperament. Such constitutional differences affect the primary laws in two ways,—first, by augmenting and extending the influence of all of them, as in the varieties of the general power of remembering, so observable in different individuals. Secondly, they modify the influence of the primary laws, by giving greater proportional vigor to one set of tendencies of suggestion than to another.

The primary laws of association, then, it appears, as far as they operate in our intellectual exertions, are greatly modified by original constitutional diversities. They are not less modified by constitutional diversities of another kind. These are the diversities of what is called temper, or disposition. It is thus we speak of one person of a *gloomy,* and another of a *cheerful* disposition; and we avoid the one, and seek the company of the other, as if with perfect confidence, that the trains of thought which rise by spontaneous suggestion to the minds of each will be different, and will be in accordance with that variety of character which we have supposed. To the cheerful, almost every object which they perceive is cheerful as themselves. In the very darkness of the storm, the cloud which hides the sunshine from their eye, does not hide it from their heart: while, to the sullen, no sky is bright, and no scene is fair. There are future fogs, which to their eyes, pollute and darken the purest airs of spring; and spring itself is known to them less as the season which follows and repairs the desolation of winter that is past, than as the season which announces its approaching return.

The next secondary law of suggestion to which I proceed, is one akin to the last which we have considered. The primary laws are modified, not by constitutional and permanent differences only, but by differences which occur in the same individual, according to the varying emotion of the hour. As there are persons, whose general character is gloomy or cheerful, we have, in like manner, our peculiar days or moments in which we pass from one of these characters to the other, and in which our trains of thought are tinctured with the corresponding varieties. A mere change of fortune is often sufficient to alter the whole cast of sentiment. Those who are in possession of public station, and power and affluence, are accustomed to represent affairs in a favorable light: the disappointed competitors for place to represent them in the most gloomy light; and though much of this difference may, unquestionably, be ascribed to wilful mis-statement in both cases, much of it is, as unquestionably, referable to that difference of colouring in which objects appear to the successful and the unsuccessful.

If even a slight momentary feeling of joy or sorrow have the power of modifying our suggestions, in accordance with it, emotions of a stronger and lasting kind must influence the trains of thought still more;—the meditations of every day rendering stronger the habitual connexions of such thoughts as accord with the peculiar frame of mind. It is in this way that every passion, which has one fixed object,—such as love, jealousy, revenge, derives nourishment from itself, suggesting images that give it in return, new force and liveliness. We see, in every thing, what we feel in ourselves; and the thought which external things seem to suggest, are thus, in part at least, suggested by the permanent emotion within.

The temporary diversities of state, that give rise to varieties of suggestion, are not mental only, but corporeal; and this difference of bodily state furnishes another secondary law, in modification of the primary. I need not refer to the extreme cases of intoxication or actual delirium,—the copious flow of follies, which a little wine, or a few grains of opium, may extract from the proudest reasoner. In circumstances less striking, how different are the trains of thought in health and in sickness,—after a temperate meal and after a luxurious excess! It is not to the animal powers only, that the burthen of digestion may become oppressive, but to the intellectual also; and often to the intellectual powers even more than to the animal. In that most delightful of all states, when the bodily frame has recovered from disease, and when in the first walk beneath the open sunshine, amid the blossoms and balmy air of summer, there is a mixture of corporeal and mental enjoyment, in which it is not easy to discriminate what images of pleasure arise from every object, that, in other states of health, might have excited no thought or emotion whatever.

There is yet another principle which modifies the primary laws of suggestion with very powerful influence. This is the principle of habit. I do not speak of its influence in suggesting images which have been already frequently suggested in a certain order,—for it would then be simpler to reduce the habit itself to the mere power of association. I speak of cases, in which the images suggested may have been of recent acquisition, but are suggested more readily in consequence of general tendencies produced by prior habits. When men of different professions observe the same circumstances, listen to the same story, or peruse the same work, their subsequent suggestions are far from being the same; and could the future differences of the associate feelings that are to rise, be foreseen by us at the time, we should probably be able to trace many of them to former professional peculiarities, which are thus always unfortunately apt to be more and more aggravated by the very suggestions to which they have themselves given rise. The most striking example, however, of the power of habit in modifying suggestion, is in the command which it gives to the orator, who has long been practiced in extemporary elocution; a command not of words merely, but of thoughts and judgments, which, at the very moment of their sudden inspiration, appear like the long-weighed calculations of deliberate reflection. The whole divisions of his subject start before him at once; image after image as he proceeds, arises to illustrate it; and proper words in proper places are all the while embodying his sentiments, as if without the slightest effort of his own.

In addition then, to the primary laws of suggestion, which are founded on the mere relations of the objects or feelings to each other, it appears that there is another set of laws, the operation of which is indispensable to account for the variety in the effects of the former. To these I have given the name of secondary laws of suggestion;—and we have seen accordingly that the suggestions are various as the original feelings have been, 1st, of longer or shorter continuance; 2dly, more or less lively; 3dly, more or less frequently present; 4thly, more or less recent; 5thly, more or less pure, if I may so express it, from the mixture of other feelings; 6thly, that they vary according to differences of original constitution; 7thly, according to differences of temporary emotion; 8thly, according to changes produced in the state of the body; and 9thly, according to general tendencies produced by prior habits.

❀

Across the Channel, associationism, essentially of a Lockean type, continued to flourish. How far it had spread is suggested by the true story of the "wild boy of Aveyron." In 1798 a group of French hunters found in Aveyron a boy without language or human ways. He was soon entrusted to Dr. Itard, a teacher of deaf-mutes, who thought that since the boy had no *ideas* he could be given ideas, according to Locke's theory, and thus gain normal intelligence. After five years Itard gave up. It might seem from the work of Condillac and later application of John Locke's work during the French Revolution by Condorcet, and by the attempt to reeducate the "wild boy of Aveyron," that associationism had just done all the work that it could possibly do. Nevertheless, we saw that Bentham was pushing it further, to make it a principle of "Morals and Legislation"; and that John Stuart Mill had developed this ethical system (see pages 187–195); and as we turn to Germany we find that associationism had proved capable of offering fresh and very different challenges.

One thing which British associationism had never done was to make ideas themselves dynamic; that is, sources of energy. Ideas acted upon one another almost as billiard balls would. There had to be a push to start a ball rolling, and it had to bump into others if it was to make them move. There remained the possibility, however, that the whole mental life is really dynamic; that the impact of the outer world is to alter the systems of stresses and strains already at work within, and that every factor from outside in the form of sensations remains within us as a memory, containing its own intrinsic push to get back into conscious life again. We have then a system of inner forces pushing and pulling one another. It is their dynamic pushes and pulls which one must understand if the process of perceiving, remembering, and thinking is to be real to us. This was the conception of Johann Friedrich Herbart. One of the many reasons for studying Herbart is to see the relation of his striving process to the later dynamism of Freud. It is, however, fascinating in its own right.

JOHANN FRIEDRICH HERBART

For Herbart, sensory impressions again constitute the basis of all experiences. But sensations are not passively linked one to another; they are active. Each sensation or its residue in the mind competes vigorously with other sensations for its place in consciousness, and in the battle of all against all some are relegated to an unconscious state, while others become dominant. (This is one of the most frequently cited forerunners of the Freudian unconscious.) The ideas, indeed, can be predicted to compete in accordance with quantitative principles, depending upon their strength. At times they join forces, so that groups of ideas battle against other groups of ideas. A new idea, in turn, which must find its place among those already existing, must be acceptable, compatible with those already established. There is an existing "apperception mass" in which the new idea must become embedded if it is to be accepted at all. This is one of the major contributions of Herbart. Through an established system of experimental schools, he saw to it that teachers understood how to add ideas slowly, one at a time, in accordance with the law of the child's development, in terms of larger and larger masses of experience which must assimilate with what is already there.

Though Herbart's major emphasis upon the dynamics of competing ideas and upon the principles of education must receive such primary emphasis, he is also important in another way. Since his ideas were quantitative, since he believed in the measurement of the intensities with which ideas compete for a place in consciousness, he suggested a "threshold" or a measurable level at which an idea gets into consciousness.* It is either above this threshold, that is, in awareness, or it sinks below this threshold of awareness into the unconscious sphere. This idea of threshold, the point separating that which gets into awareness from that which does not, we shall encounter in a long line of important modern studies; both in psychology and physiology there is scarcely a more constantly used or a more indispensable concept, if one must decide after all what is the quantity of stimulation needed to get an impression "into the mind."

* Compare Immanuel Kant, *Prolegomena to any Future Metaphysics* (Part II, Section 24):

> The first of the physical principles subsumes all phenomena, as intuitions in space and time, under the concept of quantity, and is thus a principle of the application of mathematics to experience. The second one subsumes the strictly empirical element, namely, sensation, which denotes the real in intuitions, not indeed directly under the concept of quantity, because sensation is not an intuition that *contains* either space or time, though it places the respective object corresponding to it in both. But still there is between reality (sense-representation) and the zero, or total void of intuition in time, a difference which has a quantity. For between every given degree of light and of darkness, between every degree of heat and of absolute cold, between every degree of weight and of absolute lightness, between every degree of occupancy space and of totally void space, diminishing degrees can be conceived, in the same manner as between consciousness and total unconsciousness (psychological darkness) ever-diminishing degrees obtain. Hence there is no perception that can prove an absolute absence; for instance, no psychological darkness that cannot be considered as consciousness which is only outbalanced by a stronger consciousness. This occurs in all cases of sensation, and so the understanding can anticipate even sensations, which constitute the peculiar quality of empirical representations (appearances), by means of the principle that they all have degree (and consequently that what is real in all appearance has degree). Here is the second application of mathematics (*mathesis intensorum*) to the science of nature.

Fundamental Principles *

CHAPTER I. THE CONDITION OF CONCEPTS, WHEN THEY ACT AS FORCES

10. Concepts become forces when they resist one another. This resistance occurs when two or more opposed concepts encounter one another.

At first let us take this proposition as simply as possible. In this connection, therefore, we shall not think of complex nor of compound concepts of any kind whatever; nor of such as indicate an object with several characteristics, neither of anything in time nor space, but of entirely simple concepts or sensations—e.g., red, blue, sour, sweet, etc. It is not our purpose to consider the general notions of the above-mentioned sensations, but to consider such representations as may result from an instantaneous act of sense-perception.

Again, the question concerning the origin of the sensations mentioned does not belong here, much less has the discussion to do with the consideration of anything else that might have previously existed or occurred in the soul.

The proposition as it stands is that opposed concepts resist one another. Concepts that are not opposed—e.g., a tone and a color—may exist, in which case it will be assumed that such concepts offer no resistance to one another. (Exceptions to this latter proposition may occur, of which more hereafter.)

Resistance is an expression of force. To the resisting concept, however, its action is quite accidental; it adjusts itself to the attack which is mutual among concepts, and which is determined by the degree of opposition existing between them. This opposition may be regarded as that by which they are affected collectively. In themselves, however, concepts are not forces.

11. Now, what is the result of the resistance mentioned?

Do concepts partially or wholly destroy one another, or, notwithstanding the resistance, do they remain unchanged?

Destroyed concepts are the same as none at all. However, if, notwithstanding the mutual attack, concepts remain unchanged, then one could not be removed or suppressed by another (as we see every moment that they are). Finally, if all that is conceived of each concept were changed by the contest, then this would signify nothing more than, at the beginning, quite another concept had been present in consciousness.

* From Johann Friedrich Herbart, *A Text-Book in Psychology*, trans. by Margaret K. Smith (New York: D. Appleton and Company, 1891), pp. 9–15.

The presentation (concept), then, must yield without being destroyed —i.e., the real concept is changed into an effort to present itself.

Here it is in effect stated that, as soon as the hindrance yields, the concept by its own effort will again make its appearance in consciousness. In this lies the possibility (although not for all cases the only ground) of reproduction.

12. When a concept becomes not entirely, but only in part, transformed into an effort, we must guard against considering this part as a severed portion of the whole concept. It has certainly a definite magnitude (upon the knowledge of which much depends), but this magnitude indicates only a degree of the obscuration of the whole concept. If the question be in regard to several parts of one and the same concept, these parts must not be regarded as different, severed portions, but the smaller divisions may be regarded as being contained in the larger. The same is true of the remainders after the collisions—i.e., of those parts of a concept which remain unobscured, for those parts are also degrees of the real concept.

CHAPTER II. EQUILIBRIUM AND MOVEMENT OF CONCEPTS

13. When a sufficiency of opposition exists between concepts, the latter are in equilibrium. They come only gradually to this point. The continuous change of their degree of obscuration may be called their movement.

The statics and mechanics of the mind have to do with the calculation of the equilibrium and movement of the concepts.

14. All investigations into the statics of the mind begin with two different quantitative factors, viz., the sum (or the aggregate amount) of the resistances and the ratio of their limitation. The former is the quantity which rises from their encounter, to be divided between the opposing concepts. If one knows how to state it, and knows also the ratio in which the different concepts yield in the encounter, then, by a simple calculation in proportion, the statical point of each concept—i.e., the degree of its obscuration in equilibrium—may be found.

15. The sum as well as the ratio of the mutual limitation depends upon the strength of each individual concept which is affected in inverse ratio to its strength, and upon the degree of opposition between the two concepts. For their influence upon each other stands in direct ratio to the strength of each.

The principle determining the sum of the mutual limitation is, that it shall be considered as small as possible, because all concepts strive against suppression, and certainly submit to no more of it than is absolutely necessary.

16. By actual calculation, the remarkable result is obtained that, in the case of the two concepts, the one never entirely obscures the other, but, in the case of three or more, one is very easily obscured, and can be made as ineffective—notwithstanding its continuous struggle—as if it were not present at all. Indeed, this obscuration may happen to a large number of concepts as well as to one, and may be effected through the agency of two, and even through the combined influence of concepts less strong than those which are suppressed.

Here the expression "threshold of consciousness" must be explained, as we shall have occasion to use it. A concept is in consciousness in so far as it is not suppressed, but is an actual representation. When it rises out of a condition of complete suppression, it enters into consciousness. Here, then, it is on the threshold of consciousness. It is very important to determine by calculation the degree of strength which a concept must attain in order to be able to stand beside two or more stronger ones exactly on the threshold of consciousness, so that, at the slightest yielding of the hindrance, it would begin to rise into consciousness.

NOTE.—The expression "A concept is in consciousness" must be distinguished from that, "I am conscious of my concept." To the latter belongs inner perception; to the former not. In psychology, we need a word that will indicate the totality of all simultaneous actual presentations. No word except consciousness can be found for this purpose.

Here we are obliged to be content with a circumlocution—and this all the more, because the inner perception which is usually attributed to consciousness has no fixed limit where it begins or ceases, and, moreover, the act of perceiving is not itself perceived; so that, since we are not conscious of it in ourselves, we must exclude it from consciousness, although it is an active knowing, and in no way a restricted or suppressed concept.

17. Among the many, and, for the most part, very complicated laws underlying the movement of concepts, the following is the simplest:

While the arrested portion (*Hemmungssumme*) of the concepts sinks, the sinking part is at every moment proportional to the part unsuppressed.

By this it is possible to calculate the whole course of the sinking even to the statical point.

NOTE.—Mathematically, the above law may be expressed: $\sigma = S\,(1-e^{-t})$ in which $S =$ the aggregate amount suppressed, $t =$

the time elapsed during the encounter, $\sigma =$ the suppressed portion of all the concepts in the time indicated by t.

As the latter quantity is apportioned among the individual concepts, it is found that those which fall directly beneath the statical threshold (16) are very quickly driven thence, while the rest do not reach exactly their statical point in any given finite time. On account of this latter circumstance, the concepts in the mind of a man of most equable temperament are, while he is awake, always in a state of gentle motion. This is also the primary reason why the inner perception never meets an object which holds it quite motionless.

18. When to several concepts already near equilibrium a new one comes, a movement arises which causes them to sink for a short time beneath their statical point, after which they quickly and entirely of themselves rise again—something as a liquid, when an object is thrown into it, first sinks and then rises. In this connection several remarkable circumstances occur:

19. First, upon an occasion of this kind, one of the older concepts may be removed entirely out of consciousness even by a new concept that is much weaker than itself. In this case, however, the striving of the suppressed concept is not to be considered wholly ineffective, as shown above (see 16); it works with all its force against the concepts in consciousness. Although its object is not conceived, it produces a certain condition of consciousness. The way in which these concepts are removed out of consciousness and yet are effective therein may be indicated by the expression, "They are on the mechanical threshold." The threshold mentioned above (16) is called for the sake of distinction the statical threshold.

NOTE.—If the concepts on the statical threshold acted in the same way as on the mechanical threshold we should find ourselves in a state of the most intolerable uneasiness, or rather the body would be subjected to a condition of tension that must in a few moments prove fatal, even as under present conditions sudden fright will sometimes cause death; for all the concepts which, as we are accustomed to say, the memory preserves, and which we well know can upon the slightest occasion be reproduced, are in a state of incessant striving to rise, although the condition of consciousness is not at all affected by them.

20. Second, the time during which one or more concepts linger upon the mechanical threshold can be extended if a series of new, although weaker, concepts come in succession to them.

Every employment to which we are unaccustomed puts us in this condition. The earlier concepts are pressed back of the later ones. The former, however, because they are the stronger, remain tense, affect the physical organism more and more, and finally make it necessary that the employment cease, when the old concepts immediately rise, and we experience what is called a feeling of relief which depends in part upon the physical organism, although the first cause is purely psychological.

21. Third, when several concepts are driven in succession to the mechanical threshold, several sudden successive changes in the laws of reciprocal movements arise.

In this way is to be explained the fact that the course of our thoughts is so often inconsequent, abrupt, and apparently irregular. This appearance deceives in the same way as the wandering of the planets. The conformity to law in the human mind resembles exactly that in the firmament.

PHYSIOLOGICAL APPROACHES TO THE MIND

Associationism thus became in the West a mature and commanding system of interpretations about the work of the mind, with which no serious study of the world of the mind could dispense. Herbart saw the need for dynamics in associationist psychology, the need for more than mental elements and modes of connection between them, the need, in fact, for some sort of push and pull.

In a larger sense, moreover, the whole era was one of push and pull, as we may almost translate the romantic phrase in the Germany of the times, *Sturm und Drang* (usually rendered "Storm and Stress"). Romanticism, already evident through Rousseau, in Switzerland and France, became more and more recognizable in Germany, especially in the towering romantic genius of Goethe. Haydn, Mozart, Beethoven, Schubert expressed the grace and form which had prevailed since the time of Bach, but were now suffused with an intensity of feeling which at times broke free from tradition. No human activity, like philosophy or psychology, could be free of the impact of so massive a trend.

The biological sciences went so far in this direction that some biologists actually became sentimental, and therefore at times lost their touch with the nature of science, but in many ways this reactivation of the life of impulse made for a richer psychology. The biological sciences became, in fact, more creative, partly because of, but in a large part because of the *reaction against,* the excessive preoccupation with sentiment and with subjective meaning. We cannot do justice to the rich fabric of interwoven strands, but we must say a little about the extraordinary forward movement of the biological sciences, first in France before and during the period of the French Revolution and Napoleon, and thereafter notably in Germany.

The first great expression of the vitalized biological sciences in the German-speaking world is to be found, indeed, immediately upon the end of the Napoleonic period, and specifically with physiological investigations which had a psychological aspect. As physiologists investigated the process of seeing and hearing and touching, they began to find more exact ways of describing the first psychological responses to the environment, and measuring the relation between the impact of the stimulus and the magnitude of the psychological response. Here the psychologist with a technical interest will give much time to the brilliant and creative investigations of E. H. Weber, and later G. T. Fechner, who laid the foundations of a science of *psychophysics.* Psychophysics is a science dealing with the relations of the physical impacts upon sense organs to *psychological* responses to such stimulation. At the same time, some of the physiologists of the period, aware of the more psychological trends, and protecting themselves against sentimental and mystical overelaborations of the results, began to write a systematic physiology which was at the same time the foundation for a systematic psychology.

Quite aside from his role as a precursor of the conception of the unconscious, Herbart had made two fundamental psychological contributions: (1) the conception of the *threshold;* (2) the conception that psychological magnitudes can be *measured.** Both ideas were carried forward by the physicist-philosopher-essayist Gustav Theodor Fechner, one of the founders of experimental psychology. In seeking a quantitative relation between the physical and

* Compare Kant, page 201 n.

the psychological worlds, he had hit upon the principle—just discovered by E. H. Weber—that the ability to differentiate between two stimuli depends on the *relative* intensities of the two. You may distinguish between a line of 50 cm. and a line of 51 cm., but not between a line of 500 cm. and 501 cm.; it is the relation, not the absolute difference, that counts. This seemed to Fechner to mean that in comparing stimuli you can assert that a "just noticeable difference" is one psychological *unit,* and that this unit of psychological response always depends upon the relation of two stimuli, not their absolute magnitude. He proceeded to build up the new science of "psychophysics"—based on many ingenious and systematic ways of presenting stimuli which had to be compared. These "psychophysical methods" are widely used today in fields as far apart as ophthalmology, illumination, and telephone engineering, while the idea of "measuring sensation" remains as challenging and as controversial as it was a century ago.

GUSTAV THEODOR FECHNER

The Fundamental Formula and the Measurement Formula *

Although not as yet having a measurement for sensation, still one can combine in an exact formula the relation expressed in Weber's law—that the sensation difference remains constant when the relative stimulus difference remains constant—with the law, established by the mathematical auxiliary principle, that small sensation increments are proportional to stimulus increments. Let us suppose, as has generally been done in the attempts to preserve Weber's law, that the difference between two stimuli, or, what is the same, the increase in one stimulus, is very small in proportion to the stimulus itself. Let the stimulus which is increased be called β, the small increase $d\beta$, where the letter d is to be considered not as a special magnitude, but simply as a sign that $d\beta$ is the small increment of β. This already suggests the differential sign. The relative stimulus increase therefore is $\frac{d\beta}{\beta}$. On the other hand, let the sensation

* From Gustav Theodor Fechner, *Elements of Psychophysics,* trans. by H. S. Langfeld, in Benjamin Rand (ed.), *The Classical Psychologists* (Boston: Houghton Mifflin Company, 1912). Copyright 1912 by Benjamin Rand.

which is dependent upon the stimulus be called γ, and let the small increment of the sensation which results from the increase of the stimulus by $d\beta$ be called $d\gamma$, where d again simply expresses the small increment. The terms $d\beta$ and $d\gamma$ are each to be considered as referring to an arbitrary unit of their own nature.

According to the empirical Weber's law, $d\gamma$ remains constant when $\frac{d\beta}{\beta}$ remains constant, no matter what absolute values $d\beta$ and β take; and according to the *a priori* mathematical auxiliary principle the changes $d\gamma$ and $d\beta$ remain proportional to one another so long as they remain very small. The two relations may be expressed together in the following equation: $d\gamma = \frac{\kappa d\beta}{\beta}$ (1) where κ is constant (dependent upon the units selected for γ and β). In fact, if one multiplies βd *and* β by any number, so long as it is the same number for both, the proportion remains constant, and with it also the sensation difference $d\gamma$. This is Weber's law. If one doubles or triples the value of the variation $d\beta$ without changing the initial value β, then the value of the change $d\gamma$ is also doubled or tripled. This is the mathematical principle. The equation $d\gamma = \frac{\kappa d\beta}{\beta}$ therefore entirely satisfies both Weber's law and this principle; and no other equation satisfies both together. This is to be called the *fundamental formula,* in that the deduction of all consequent formulas will be based upon it.

The fundamental formula does not presuppose the measurement of sensation, nor does it establish any; it simply expresses the relation holding between small relative stimulus increments and sensations increments. In short, it is nothing more than Weber's law and the mathematical auxiliary principle united and expressed in mathematical symbols.

There is, however, another formula connected with this formula by infinitesimal calculus, which expresses a general quantitative relation between the stimulus magnitude as a summation of stimulus increments, and the sensation magnitude as a summation of sensation increments, in such a way, that with the validity of the first formula, together with the assumption of the fact of limen, the validity of this latter formula is also given.

Reserving for the future a more exact deduction, I shall attempt first to make clear in a general way the connection of the two formulas.

One can readily see, that the relation between the increments $d\gamma$ and $d\beta$ in the fundamental formula corresponds to the relation between the increments of a logarithm and the increments of the corresponding number. For as one can easily convince oneself, either from theory or from the table, the logarithm does not increase by equal increments when the corresponding number increases by equal increments, but rather when the latter increases by equal amounts; in other words, the increases in the logarithms remain equal, when the relative increases of the numbers remain equal. Thus, for example, the following numbers and logarithms belong together:

Number	Logarithm
10	1.000000
11	1.0413927
100	2.000000
110	2.0413927
1000	3.000000
1100	3.0413927

where an increase of the number 10 by 1 brings with it just as great an increase in the corresponding logarithm, as the increase of the number 100 by 10 or 1000 by 100. In each instance the increases in the logarithm is 0.0413927. Further, as was already shown in explaining the mathematical auxiliary principle, the increases in the logarithms are proportional to the increases of the numbers, so long as they remain very small. Therefore one can say, that Weber's law and the mathematical auxiliary principle are just as valid for the increases of logarithms and numbers in their relation to one another, as they are for the increases of sensation and stimulus.

The fact of the threshold appears just as much in the relation of a logarithm to its number as in the relation of sensation to stimulus. The sensation begins with values above zero, not with zero, but with a finite value of the stimulus—the threshold; and so does the logarithm begin with values above zero, not with a zero value of the number, but with a finite value of the number, the value 1, inasmuch as the logarithm of 1 is equal to zero.

If now, as was shown above, the increase of sensation and stimulus stands in a relation similar to that of the increase of logarithm and number, and, the point at which the sensation begins to assume a noticeable value stands in a relation to the stimulus similar to that which the point at which the logarithm attains positive value stands to the number, then one may also expect that sensation and stimulus themselves stand in a relation to one another similar to that of logarithm to number, which, just as the former (sensation and stimulus) may be regarded as made up of a sum of successive increments.

Sensations thus still seem to be central to the psychologist's world; but here they are becoming ponderable and *measurable* quantities. Perhaps there is here the beginning of a quantitative science of the subjective world? We shall be back with this question when we come to contemporary psychology.

GERMAN PHYSIOLOGY

In the mid-nineteenth century, German science reached great heights, and nowhere more than in the development of experimental physiology—an experimental physiology destined soon to give birth to experimental psychology. The contributions of two great figures in this period still play a large part in the psychology of today: Johannes Müller and Hermann von Helmholtz. We shall sample briefly from each of these men.

Johannes Müller, drawing students from all over Europe to his laboratory in Berlin, began to write a physiology of the sensory processes. One of his memorable principles, the principle of "specific energies," ran as follows: the subjective quality of each experience, whether it be a red or a blue, a sweet or a sour, is given by the local and specific qualities of those portions of the central nervous system which are being excited. Thus you excite a *particular region* in the nervous system and you arouse a specific experience of red. No *other* region when excited can ever give this result. There is a specific region for each of the hues. There is a region in the nervous system for each quality of hearing, or of touch or of the other sense modalities. This principle, as used by Johannes Müller, was taken over by his great pupil, Helmholtz, who in the midst of a spectacular array of investigations of seeing, hearing, and other psychological problems, relied upon the principle that each subjective experience, or experience known to the experimental subject, is the reflection in our awareness of the particular local character of the brain excitation involved. In the dramatic language of William James, if you should splice the nerves so that the excitation of the ear led to the brain center which is concerned with seeing, and the inner fibers from the eyes led to the nerve centers concerned with hearing, we should "hear the lightning and see the thunder." *

Turning to the great giant of physiological psychology in that period, Hermann von Helmholtz, we cannot do justice to the range of his contributions to the study of hearing and of sight, his measurement of the speed of human response, his conception of the role of association in perception and judgment. All that we can do is to give a sample of his lucid and cogent presentation of a scientific issue—his development of Thomas Young's theory of color in a form fundamental for modern studies of the sources of our elementary human experiences.

HERMANN VON HELMHOLTZ

Theory of Color Vision †

Hypotheses. The facts to be deduced from the laws of color-mixture, that three constituents of sensation which proceed independently of one another are produced by external stimulation, have received their more definite and more significant expression in the hypotheses, which assume, that these different constituents are excited and transmitted in different portions of the optic nerve; but that they simultaneously attain to consciousness, and thereby, so far as they have become excited from the same place of the retina, they are also localized in the same place of the field of vision.

Such a theory was first proposed by Thomas Young.[1] The more

* Müller guessed that the specific points in the nervous system related to specific kinds of experience lie in the terminals of the *sensory* or incoming pathways. In this he guessed wrong. His theory works, however, just as well when applied to higher (cortical) *brain* regions.

† From Hermann von Helmholtz, *A Manual of Physiological Optics,* trans. by Benjamin Rand, in Benjamin Rand (ed.), *The Classical Psychologists* (Boston: Houghton Mifflin Company, 1912), pp. 573–577. Copyright 1912 by Benjamin Rand.

[1] Thomas Young's theory of color vision is as follows: "From three simple sensations, with their combinations, we obtain seven primitive distinctions of colours; but the different proportions, in which they may be combined, afford a variety of traits beyond all calculation. The three simple sensations being red, green, and violet, the three binary combinations are yellow, consisting of red and green; crimson, of red and violet; and blue, of green and violet; and the seventh in order is white light, composed by all three united. But the blue thus produced, by com-

detailed development of it is essentially conditioned by the fact, that its author would ascribe to the sensitive nerves of the eye only the properties and capacities, which we positively know as belonging to the motor nerves of men and of animals. We have a much more favorable opportunity to discover these latter by experiment than is the case with the nerves of sensation, since we are able comparatively easily and definitely both to discern and to measure the finest changes of their excitation and excitability by means of the contractions occurring in the muscles, and their changes. What we furthermore have been able to ascertain concerning the structure, the chemical constitution, the excitability, the conductivity, and the electrical behavior of the sensitive nerves, harmonises so perfectly with the corresponding behavior of the motor nerves, that fundamental differences in the nature of their activity are extremely improbable, at least so far as these do not depend upon the other organic apparatus connected with them, upon which they exert their influence.

Now we know in regard to motor nerves only the contrast between the state of rest and of activity. In the former state the nerve can remain unaltered a long time without important chemical change or development of heat; and at the same time the muscle dependent upon the nerve remains lax. If we stimulate the nerve, heat develops in it material changes, electrical oscillations are shown, and the muscle is contracted. In a cut nerve-preparation the sensitiveness is quickly lost, probably on account of the expansion of the chemical constituents necessary for activity. Under the action of atmospheric oxygen, or better still of the arterial blood containing oxygen, the sensitiveness is wholly or partially slowly restored, save that these processes of restoration excite contractions of the muscle, or changes of electrical relation in nerve and muscle coincident with the activity. We are acquainted also with no external means which can produce this process of restoration so quickly and intensively, and which can permit it at the same time so suddenly to appear and again to cease, as would be necessary, if this process were to serve as the physiological basis of a powerful sensation occurring with precision.

If we confine our assumptions concerning the development of a theory of color vision to the properties belonging with certainty to the

bining the whole of the green and violet rays, is not the blue of the spectrum, for four parts of green and one of violet make a blue differing very little from green; while the blue of the spectrum appears to contain as much violet as green: and it is for this reason that red and blue usually make a purple, deriving its hue from the predominance of the violet." (Thomas Young, *A Course of Lectures on Natural Philosophy,* 1807, Vol. I, p. 440.)

nerves, there is presented in fairly secure outline the theory of Thomas Young.

The sensation of dark corresponds to the state of rest of the optic nerve, that of colored or white light to an excitement of it. The three simple sensations which correspond to the excitement only of a single one of the three nerve systems, and from which all the others can be composed, must correspond in the table of colors to the three angles of the color triangle.

In order to assume the finest possible color sensations not demonstrable by objective stimulus, it appears appropriate so to select the angles of the color triangle that its sides include in the closest possible way the curves of the colors of the spectrum.

Thomas Young has therefore assumed:

1. There are in the eye three kinds of nerve fibres. The excitation of the first produces the sensation of red; the excitation of the second, the sensation of green; the excitation of the third, the sensation of violet.

2. Objective homogeneous light excites these three kinds of fibres with an intensity which varies according to the length of the wave. The fibres sensitive to red are excited most strongly by light of the greatest wave-length; and those sensitive to violet by light of the smallest wave-length. Nevertheless, it is not precluded, but rather to be assumed, for the explanation of a series of phenomena, that each color of the spectrum excites all the kinds of fibres, but with different intensity. If we suppose in *Fig. 1* the spectrum colors placed horizontally and in their natural order, beginning from red R up to violet V, the three curves may represent more or less exactly the strength of the excitation of the three kinds of fibres: no. 1 those sensitive to red; no. 2 those sensitive to green; and no. 3 those sensitive to violet.

The simple red excites strongly the fibres sensitive to red, and weakly the two other kinds of fibres; sensation: red.

The simple yellow excites moderately the fibers sensitive to red, and green, weakly the violet; sensation: red.

The simple green excites strongly the fibres sensitive to green, much more weakly the two other kinds; sensation: green.

The simple blue excites moderately the fibres sensitive to green and violet, weakly the red; sensation: blue.

The simple violet excites strongly the fibres which belong to it, and weakly the others; sensation: violet.

The excitation of all the fibres of nearly equal strength gives the sensation of white, or of whitish colors.

Perhaps it may be objected at first view to this hypothesis, that three times the number of nerve fibres and nerve endings must be presumed than in the older assumption, according to which each separate nerve fibre was thought capable of transmitting all kinds of chromatic excitations. But I do not believe, that in this connection the supposition of Young is in contradiction with the anatomical facts. An hypothesis was previously discussed, which explains the accuracy of sight by the aid of a much smaller number of visual nerve fibres, than the number of distinguishable places in the field of vision.

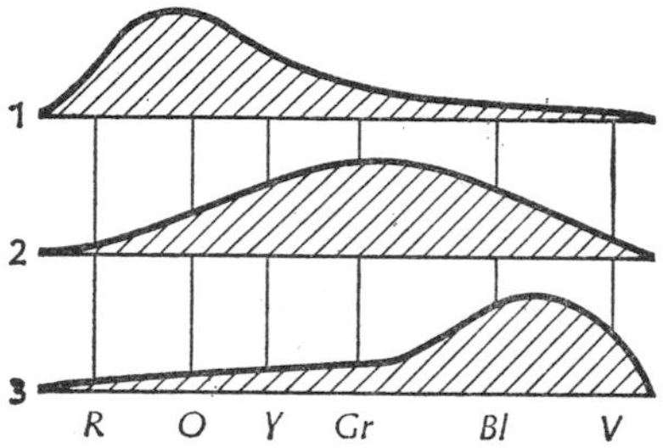

Fig. 1

The choice of the three fundamental colors seems at first, as we have observed, somewhat arbitrary. Any other three colors might be chosen from which white can be composed. Young was guided probably by the consideration that the colors at the end of the spectrum appear to claim a privileged position. If we were not to select these it would be necessary to take for one of the fundamental colors a purple shade, and the curve which corresponds to it in the foregoing figure (*Fig. 1*) would have two maxima: one in red, and the other in violet.

The single circumstance, which is of direct importance in the mode of sensation and appears to give a clue for the determination of the fundamental colors, is the apparent greater color-saturation of the red and violet; a thing which also manifests inself, although indeed less markedly, for green. Since we style colors the more saturated the farther they are removed from white, we must expect that great saturation must belong particularly to those colors of the spectrum which produce most purely the simplest sensations of color. In fact, these colors, if they are very pure, have even with inferior brilliancy, something of an intensively glowing, almost dazzling quality. There are especially red, violet, or blue violet flowers, e.g. of the cameraria, whose colors display this characteristic blending of darkness and brilliancy. Young's hypothesis affords for this a simple explanation. A dark color can cause an intensive excitation of one of the three nerve systems, while the corresponding bright white causes a much weaker excitation of the same. The difference appears analogous to that between the sensation of very hot water upon a small portion of the skin and lukewarm water striking a greater surface.

In particular violet makes upon me this impression of a deeply saturated color. But inasmuch as the strictly violet rays, even when they occur in sunlight, are of slight intensity and are modified by fluorescence, ultramarine blue, which has far the advantage of greater intensity of light, produces an effect approximately equal to it. The strictly pure violet of the spectrum is very little known among the laity, since the violet pigments give nearly always the effect of a slight admixture of red, or appear very dark. For that very reason, the shades of the ultramarine blue coming near to the violet excite the general attention much more, are much better known, and are designated by a much older name—that of blue—than the violet strictly so called. In addition one has in the deep ultramarine blue of the cloudless sky a highly imposing, well known, and constant example of this color.

Thus, side by side with Johannes Müller's idea that such elementary experiences as red or blue come from specific regions in the nervous system, we have Young's and Helmholtz's conception that they are related also to specific sense organs in the retina. So why not put the two ideas together? Any color stimulus, such as red, excites its appropriate receptor, and from its receptor a nerve pathway leads to the visual center in the brain: specifically, to that spot in the brain which always gives rise to red. Red as an experience is simply the response of a specific brain area and it cannot ordinarily be aroused except in this way. In modern times it has been found that specific regions in the cortex ("bark" or surface) of the brain will yield color experiences whether aroused electrically, or chemically (by drugs or poisons, or the toxins of infectious disease), or by pressure (of tumors), or shock; and, indeed, that the same specific memories may sometimes be repeatedly called back if the surgeon electrically excites the same region.

Five

EVOLUTIONARY PSYCHOLOGY

INTRODUCTION *

In the work of Johannes Müller and Helmholtz, we find German physiology rising to a high pitch, and with it come a wide array of new psychological discoveries and a growing conviction that psychological problems were amenable to experimental attack. It was still experimental physiology, but a generous physiology, which had under its wing many of the traditional psychological problems about the nature of the process of perceiving. One might have predicted that the rest of the century could well be spent in the uses of the physiological laboratory in illuminating one psychological problem after another: the nature of memory, thought, emotion, and the will.

Actually, history had in its womb a child which could compete with them in terms of scientific and general human interest, especially in terms of implications for humanity. This was the evolutionary conception that all things grow into something new; that life itself is a succession of new stages and forms; that the higher forms are derived from the simpler; and that humanity itself is the expression of a very long and very complex evolutionary process.

The Renaissance spirit of rediscovery of the ancient world and fresh delight in the principles of order and rationality had led on into more and more rationalism, until the thoughtful man of the eighteenth century thought of himself as achieving a great "enlightenment." He began to enter upon what Tom Paine and many of the French and the British regarded as truly an Age of Reason. The

* Parts of the following section on evolutionary psychology appeared in slightly different form in the *Bulletin of the Menninger Clinic,* Vol. XXXII (1968). © 1968 by the Menninger Foundation.

symbols of such rationality were, of course, eagerly welcomed in the new conquests made by the physical sciences, especially in the orderly beauty of the rationalist astronomy. How far astronomy had moved, from Phoebus Apollo driving his chariot across the sky, and the cycling planets singing the "harmony of the spheres," to the cold and orderly movements of celestial bodies—cold, but beautiful, as expressed in Laplace's *System of the World!* The rationalism of Locke and of Descartes, swelling with the new pride of the advancing sciences, led many to think of the eighteenth century as an age of intellectualist triumph.

But as early as the middle of the eighteenth century many signs of a new stirring appeared. As men traveled, they began to delight in the new world which they saw, and to write about it; heroic couplets changed rapidly into romantic expression. The troubled young Swiss, Jean Jacques Rousseau, began to protest the dry, mechanical, and authoritative spirit in education and to insist on setting free the young mind, encouraging it to explore, and giving it for nourishment all that it delighted to discover and devour. Robert Burns, scornful of discipline and authority, swore that "a man's a man for a' that." As Wordsworth turned to the radiant beauty of lake and stream, the new romanticism began suddenly to rock Germany, as we have noted (pages 206–207) in a movement of "storm and stress," which we recognize in the great music of the early nineteenth century.

Not so much a *cause* of this as a parallel expression of it: the life sciences began suddenly to make strides. The development of the microscope, and the development of interest in field exploration and the gathering of specimens, were accompanied by a sense of growth, a need to see in nature the constant reawakening to newer and higher forms of expression. Both in sober laboratory devotion to careful observation, and in the literary heights of a "philosophy of nature" which sought spiritual meanings in every life principle revealed in animal or plant, we soon find ourselves among a host of theories of evolution.

The radical conception of the dynamics of the development of species came in a context of a new and profound emphasis upon the struggle, the success-and-failure aspect of life, the feelings and impulses that went with fears, hates, and strivings. Ultimately (just as the philosopher Schopenhauer had suggested at the beginning of the nineteenth century), the biologist saw that impulses come before thoughts, that thoughts indeed arise out of the very tissue of impulse. Impulse may be the raw struggle for air, water, or mates, or it may take on the form of increasing struggle to master a complex environment: to learn, understand, and control. The modern psychology which we are going to try now to portray is modern not only in the sense that it finds a place for man's evolutionary past, but more especially because it finds a place for a life of struggle, feeling, impulse, and action, which is not only just as important as thought, but which historically precedes and in a deep sense always preconditions and underlies the higher phenomena of mind. We make a real break then as we turn to the evolutionary psychologies of the latter half of the nineteenth century and of our own twentieth century.

The primary problem for the biologist was the transmutation of species—the capacity of species to develop from other species, rather than arising, once and for all, independently of other species (as in the creation story in the Book of Genesis). The problem had been recognized, but not solved, by the ancients.

As with Lucretius (pages 83–93), the new evolutionary doctrines seemed to lend themselves to poetic form. Buffon speculated poetically about evolutionary change in the mid-eighteenth century, and at the beginning of the nineteenth Erasmus Darwin, the grandfather of Charles Darwin, made a similar bold stroke in a poem entitled "Zoonomia." French and British biologists argued unconvincingly, pro and con, many of them seeing how an evolutionary principle would clarify their subject matter. With the vast accumulation of knowledge about the forms of animals and plants spread over the earth and in the air and under the sea, and with rapidly increasing skills in the discovery and interpretation of fossil remains, it began to appear, by the second quarter of the nineteenth century, that the cardinal question was the "transmutation of species," the derivation of one species from another. Aristotle had agreed that forms of life can be arranged in an order, but he could not agree that one could change into another. It was this very question, the possibility that one form of life *could* change into another, which became the center of the controversy. There was need for more evidence; but the matter could not be settled by the sheer accumulation of more and more massive evidence on the part of the collectors and the dissectors, the interpreters and the debaters. There had to be at the same time a reasonable interpretation of the process, the enunciation of a principle by which new species could come into existence. We see the story unfolding in the life of Charles Darwin.

The story makes clear why the impact of his work was so great. The reading public had been made ready by romantic and speculative efforts of many sorts. Herbert Spencer's theory of evolution was already becoming known during the 1850's: stars, the earth, and life were all products of a gradual process of differentiation from an undifferentiated whole. Changes in the earth, and the problem of fossil remains of forms that must have lived long ago but had become extinct, excited attention. In all this, however, evolution was still a matter of talk, a matter of opinion, something on which serious people could arguc inconclusively. Darwin's paper before the Linnean Society in 1858 had offered something more; it offered a structured system buttressed heavily upon a wide range of solid facts. The 1,500 copies of the new book available in the retail bookstores were exhausted on the day of publication. Right and left the excitement rose. Bishop Wilberforce thought it was disgraceful to be descended from a monkey. (It was none other than the great empire builder, Disraeli, who said, in 1864, "Is man an ape or an angel? I, my Lord, I am on the side of the angels. I repudiate with indignation and abhorrence those new-fangled theories.") It was hard riding. The great Harvard zoologist Louis Agassiz, teacher of William James, died without accepting Darwin's evidence. The pressure of more and more facts closed in upon the reluctant and the doubters, and by the end of the century most biologists and, indeed, most thoughtful persons had begun not only to take the evolutionary principle, the principle of the transmutation of species, as a new cardinal foundation for the life sciences, but had begun to see the implications for human life, and in particular for human psychology. Charles Darwin himself, in *The Descent of Man,* had shown that mammals are not necessarily as dumb as they seem, nor man as bright, and that transitional forms of learning between animal learning and human learning can be found, with implications for the animal character of at least much of the human mind. Perhaps the constitution of the human mind can be understood in the light of its long development, through ages of adaptation. While Kant had thought of constitutional limits in man's capacity to know reality, Darwin had come to the view that the limits are given by the instinct and intelligence born with us; James was to make this a cardinal principle for the understanding of the broad dimensions of human existence. James's relativism and pragmatism are based on the one hand upon skepticism regarding all absolutes, but on the other hand premised more specifically upon the recognition that what the mind, the heart, the feelings, the will can be must at least be seen in terms of simpler structures. In Emerson's words

> Striving to be man, the worm
> mounts through all the spires of form.

Such an evolutionism was not pessimistic; it was not a derogation of human dignity. On the contrary, it accepted man's status as the finest end product of civilization, and for a while at least it pointed to an unceasing upward continuation along the lines defined in this same Emersonian spiral of majestic growth.

But Charles Darwin was not only the founder of a new biology. He was very specifically and very effectively an observer, an interpreter, of human and of animal powers and functions. His best-known psychological contribution is his celebrated *Expression of the Emotions in Man and in Animals.* This is an attempt to view in a large perspective the development of primitive instinctive tendencies which aid the survival of the animal possessing them. Take, for example, the biting and clawing which go with successful attack, and the bristling, trembling, and flight which mark the behavior repertories of those that survive and pass through moments of danger rather than being overwhelmed. The action patterns are inborn, and those in whom their inborn quality is poorly defined are constantly being eliminated, while the more effective in attack or defense tend to be preserved.

But let us suppose that the situation does not actually demand teeth and claws; suppose that one can defend one's food by baring the teeth and snarling; or suppose, indeed, that one can preserve one's own identity by scaring off those who offer such threats. We can see how the incomplete or truncated expression of primitive rage or flight may easily survive, and how *a wide variety of emotional expressions may be explained as residual expressions which are the same, except in degree, as the overt movements of attack or defense.* Some of the emotions may be essentially expressions of overflow or excitement, but here too they would have the background derived from the stirred-up state of the organism which is regularly present among strains which have been successful in the struggle for existence.

A celebrated example is Fabre's study of the sand-wasp, which stings its prey near a great nerve center so that the prey remains paralyzed and immobile, capable of giving sustenance to the growing sand-wasps of the next generation. (After decades of controversy, Fabre's ideas, with vivid documentation, are to be seen expressed today in a Walt Disney film.)

But it was not only in insects that such functions were observed. Lloyd Morgan intrigued a whole generation of psychologists by his observations of the manner in which the moor-hen dives when startled, and with his discussion of the innate neuromuscular structure which makes this perfect behavior possible in an inexperienced bird. (This never-ending question of innate behavior patterns—whether they could really be simply "learned behavior"—is one to which we shall return again and again.)

Soon more and more aspects of psychology, more clearly anchored to the physiological life of man, began to be affected. In time it became evident that there was just nothing in the psychological view of man that was not going to be influenced by the evolutionary principle in one way or another. One might, with Aristotle and with Descartes, lift out a certain group of functions—"active reason" and the like—from the context within which the rest of the living system is judged. One might have an intellectual principle that is not derived from an evolutionary background. There are philosophers who still defend such a position. This special exemption, however, creates problems, and these must be faced at the level of the severest and most exacting demands which philosophers impose upon one another. These are not, we believe, the kinds of issues when can be fully debated back and forth in a presentation of modern psychology. It would be nearer to the truth to say that, in the hundred years since *The Origin of Species,* psychology has been moving toward a generalized and fundamental evolutionism.

CHARLES DARWIN *

By the time I went to this day-school my taste for natural history, and more especially for collecting, was well developed. I tried to make out the names of plants, and collected all sorts of things, shells, seals, franks, coins, and minerals. The passion for collecting which leads a man to be a systematic naturalist, a virtuoso, or a miser, was very strong in me, and was clearly innate, as none of my sisters or brother ever had this taste.

One little event during this year has fixed itself very firmly in my mind, and I hope that it has done so from my conscience having been afterwards sorely troubled by it; it is curious as showing that apparently I was interested at this early age in the variability of plants! I told another little boy that I could produce variously coloured polyanthuses and primroses by watering them with certain coloured fluids, which was of course a monstrous fable, and had never been tried by me. I may here also confess that as a little boy I was much given to inventing deliberate falsehoods, and this was always done for the sake of causing excitement. For instance, I once gathered much valuable fruit from my father's trees and hid it in the shrubbery, and then ran in breathless haste to spread the news that I had discovered a hoard of stolen fruit.

. . .

* From Charles Darwin, *The Autobiography of Charles Darwin and Selected Letters,* edited by Francis Darwin (New York: Dover Publications, 1958), pp. 6, 10–11, 15, 21, 25–32, 34–35, 41–45, 50, 58.

With respect to science, I continued collecting minerals with much zeal, but quite unscientifically—all that I cared about was a new-named mineral, and I hardly attempted to classify them. I must have observed insects with some little care, for when ten years old (1819) I went for three weeks to Plas Edwards on the sea-coast in Wales, I was very much interested and surprised at seeing a large black and scarlet Hemipterous insect, many moths (Zygœna), and a Cicindela, which are not found in Shropshire. I almost made up my mind to begin collecting all the insects which I could find dead, for on consulting my sister, I concluded that it was not right to kill insects for the sake of making a collection. From reading White's *Selborne,* I took much pleasure in watching the habits of birds, and even made notes on the subject. In my simplicity, I remember wondering why every gentleman did not become an ornithologist.

Towards the close of my school life, my brother worked hard at chemistry, and made a fair laboratory with proper apparatus in the tool-house in the garden, and I was allowed to aid him as a servant in most of his experiments. He made all the gases and many compounds, and I read with care several books on chemistry, such as Henry and Parkes' *Chemical Catechism.* The subject interested me greatly, and we often used to go on working till rather late at night. This was the best part of my education at school, for it showed me practically the meaning of experimental science. The fact that we worked at chemistry somehow got known at school, and as it was an unprecedented fact, I was nick-named "Gas." I was also once publicly rebuked by the head-master, Dr. Butler, for thus wasting my time on such useless subjects; and he called me very unjustly a "poco curante," and as I did not understand what he meant, it seemed to me a fearful reproach. . . .

During my second year at Edinburgh I attended Jameson's lectures on Geology and Zoology, but they were incredibly dull. The sole effect they produced on me was the determination never as long as I lived to read a book on Geology, or in any way to study the science. Yet I feel sure that I was prepared for a philosophical treatment of the subject; for an old Mr. Cotton, in Shropshire, who knew a good deal about rocks, had pointed out to me two or three years previously a well-known large erratic boulder in the town of Shrewsbury, called the "bell-stone"; he told me that there was no rock of the same kind nearer than Cumberland or Scotland, and he solemnly assured me that the world would come to an end before any one would be able to explain how this stone came where it now lay. This produced a deep impression on me, and I meditated over this wonderful stone. So that I felt the keenest delight when I first read of the action of icebergs in transporting boulders, and I gloried in the progress of Geology. Equally striking is the fact that I, though now only sixty-seven years old, heard the Professor, in a field lecture at Salisbury Craigs, discoursing on a trap-dyke, with amygdaloidal margins and the strata indurated on each side, with volcanic rocks all around us, say that it was a fissure filled with sediment from above, adding with a sneer that there were men who maintained that it had been injected from beneath in a molten condition. When I think of this lecture, I do not wonder that I determined never to attend to Geology. . . .

But no pursuit at Cambridge was followed with nearly so much eagerness or gave me so much pleasure as collecting beetles. . . .

A short conversation with him during this evening produced a strong impression on my mind. Whilst examining an old gravel-pit near Shrewsbury, a labourer told me that he had found in it a large worn tropical Volute shell, such as may be seen on chimney-pieces of cottages; and as he would not sell the shell, I was convinced that he had really found it in the pit. I told Sedgwick of the fact, and he at once said (no doubt truly) that it must have been thrown away by some one into the pit; but then added, if really embedded there it would be the greatest misfortune to geology, as it would overthrow all that we know about the superficial deposits of the Midland Counties. These gravel-beds belong in fact to the glacial period, and in after years I found in them broken arctic shells. But I was then utterly astonished at Sedgwick not being delighted at so wonderful a fact as a tropical shell being found near the surface in the middle of England. Nothing before had ever made me thoroughly realise, though I had read various scientific books, that science consists in grouping facts so that general laws or conclusions may be drawn from them. . . .

Voyage of the "Beagle": from December 27, 1831, to October 2, 1836.

On returning home from my short geological tour in North Wales, I found a letter from Henslow, informing me that Captain Fitz-Roy was willing to give up part of his own cabin to any young man who would volunteer to go with him without pay as naturalist to the Voyage of the *Beagle.* I have given, as I believe, in my MS. Journal an account of all the circumstances which then occurred; I will here only say that I was instantly eager to accept the offer, but my father strongly objected, adding the words, fortunate for me, "If you can find any man of common-sense who advises you to go I will give my consent." So I wrote that evening and refused the offer. On the next morning I went to Maer to be ready for September 1st, and whilst out shooting, my uncle sent for me, offering to drive me over to Shrewsbury and talk with my father, as my uncle thought it would be wise in me to accept the offer.

My father always maintained that [my uncle] was one of the most sensible men in the world, and he at once consented in the kindest manner. I had been rather extravagant at Cambridge, and to console my father, said, "that I should be deuced clever to spend more than my allowance whilst on board the *Beagle*"; but he answered with a smile, "But they tell me you are very clever."

Next day I started for Cambridge to see Henslow, and thence to London to see Fitz-Roy, and all was soon arranged. Afterwards, on becoming very intimate with Fitz-Roy, I heard that I had run a very narrow risk of being rejected on account of the shape of my nose! He was an ardent disciple of Lavater, and was convinced that he could judge of a man's character by the outline of his features; and he doubted whether any one with my nose could possess sufficient energy and determination for the voyage. But I think he was afterwards well satisfied that my nose had spoken falsely. . . .

The voyage of the *Beagle* has been by far the most important event in my life, and has determined my whole career; yet it depended on so small a circumstance as my uncle offering to drive me thirty miles to Shrewsbury, which few uncles would have done, and on such a trifle as the shape of my nose. I have always felt that I owe to the voyage the first real training or education of my mind; I was led to attend closely to several branches of natural history, and thus my powers of observation were improved, though they were always fairly developed.

The investigation of the geology of all the places visited was far more important, as reasoning here comes into play.

On first examining a new district, nothing can appear more hopeless than the chaos of rocks; but by recording the stratification and nature of the rocks and fossils at many points, always reasoning and predicting what will be found elsewhere, light soon begins to dawn on the district, and the structure of the whole becomes more or less intelligible. I had brought with me the first volume of Lyell's *Principles of Geology,* which I studied attentively; and the book was of the highest service to me in many ways. The very first place which I examined, namely, St. Jago, in the Cape de Verde islands, showed me clearly the wonderful superiority of Lyell's manner of treating geology, compared with that of any other author whose works I had with me or ever afterwards read.

Another of my occupations was collecting animals of all classes, briefly describing and roughly dissecting many of the marine ones; but from not being able to draw, and from not having sufficient anatomical knowledge, a great pile of MS. which I had made during the voyage has proved almost useless. I thus lost much time, with the exception of that spent in acquiring some knowledge of the Crustaceans, as this was of service when in after years I undertook a monograph of the Cirripedia.

During some part of the day I wrote my Journal, and took much pains in describing carefully and vividly all that I had seen; and this was good practice. My Journal served also, in part, as letters to my home, and portions were sent to England whenever there was an opportunity.

The above various special studies were, however, of no importance compared with the habit of energetic industry and of concentrated attention to whatever I was engaged in, which I then acquired. Everything about which I thought or read was made to bear directly on what I had seen or was likely to see; and this habit of mind was continued during the five years of the voyage. I feel sure that it was this training which has enabled me to do whatever I have done in science.

Looking backwards, I can now perceive how my love for science gradually preponderated over every other taste. During the first two years my old passion for shooting survived in nearly full force, and I shot myself all the birds and animals for my collection; but gradually I gave up my gun more and more, and finally altogether, to my servant, as shooting interfered with my work, more especially with making out the geological structure of a country. I discovered, though unconsciously and insensibly, that the pleasure of observing and reasoning was a much higher one than that of skill and sport. That my mind became developed through my pursuits during the voyage is rendered probable by a remark made by my father, who was the most acute observer whom I ever saw, of a sceptical disposition, and far from being a believer in phrenology; for on first seeing me after the voyage, he turned round to my sisters, and exclaimed, "Why, the shape of his head is quite altered." . . .

I need not here refer to the events of the voyage—where we went and what we did as I have given a sufficiently full account in my published Journal. The glories of the vegetation of the Tropics rise before my mind at the present time more vividly than anything else; though the sense of sublimity, which the great deserts of Patagonia and the forest-clad mountains of Tierra del Fuego excited in me, has left an indelible impression on my mind. The sight of a naked savage in his native land is an event which can never be forgotten. Many of my excursions on horseback through wild countries, or in the boats, some of which lasted several weeks, were deeply interesting; their discomfort and some degree of danger were at that time hardly a drawback, and none at all afterwards. I also reflect with high satisfaction on some of my scientific work, such as solving the problem of coral islands, and making out the geological structure of certain islands, for instance, St. Helena. Nor must I pass over the discovery of the singular relations of the animals and plants inhabiting the several islands of the Galapagos archipelago, and of all of them to the inhabitants of South America.

As far as I can judge of myself, I worked to the utmost during the voyage from the mere pleasure of investigation, and from my strong desire to add a few facts to the great mass of facts in Natural Science. But I was also ambitious to take a fair place among scientific men,—whether more ambitious or less so than most of my fellow-workers, I can form no opinion. . . .

Towards the close of our voyage I received a letter whilst at Ascension, in which my sisters told me that Sedgwick had called on my father, and said that I should take a place among the leading scientific men. I could not at the time understand how he could have learnt anything of my proceedings, but I heard (I believe afterwards) that Henslow had read some of the letters which I wrote to him before the Philosophical Society of Cambridge, and had printed them for private distribution. My collection of fossil bones, which had been sent to Henslow, also excited considerable attention amongst palæontologists. After reading this letter, I clambered over the mountains of Ascension with a bounding step, and made the volcanic rocks resound under my geological hammer. All this shows how ambitious I was; but I think that I can say with truth that in after years, though I cared in the highest degree for the approbation of such men as Lyell and Hooker, who were my friends, I did not care much about the general public. I do not mean to say that a favourable review or a large sale of my books did not please me greatly, but the pleasure was a fleeting one, and I am sure that I have never turned one inch out of my course to gain fame.

From my return to England (October 2, 1836) to my marriage (January 29, 1839).

These two years and three months were the most active ones which I ever spent, though I was occasionally unwell, and so lost some time. After going backwards and forwards several times between Shrewsbury, Maer, Cambridge, and London, I settled in lodgings at Cambridge on December 13th, where all my collections were under the care of Henslow. I stayed here three months, and got my minerals and rocks examined by the aid of Professor Miller.

I began preparing my *Journal of Travels,* which was not hard work, as my MS. Journal had been written with care, and my chief labour was making an abstract of my more interesting scientific results. I sent also, at the request of Lyell, a short account of my observations on the elevation of the coast of Chili to the Geological Society.

On March 7th, 1837, I took lodgings in Great Marlborough Street in London, and remained there for nearly two years, until I was married. During these two years I finished my Journal, read several papers before the Geological Society, began preparing the MS. for my *Geological Observations,* and arranged for the publication of the *Zoology of the Voyage of the Beagle.* In July I opened my first notebook for facts in relation to the *Origin of Species,* about which I had long reflected, and never ceased working for the next twenty years. . . .

Besides my work on coral-reefs, during my residence in London, I read before the Geological Society papers on the Erratic Boulders of South America, on Earthquakes, and on the Formation by the Agency of Earth-worms of Mould. I also continued to superintend the publication of the *Zoology of the Voyage of the Beagle.* Nor did I ever intermit collecting facts bearing on the origin of species; and I could sometimes do this when I could do nothing else from illness. . . .

I saw more of Lyell than of any other man, both before and after my marriage. His mind was characterised, as it appeared to me, by clearness, caution, sound judgment, and a good deal of originality. When I made any remark to him on Geology, he never rested until he saw the whole case clearly, and often made me see it more clearly than I had done before. He would advance all possible objections to my suggestion, and even after these were exhausted would long remain dubious. A second characteristic was his hearty sympathy with the work of other scientific men.

On my return from the voyage of the *Beagle,* I explained to him my views on coral-reefs, which differed from his, and I was greatly surprised and encouraged by the vivid interest which he showed. His delight in science was ardent, and he felt the keenest interest in the future progress of mankind. He was very kind-hearted, and thoroughly liberal in his religious beliefs, or rather disbeliefs; but he was a strong theist. His candour was highly remarkable. He exhibited this by becoming a convert to the Descent theory, though he had gained much fame by opposing Lamarck's views, and this after he had grown old. He reminded me that I had many years before said to him, when discussing the opposition of the old school of geologists to his new views, "What a good thing it would be if every scientific man was to die when sixty years old, as afterwards he would be sure to oppose all new doctrines." But he hoped that now he might be allowed to live. . . .

From September 1854 I devoted my whole time to arranging my huge pile of notes, to observing, and to experimenting in relation to the transmutation of species. During the voyage of the *Beagle* I had been deeply impressed by discovering in the Pampean formation great fossil animals covered with armour like that on the existing armadillos; secondly, by the manner in which closely allied animals replace one another in proceeding southwards over the Continent; and thirdly, by the South American character of most of the productions of the Galapagos archipelago, and more especially by the manner in which they differ slightly on each island of the group; none of the islands appearing to be very ancient in a geological sense.

It was evident that such facts as these, as well as many others, could only be explained on the supposition that species gradually become modified; and the subject haunted me. But it was equally evident that neither the action of the surrounding conditions, nor the will of the organisms (especially in the case of plants) could account for the innumerable cases in which organisms of every kind are beautifully adapted to their habits of life—for instance, a woodpecker or a tree-frog to climb trees, or a seed for dispersal by hooks or plumes. I had always been much struck by such adaptations, and until these could be explained it seemed to me almost useless to endeavour to prove by indirect evidence that species have been modified.

After my return to England it appeared to me that by following the example of Lyell in Geology, and by collecting all facts which bore in any way on the variation of animals and plants under domestication and nature, some light might perhaps be thrown on the whole subject. My first note-book was opened in July 1837. I worked on true Baconian principles, and without any theory collected facts on a wholesale scale, more especially with respect to domesticated productions, by printed enquiries, by conversation with skilful breeders and gardeners, and by extensive reading. When I see the list of books of all kinds which I read and abstracted, including whole series of Journals and Transactions, I am surprised at my industry. I soon perceived that selection was the keystone of man's success in making useful races of animals and plants. But how selection could be applied to organisms living in a state of nature remained for some time a mystery to me.

In October 1838, that is, fifteen months after I had begun my systematic enquiry, I happened to read for amusement Malthus on *Population,* and being well prepared to appreciate the struggle for existence which everywhere goes on from long-continued observation of the habits of animals and plants, it at once struck me that under these circumstances favourable variations would tend to be preserved and unfavourable ones to be destroyed. The result of this would be the formation of new species. Here, then, I had at last got a theory by which to work; but I was so anxious to avoid prejudice, that I determined not for some time to write even the briefest sketch of it. In June 1842 I first allowed myself the satisfaction of writing a very brief abstract of my theory in pencil in 35 pages; and this was enlarged during the summer of 1844 into one of 230 pages, which I had fairly copied out and still possess.

But at that time I overlooked one problem of great importance; and it is astonishing to me, except on the principle of Columbus and his egg, how I could have overlooked it and its solution. This problem is the tendency in organic beings descended from the same stock to diverge in character as they become modified. That they have diverged greatly is obvious from the manner in which species of all kinds can be classed under genera, genera under families, families under sub-orders, and so forth; and I can remember the very spot in the road, whilst in my carriage, when to my joy the solution occurred to me; and this was long after I had come to Down. The solution, as I believe, is that the modified offspring of all dominant and increasing forms tend to become adapted to many and highly diversified places in the economy of nature.

Early in 1856 Lyell advised me to write out my views pretty fully, and I began at once to do so on a scale three or four times as extensive as that which was afterwards followed in my *Origin of Species;* yet it was only an abstract of the materials which I had collected, and I got through about half the work on this scale. But my plans were overthrown, for early in the summer of 1858 Mr. Wallace, who was then in the Malay archipelago, sent me an essay *On the Tendency of Varieties to depart indefinitely from the Original Type;* and this essay contained exactly the same theory as mine. Mr. Wallace expressed the wish that if I thought well of his essay, I should send it to Lyell for perusal.

The circumstances under which I consented at the request of Lyell and Hooker to allow of an abstract from my MS., together with a letter to Asa Gray, dated September 5, 1857, to be published at the same time with Wallace's Essay, are given in the *Journal of the Proceedings of the Linnean Society,* 1858, p. 45. I was at first very unwilling to consent, as I thought Mr. Wallace might consider my doing so unjustifiable, for I did not then know how generous and noble was his disposition. The extract from my MS. and the letter to Asa Gray had neither been intended for publication, and were badly written. Mr. Wallace's essay, on the other hand, was admirably expressed and quite clear. Nevertheless, our joint productions excited very little attention, and the only published notice of them which I can remember was by Professor Haughton of Dublin, whose verdict was that all that was new in them was false, and what was true was old. This shows how necessary it is that any new view should be explained at considerable length in order to arouse public attention.

In September 1858 I set to work by the strong advice of Lyell and

Hooker to prepare a volume on the transmutation of species, but was often interrupted by ill-health, and short visits to Dr. Lane's delightful hydropathic establishment at Moor Park. I abstracted the MS. begun on a much larger scale in 1856, and completed the volume on the same reduced scale. It cost me thirteen months and ten days' hard labour. It was published under the title of the *Origin of Species,* in November 1859. Though considerably added to and corrected in the later editions, it has remained substantially the same book. . . .

The success of the *Origin* may, I think, be attributed in large part to my having long before written two condensed sketches, and to my having finally abstracted a much larger manuscript, which was itself an abstract. By this means I was enabled to select the more striking facts and conclusions. I had, also, during many years, followed a golden rule, namely, that whenever a published fact, a new observation or thought came across me, which was opposed to my general results, to make a memorandum of it without fail and at once: for I had found by experience that such facts and thoughts were far more apt to escape from the memory than favourable ones. Owing to this habit, very few objections were raised against my views which I had not at least noticed and attempted to answer.

It has sometimes been said that the success of the *Origin* proved "that the subject was in the air," or "that men's minds were prepared for it." I do not think that this is strictly true, for I occasionally sounded not a few naturalists, and never happened to come across a single one who seemed to doubt about the permanence of species. Even Lyell and Hooker, though they would listen with interest to me, never seemed to agree. I tried once or twice to explain to able men what I meant by Natural selection, but signally failed. What I believe was strictly true is that innumerable well-observed facts were stored in the minds of naturalists ready to take their proper places as soon as any theory which would receive them was sufficiently explained. Another element in the success of the book was its moderate size; and this I owe to the appearance of Mr. Wallace's essay; had I published on the scale in which I began to write in 1856, the book would have been four or five times as large as the *Origin,* and very few would have had the patience to read it.

I gained much by my delay in publishing from about 1839, when the theory was clearly conceived, to 1859; and I lost nothing by it, for I cared very little whether men attributed most originality to me or Wallace; and his essay no doubt aided in the reception of the theory. I was forestalled in only one important point, which my vanity has always made me regret, namely, the explanation by means of the Glacial period of the presence of the same species of plants and of some few animals on distant mountain summits and in the arctic regions. . . .

My first child was born on December 27, 1839, and I at once commenced to make notes on the first dawn of the various expressions which he exhibited, for I felt convinced, even at this early period, that the most complex and fine shades of expression must all have had a gradual and natural origin. During the summer of the following year, 1840, I read Sir C. Bell's admirable work on expression, and this greatly increased the interest which I felt in the subject, though I could not at all agree with his belief that various muscles had been specially created for the sake of expression. From this time forward I occasionally attended to the subject, both with respect to man and our domesticated animals. My book sold largely; 5267 copies having been disposed of on the day of publication. . . .

Therefore, my success as a man of science, whatever this may have amounted to, has been determined, as far as I can judge, by complex and diversified mental qualities and conditions. Of these, the most important have been—the love of science—unbounded patience in long reflecting over any subject— industry in observing and collecting facts—and a fair share of invention as well as of common-sense. With such moderate abilities as I possess, it is truly surprising that I should have influenced to a considerable extent the belief of scientific men on some important points.

First cousin to Charles Darwin, the ingenious Francis Galton saw the basis for a whole system of evolutionary psychology, based on *individual differences.* At first sight his facility in devising new methods may make us think of him as a consummate tinker, a man intrigued by little practical immediate realities which he can manipulate, rearrange, tinker with, patch up, and make into a new pattern: a sort of Benjamin Franklin, we might say, who invents a Franklin stove, and draws a spark from a thunderstorm, as he creates the homely wisdom of *Poor Richard.* We have several such practical tinkering psychologists in our notebook. Some are great psychologists, others are not, but all, insofar as we care for the world of mechanics and invention, *Better Homes and Gardens,* improvements of ways of drawing a cork or laying linoleum, make psychology come to life as a series of processes to be realistically observed, taken apart and put together again in terms of some practical objective. But in time's perspective we recognize here the first great psychological student of individuality, and the first great division of methods for the study of individuality.

Galton wanted to know, for example, what goes on in the mind's eye, in the world of images. He prepared a little questionnaire to ask people how they visualized the breakfast table as they had sat down to it that day, and devised a method of scaling the vividness of images from 0 to 100. For there were indeed people who denied that they had any mental pictures whatever. Some had them faint, some stronger, and some insisted that the images were true hallucinatory form; they could be scaled at 100, the image being indistinguishable in intensity from the sight of the object. He compared images in the visual field with those in the auditory and other fields. He managed to convince a large portion of his colleagues that the whole world of painters, scientists, inventors, mathematicians, actually carried around in their experience images of various sorts. He showed the apparent weakening of imagery as a product of training in abstract subjects such as mathematics. He showed that one could carry out effective activity without needing images. There were, for example, painters in the Royal Academy of Fine Arts who did not have visual images at all. He showed that the world of images was rich, complex, and above all accessible. It was the accessibility, the practicality, the effort to get materials out where they can be observed and measured, that intrigued him the most.

Quantitative method regularly goes with this posture of the inventor. He decided that all observations could take the form: "greater than," "equal to," or "less than." All right, he thought, we will learn to use this method in the measurement of British noses. He made himself a little paper cross-shaped figure with one long arm, three short ones, hid this in his vest, attached a little pricking instrument to his thumb. As he walked along the Strand, he saw a man whose nose was plainly longer than that of the average or norm which he had in mind, so the right hand of the cross would be pricked. Then there was a man whose nose was shorter than the norm and the left hand would be pricked. Then a man whose nose was about "standard" size and the middle arm would be pricked. Before very long he had gathered enough material to permit decision whether he had chosen a norm which was excessively high so that most of the estimates indicated a "short" nose, or whether he should set the average or norm so there would be approximately equal numbers who would be above and below this norm. When once you work out a method of this sort, you can compare noses of different populations; and what is vastly more important, you can develop a simple quantitative method by which all data can be ranked or ordered in terms of one, two, and three. Today the public opinion pollster may want to know in a time of financial crisis how people feel about the business situation, and he may class people as more optimistic, less optimistic, or about at the average level of optimism at a particular period, and may systematically measure shifts in the direction of optimism or pessimism, as he repeats his measures month by month. In the same way estimates of the competence of students or teachers may be set up.

Galton went on to study the associations between words. He put words on slips of paper which were hidden under books and later, after a chance to forget, he used a spring chronometer, primitive stopwatch, to measure how long it took for words to form in association with those suddenly presented. This was the beginning of the association test, and one of the beginnings of the measurement of the speed of mental responses.

Naturally enough he went on to devise a method of correlation to show the relative dependence of one group of measurements upon another. If, for example, within a particular population walking the sidewalks of the Strand, the long-nosed men tended to have mustaches, he could devise a method of showing the degree of connection between the two. Or he could even go on to a refined measure like ability in engineering as related to scores on mathematics tests. He took time off to develop fingerprinting and composite photography and other Franklin-like practical techniques.

All this is a psychology of the man of action who is also a man of thought. Indeed, what Galton wrote out as a theory was not particularly original or valuable in contrast with these highly practical suggestions as to new methods. He was a lover of things, a lover of manipulations, and a lover of results. We may compare all these with the kinds of sensory and intellectual satisfactions that we have already considered in psychologists of earlier periods. If, however, there is such a thing as rich and exuberant delight in sheer things to see, handle, and use, Galton is a perfect exemplification of them. You can perfectly well write the psychology of a psychologist if you start with the empirical material of what he produced, look to see the love of the task, in other words, the motivation driving him, the form of the skill which he uses in fulfilling the task, and the nature of the systematic product which is the personal psychology which the man produced.

Some such psychologists will be superficial, others profound. Were Alfred Adler living, he could certainly maintain that the interpretation of Nietzsche given below is a more profound interpretation than the one of Galton offered now. To say that it is more profound does not say, however, that it is the only legitimate approach. Psychology springs from all that is in human beings, whether at deeper or at less profound levels, and whether scattered or unified, highly integrated as in the work of Nietzsche, scattered, as in the work of James, or grubby, molelike, particularistic, anchored on immediate reality, as in the case of Galton.

We may use five figures to serve as symbols for the great transition to evolutionary psychology:

1. Charles Darwin, naturalist, traveler, recluse, innovator, ruthless self-critic, modest philosopher of the glory and tragedy of the individual.

2. Francis Galton, the first thorough-going psychologist of individuality.

3. The prophetic Friedrich Nietzsche, lover of beauty and of spontaneity, who in his solitude dreamed the most magnificent and towering dreams of the natural man which becomes the more than now conceivable man, the superman, the ultimate fulfillment of the will to majesty and power.

4. A moment later came the far-roaming, psychological and philosophical genius William James, who, in an intellectual world of aristocracy, simplicity, earnestness, and almost reckless imagination, built a solid psychology upon biology, medicine, the arts, and the new cosmic evolutionary conception, and in countless brilliant passages showed the perennial source of human mind and thought in the deep impulses that lie within the tissues.

5. Sigmund Freud, the research biologist turned physician and psychiatrist, saw the broad sweep of the deeper impulse life and its vast implications for the entire spectrum of human expression through mind, heart, and will, creating almost single-handed a psychological system; the biology of instinct expressed through all the tissues of the body becomes a key even to the most complex, subtle, and elaborate operations of the mind.

Darwin and Galton have been presented. Freud's impact is so great that his work will dominate another volume of our work. The other great evolutionists—Nietzsche and James—we shall now try to make real to our readers.

FRIEDRICH NIETZSCHE

If Charles Darwin was the first to establish the evolutionary principle to the satisfaction of biologists, and if William James was the first to write a psychology which was awake to the evolutionary implications, then Friedrich Nietzsche was the first philosopher to penetrate to the implications of the new biology for human life and thought. Not that Nietzsche attributed any great personal importance to Charles Darwin; rather, he thought that the gathering of "little facts" was an English affair for which he had no taste. Nietzsche, however, grasped profoundly the meaning of evolution, grasped the conception that instinct is the precursor, the life, the basis, the substrate of thought, and indeed of consciousness itself; that man is constantly striving to pass beyond his humanness into a life of the superman; that the social order (as expressed in *The Genealogy of Morals*) is the expression of a struggle eventuating in a "master morality and slave morality," with the will to power driving life into new dimensions "beyond good and evil"; and with the arts, the sciences, and the philosophies expressive of that which is too deep for words, too deep, indeed, for the kind of "pure reason" to which Kant, in the brilliant age of the transcendental, had paid tribute. It is easy to grasp in retrospect why Freud, after a glance at Nietzsche, did not allow himself to read Nietzsche's work. This was too much like himself, too close to himself; he could not breathe. To read Nietzsche would be to prevent his own quest for his own individuality.

What we offer from Nietzsche is, of course, insufficient. It is offered first to show the evolutionary quality pulsing in the thought patterns of the era, and secondly to show Nietzsche as the great protagonist of that doctrine which was to sweep over our modern thought in the next half century: the conception that our thought is itself an expression of what we are, as evolving forms of life adapted to our terrestrial habitat, shaping our life not in terms of the transcendent but in terms of the stuff of which the cosmos and ourselves alike are made.

Nietzsche's scholarly life began well. He made himself competent in the Indo-European languages and literatures, and in the civilizations which reached from the high Persian plateau to the seas and islands of the eastern Mediterranean world. The glory that was Greece took hold of him in an agony of worship for these men of beauty and power. At the same time he saw that their passion was balanced by their devotion to order; they had to have both Dionysus, god of frenzy, and Apollo, god of the divine and classical beauty.

What was at work within him? The long and terrible walks in which he tried to shake off the long and terrible gastric pains, the lonely hours of study in which apparently friendship and comradeship were belittled or found impossible, strongly suggest constitutional frailty and a basic lack of that heroic mold which he was at the time so profoundly admiring. In a period of confused sexuality, he apparently contracted syphilis, which for a period of some twenty years worked first an insidious and then a more open conquest over his failing strength. It is just no "explanation" of

Nietzsche to say that he became grandiose or excited. On the contrary, the magnificent vision of Dionysus and Apollo belongs to his early manhood, his finest flower. But this arose from a period of devotion to an ideal model, together with an utter incapacity to make a real flesh and blood hero among men as he would have craved it. His brief contact with the fighting in the Franco-Prussian War was again a grandiose bit of theatrical excitement. When later he became a passionate devotee of Wagner's Germanic heroes, he was doing exactly what other sickly or puny young men were doing, and when he turned violently upon Wagner because of Wagner's espousal of the Christian epic in *Parsifal,* he was protesting the mawkish sentimentality of a "slave morality," unworthy of a superman. The final expression of the compensation for inferiority, as Adler would call it, was *The Will to Power.* There had been much love in Nietzsche, notably in *The Birth of Tragedy* and in *Thus Spake Zarathustra,* but the forces of compensation over weakness drove home to their final conquest, and a megalomanic philosophy of overweaning self-assertion won the day.

When George Bernard Shaw wrote *Man and Superman* he saw much of this. Indeed, in the extraordinary dialogue from that play, which became Charles Laughton's stage reading of *Don Juan in Hell,* the simple goodness of the Christian is given a nudge in the ribs, with a titter which accuses the right good world of hypocrisy, while men of strength and directness are made interesting. It is exactly in keeping with the fact that the black representative of evil, Ahriman, in the Zoroastrian religious schema, is made more interesting than Ormuzd or Ahura-mazda, god of the bright sky, and just as Milton's Satan and Goethe's Mephistopheles are made interesting through their combination of physical and intellectual power, and indeed, paradoxically, their moral power, since they are free of the inherent self-contradictions of weakness and slave morality.

Nietzsche can thus be made the signer of his own death warrant; the law of compensation can be shown to be compellingly valid, and failure to create true compensatory strength of mind and body can be shown to lead only to disaster. Nietzsche, in point of fact, first won enormous strength. The evil fate which befell his brain, within the years of the forties, must not blind us to the fact that he was one of the three or four great exponents of the evolutionary doctrine within the world of thinking man. He was the true prophet of the superman; his was the ruthless and penetrating vision of man's deep unconscious strivings. Freud, as we have said, refused to read Nietzsche, for after one taste Freud saw that this would stand in the way of his own original thoughts. The compelling universal theme of power, so often neglected, came into Western psychology through Nietzsche to Adler.

Beyond Good and Evil *

3.

After keeping an eye on and reading between the lines of the philosophers for a long time, I find that I must tell myself the following: the largest part of conscious thinking must be considered an instinctual activity, even in the case of philosophical thinking. We must simply re-learn, as we have had to re-learn about heredity and "inborn" qualities. As little as the act of birth is of consequence in the whole process and progress of heredity, so little is consciousness in any decisive sense opposed to instinct. Most of the conscious thinking of a philosopher is secretly guided by his instincts and forced along certain lines. Even behind logic and its apparent sovereignty of development stand value judgments, or, to speak more plainly, physiological demands for preserving a certain type of life. Such as for example, that the definite is worth more than the indefinite, that appearance is less valuable than "the truth." Such valuations, all their regulative importance notwithstanding, can for *us* be only foreground-valuations, a definite type of ridiculous simplicity, possibly necessary for the preservation of the creature we happen to be. Assuming, to be sure, that man does not happen to be "the measure of all things."

. . .

6.

Gradually I have come to realize what every great philosophy up to now has been: the personal confession of its originator, a type of invol-

* From Friedrich Nietzsche, *Beyond Good and Evil,* trans. by Marianne Cowan (Chicago: Henry Regnery Company, 1955), pp. 3–4, 6–7, 15, 19, 20–22, 27–28, 64, 75–76, 78–82, 87–89, 233.

untary and unaware memoirs; also that the moral (or amoral) intentions of each philosophy constitute the protoplasm from which each entire plant has grown. Indeed, one will do well (and wisely), if one wishes to explain to himself how on earth the more remote metaphysical assertions of a philosopher ever arose, to ask each time: What sort of morality is this (is *he*) aiming at? Thus I do not believe that a "desire for comprehension" is the father of philosophy, but rather that a quite different desire has here as elsewhere used comprehension (together with miscomprehension) as tools to serve its own ends. Anyone who looks at the basic desires of man with a view to finding out how well they have played their part in precisely this field as inspirational genii (or demons or hobgoblins) will note that they have all philosophized at one time or another. Each individual desire wants badly to represent itself as *the* final aim of existence and as rightful master of all the others. For each desire is autocratic and *as such* it attempts to philosophize. In the case of scholars, to be sure, the specifically "scientific" men, it may be different—"better" if you wish. They may really have something like a "desire for comprehension," some small independent clockwork mechanism which, when properly wound, works bravely on *without* involving the remaining desires of the scholars. The real "interests," therefore, of the scholars lie in quite another field—in their family, perhaps, or their livelihood, or in politics. It makes almost no difference, in fact, whether the little machine is employed in one place or another to serve science, and whether the "promising" young worker makes of himself a philologist or a mushroom-fancier or a chemist—his becoming this or that does not *characterize him.* Conversely, there is nothing impersonal whatever in the philosopher. And particularly his morality testifies decidedly and decisively as to *who he is*—that is, what order of rank the innermost desires of his nature occupy.

. . .

13.

The physiologists should take heed before they assume self-preservation as the cardinal drive of an organic being. Above all, a living thing wants to *discharge* its energy: life as such is will to power. Self-preservation is only one of its indirect and most frequent *consequences.* In short, here as elsewhere, beware of superfluous teleological principles, such as the instinct for self-preservation. (We owe it to Spinoza's inconsistency.) This is the first demand of methodology, which must in its essence be economy of principles.

. . .

17.

So far as the superstitiousness of logicians is concerned, I do not tire of emphasizing again and again one little briefly stated fact which these superstitious ones do not like to admit. It is simply this: A thought comes when "it" will and not when "I" will. It is thus a *falsification* of the evidence to say that the subject "I" conditions the predicate "think." *It* is thought, to be sure, but that this "it" should be that old famous "I" is, to put it mildly, only a supposition, an assertion. Above all it is not an "immediate certainty." In the end even "it is thought" says too much. Even this "it" contains an *interpretation* of the process and does not belong to the process itself. Our conclusion is here formulated out of our grammatical custom: "Thinking is an activity; every activity presumes something which is active, hence. . . ." According to this same approximate scheme, our older "atomism" was looking for the "force" that has an effect, for that little clod of matter that it inhabits, from which it acts; in short, the atom. More rigorous minds finally learned to get along without such "earthly remains," and perhaps in logic too we will some day become accustomed to getting along without that little "it" (into which the good old honest "I" has evaporated).

19.

Philosophers are in the habit of speaking of "will" as though it were the best-known thing in the world. Schopenhauer in fact gave us to understand that will alone is really known to us, completely known, known without deduction or addition. But it seems to me once again that Schopenhauer in this case too did only what philosophers are always doing: he took over and exaggerated a *popular judgment.* Willing seems to me to be, above all, something *complicated,* something that is a unity in word only. The popular judgment lies just in this word "only," and it has become master of the forever incautious philosophers. Let us be more cautious, then; let us be "unphilosophical"; let us say: in every willing there is first of all a multiplicity of feelings: the feeling of a condition to get *away* from, the feeling of a condition to get *to;* then the feeling of this "away" and "to"; furthermore, an accompanying muscular feeling which, from a sort of habit, begins a game of its own as soon as we "will"—even without our moving our "arms and legs." In the first place, then, feeling—many kinds of feeling—is to be recognized as an ingredient in willing. Secondly, there is thinking: in every act of the will there is a thought which gives commands—and we must not imagine that we can separate this thought out of "willing" and still have something like will left! Thirdly, the will is not merely a complex of feeling and thinking but above all it is a passion—the passion of commanding. What is called "freedom of the will" is essentially a passionate superiority toward a someone who must obey. "I am free; 'he' must obey"—the consciousness of this is the very willing; likewise that tension of alertness, that straightforward look which fixes on one thing exclusively, that absolute valuation which means "just now this, and nothing else, is necessary," that inner certainty that there will be obedience—all this and whatever else is part of the condition of one who is in command. A man who *wills* is giving a command to something in himself that obeys, or which he believes will obey. But now let us note the oddest thing about the will, this manifold something for which the people have only one word: because we, in a given case, are simultaneously the commanders *and* the obeyers and, as obeyers, know the feelings of forcing, crowding, pressing, resisting, and moving which begin immediately after the act of the will: because, on the other hand, we are in the habit of glossing over this duality with the help of the synthetic concept "I"—for these reasons a whole chain of erroneous conclusions, and consequently false valuations of the will, has weighted down our notion of willing, so much so that the willer believes in good faith that willing *suffices* to produce action. Because in the majority of cases there was a willing only where the effect of the command, the obedience, i.e. the action, was an *expected* one, the *appearance* translated itself into the feeling that there had been a *necessary effect.* In short, the willer believes, with a considerable degree of certainty, that will and action are somehow one. He credits the success, the execution of the willing, to the will itself, therewith luxuriating in an increase of the feeling of power which all success produces. "Freedom of the will" is the word for that manifold pleasurable condition of the willer who is in command and at the same time considers himself as one with the executor of the command—as such enjoying the triumph over the resistance, but possessed of the judgment that it is his will itself that is overcoming the resistance. In this fashion the willer adds the pleasurable feelings of the executing, successful instruments, the subservient "lower wills" or "lower souls" (for our body is nothing but a social structure of many souls) to his pleasurable feeling as Commander. *L'effet c'est moi*—the same thing happens here that happens in any well constructed and happy community: the ruling class identifies itself with the success of the community. In all willing, then, there is commanding and obeying on the basis, as we have seen, of a social structure of many "souls." This is why a philosopher should consider himself justified in including willing within the general sphere of morality—morality understood as the doctrine of the rank-relations that produce the phenomenon we call "life."

• • •

23.

All psychology hitherto has become stuck in moral prejudices and fears: none has ventured into the depths. To consider psychology as the morphology and evolutionary doctrine of the will to power—as I consider it—this no one has touched upon even in thought (insofar as it is allowable to recognize in what has been written the symptoms of what has been kept dark). The force of moral prejudices has penetrated deeply into the most spiritual, the seemingly coldest and most open-minded world, and, as one may imagine, with harmful, obstructionist, blinding, and distorting results. A proper physio-psychology must battle with unconscious resistances in the heart of the investigator; his "heart" sides against it. Even a doctrine of the reciprocally limiting interaction of the "good" and "wicked" impulses causes, as being a subtle form of immorality, some distress and aversion in a still strong and hearty conscience. Even worse is a doctrine that all the good impulses are derived from the wicked ones. But imagine someone who takes the very passions —hatred, envy, greed, domineering—to be the passions upon which life is conditioned, as things which must be present in the total household of life. Takes them to be necessary in order to preserve the very nature of life, to be further developed if life is to be further developed! Such a man suffers from the inclination of his judgment as though from seasickness! But even this hypothesis is by no means the most painful or the strangest in this enormous, almost totally unknown domain of dangerous insights. Indeed, there are a hundred good reasons for staying away from it if one—can! On the other hand, if our ship has once taken us there—very well, let us go ahead, grit our teeth, open our eyes, grip the rudder and—ride out morality! Perhaps we will crush and destroy our own remaining morality, but what do *we* matter! Never yet has a *deeper* world of insight been opened to bold travellers and adventurers. And the psychologist who can make this sort of "sacrifice" (it is not the *sacrifizio dell' intelletto*—on the contrary!) will at least be in a position to demand that psychology be acknowledged once more as the mistress of the sciences, for whose service and preparation the other sciences exist. For psychology is now again the road to the basic problems.

• • •

56.

Whoever, like myself, has because of some unknown desire long struggled to think Pessimism to a greater depth and to release it from the half-Christian, half-German narrowness and simple-mindedness with which it was exhibited during this past century in the form of Schopenhauerian philosophy—whoever has really looked at the most world-negating of all possible ways of thinking with Asiatic and ultra-Asiatic eyes—truly beyond good and evil and no longer, like Buddha and Schopenhauer, under the spell and illusion of morality—such a man has perhaps had his eyes opened, even without having wanted it, to the opposite ideal, the ideal of the truly exuberant, alive, and world-affirming man who does not merely resign himself to and learn to get along with all that was and is, but who wants everything *as it was and is* back again, back forever and ever, insatiably calling *da capo,* not only to himself but to the whole spectacle and performance, and not only to the performance but basically to that which necessitates and needs the performance because it forever and ever necessitates and needs iteslf! What did we say? Is this not the *circulus vitiosus deus?*

. . .

68.

"I did this," says my memory. "I cannot have done this," says my pride, remaining inexorable. Eventually, my memory yields.

. . .

78.

Whoever despises himself still esteems the despiser within himself.

. . .

94.

Man's maturity: to have regained the seriousness that he had as a child at play.

. . .

98.

When we coach our conscience, it kisses us as it bites.

. . .

99.

The disappointed one says: I hoped for a response and heard merely praise.

. . .

102.

When love is returned, it should really disenchant the lover with the beloved creature. "What? She is so modest in her demands as to love even you? Or so dumb? Or, or. . . ."

. . .

103.

The danger in happiness: Now everything I touch turns out to be wonderful. Now I love any fate that comes along. Who feels like being my fate?

. . .

107.

When the mind is made up, the ear is deaf to even the best arguments. This is the sign of a strong character. In other words, an occasional will to stupidity.

. . .

117.

The will to overcome a passion is in the end merely the will of another or several other passions.

. . .

119.

Disgust at dirt can be so great that it keeps us from cleaning ourselves up—from "justifying" ourselves.

. . .

124.

Whoever is joyous when burning at the stake is not triumphant over pain, but over the fact that there is no pain where he expected it. A parable.

. . .

125.

When we must change our minds about someone, we charge the inconvenience he causes us heavily to his account.

. . .

126.

A people is nature's detour to six or seven great men. Yes, and then the means to get around even them.

. . .

168.

Christianity gave Eros poison to drink; he did not die of it but he degenerated into vice.

. . .

170.

There is more obtrusiveness in praise than in blame.

. . .

175.

Ultimately one loves one's desire, not the desired object.

. . .

182.

The familiarity of one's superior makes one bitter because it cannot be reciprocated.

. . .

291.

Man, a complex, lying, artificial, and inscrutable animal, weird-looking to the other animals not so much because of his power but rather because of his guile and shrewdness, has invented the clear conscience, so that he might have the sensation, for once, that his psyche is a *simple* thing. All of morality is a continuous courageous forgery, without which an enjoyment of the sight of man's soul would be impossible. From this point of view, the concept "art" may be much more comprehensive than one commonly believes.

The Genealogy of Morals: An Attack *

PREFACE

I

We knowers are unknown to ourselves, and for a good reason: how can we ever hope to find what we have never looked for? There is a sound adage which runs: "Where a man's treasure lies, there lies his heart." Our treasure lies in the beehives of our knowledge. We are perpetually on our way thither, being by nature winged insects and honey gatherers of the mind. The only thing that lies close to our heart is the desire to bring something home to the hive. As for the rest of life—so-called "experience"—who among us is serious enough for that? Or has time enough? When it comes to such matters, our heart is simply not in it—we don't even lend our ear. Rather, as a man divinely abstracted and self-absorbed into whose ears the bell has just drummed the twelve strokes of noon will suddenly awake with a start and ask himself what hour has actually struck, we sometimes rub our ears after the event and ask ourselves, astonished and at a loss, "What have we really experienced?"—or rather, "Who are we, really?" And we recount the twelve tremulous strokes of our experience, our life, our being, but unfortunately count wrong. The sad truth is that we remain necessarily strangers to ourselves, we don't understand our own substance, we *must* mistake ourselves; the axiom, "Each man is farthest from himself," will hold for us to all eternity. Of ourselves we are not "knowers." . . .

II

My ideas about the provenance of our moral prejudices (for that is to be the subject of the present work) found their first brief and tentative

* From Friedrich Nietzsche, *The Birth of Tragedy and The Genealogy of Morals,* trans. by Francis Goffing (New York: Doubleday & Company, 1956), pp. 149–154, 158–162, 170–173. © 1956 by Doubleday & Company. Reprinted by permission of the publishers.

formulation in a collection of aphorisms called *Human, All Too Human: A Book for Free Spirits.* I began that book one winter in Sorrento, at a moment when it was given me to pause, as a wanderer might pause, and to look back over the wild and dangerous territory my mind had crossed. It was the winter of 1876–77; the ideas themselves had come to me earlier, however. And it is those same ideas I wish to take up in the present treatise: let us hope that the long interval has done them good, making them stronger and more luminous. At all events, the fact that I still hold them fast today, that through all these years they have continued to intertwine and draw nourishment from each other, encourages me to believe that from the very beginning they were not isolated thoughts, nor random or sporadic ones, but sprang from a common root, from a primary desire for knowledge, legislating from deep down in increasingly precise terms, increasingly precise demands. A philosopher should proceed in no other way. We have no right to isolated thoughts, whether truthful or erroneous. Our thoughts should grow out of our values with the same necessity as the fruit out of the tree. Our yeas and nays, our ifs and buts should all be intimately related and bear testimony to one will, one health, one soil, one sun. Supposing you find these fruits unpalatable? What concern is that of the trees—or of us, the philosophers?

III

Because of a qualm peculiar to me and which I am loath to admit, since it refers to morals, or rather to anything that has ever been cried up as ethics—a qualm which, unbidden and irresistible, put me so at variance, from my earliest childhood, with environment, age, precepts, tradition that I feel almost entitled to call it my *a priori*—both my curiosity and my suspicions were focused betimes on the provenance of our notions of good and evil. Already at the age of thirteen I was exercised by the problem of evil. At an age when one's interests are "divided between childish games and God" I wrote my first essay on ethics. My solution of the problem was to give the honor to God, as is only just, and make him the father of evil. Was this what my *a priori* demanded of me—that new, immoral, or at any rate non-moral *a priori* —and that mysterious anti-Kantian "categorical imperative" to which I have hearkened more and more ever since, and not only hearkened? Fortunately I learned in good time to divorce the theological prejudice from the moral and no longer to seek the origin of evil *behind* the world. A certain amount of historical and philological training, together with a native fastidiousness in matters of psychology, before long transformed this problem into another, to wit, "Under what conditions did man construct the value judgments *good* and *evil?*" And what is their intrinsic worth? Have they thus far benefited or retarded mankind? Do they betoken misery, curtailment, degeneracy or, on the contrary, power, fullness of being, energy, courage in the face of life, and confidence in the future? A great variety of answers suggested themselves. I began to distinguish among periods, nations, individuals; I narrowed the problem down; the answers grew into new questions, investigations, suppositions, probabilities, until I had staked off at last my own domain, a whole hidden, growing and blooming world, secret gardens as it were, of whose existence no one must have an inkling. . . . How blessed are we knowers, provided we know how to keep silent long enough!

V

At bottom, I was concerned at that time with something much more important than either my own or someone else's hypotheses about the origin of ethics—more precisely, this origin mattered to me only as one of the means toward an end. The end was the *value* of ethics, and I had to fight this issue out almost alone with my great teacher Schopenhauer, to whom *Human, All Too Human,* with all its passion and hidden contradictions, addresses itself as though he were still alive. That book, be it observed, was likewise an attack. The point at issue was the value of the non-egotistical instincts, the instincts of compassion, self-denial, and self-sacrifice, which Schopenhauer above all others had consistently gilded, glorified, "transcendentalized" until he came to see them as *absolute* values allowing him to deny life and even himself. Yet it was these very same instincts which aroused my suspicion, and that suspicion deepened as time went on. It was here, precisely, that I sensed the greatest danger for humanity, its sublimest delusion and temptation—leading it whither? into nothingness? Here I sensed the beginning of the end, stagnation, nostalgic fatigue, a will that had turned *against* life. I began to understand that the constantly spreading ethics of pity, which had tainted and debilitated even the philosophers, was the most sinister symptom of our sinister European civilization—a detour to a new Buddhism? to a European species of Buddhism? to nihilism? This preference for and overestimation of pity, among philosophers, is an entirely new development in Western civilization. The philosophers of the past deny, to a man, all value to pity. I need only instance Plato, Spinoza, La Rochefoucauld, and Kant, four minds as different from each other as possible yet agreeing in this one regard, the low esteem in which they hold pity.

VI

At first sight, this problem of pity and the ethics of pity (I am strongly opposed to our modern sentimentality in these matters) may seem very special, a marginal issue. But whoever sticks with it and learns how to ask questions will have the same experience that I had: a vast new panorama will open up before him; strange and vertiginous possibilities will invade him; every variety of suspicion, distrust, fear will come to the surface; his belief in ethics of any kind will begin to be shaken. Finally he will be forced to listen to a new claim. Let us articulate that new claim: we need a critique of all moral values; the intrinsic worth of these values must, first of all, be called in question. To this end we need to know the conditions from which those values have sprung and how they have developed and changed: morality as consequence, symptom, mask, *tartufferie,* sickness, misunderstanding; but, also, morality as cause, remedy, stimulant, inhibition, poison. Hitherto such knowledge has neither been forthcoming nor considered a desideratum. The intrinsic worth of these values was taken for granted as a fact of experience and put beyond question. Nobody, up to now, has doubted that the "good" man represents a higher value than the "evil," in terms of promoting and benefiting mankind generally, even taking the long view. But suppose the exact opposite were true. What if the "good" man represents not merely a retrogression but even a danger, a temptation, a narcotic drug enabling the present to live at the expense of the future? More comfortable, less hazardous, perhaps, but also baser, more petty —so that morality itself would be responsible for man, as a species, failing to reach the peak of magnificence of which he is capable? What if morality should turn out to be the danger of dangers? . . .

FIRST ESSAY. "GOOD AND EVIL," "GOOD AND BAD"

I

The English psychologists to whom we owe the only attempts that have thus far been made to write a genealogy of morals are no mean posers of riddles, but the riddles they pose are themselves, and being incarnate have one advantage over their books—they are interesting. What are these English psychologists really after? One finds them always, whether intentionally or not, engaged in the same task of pushing into the foreground the nasty part of the psyche, looking for the effective motive forces of human development in the very last place we would wish to have them found, e.g., in the inertia of habit, in forgetfulness, in the blind and fortuitous association of ideas: always in something that is purely passive, automatic, reflexive, molecular, and, moreover, profoundly stupid. What drives these psychologists forever in the same direction? A secret, malicious desire to belittle humanity, which they do not acknowledge even to themselves? A pessimistic distrust, the suspiciousness of the soured idealist? Some petty resentment of Christianity (and Plato) which does not rise above the threshold of consciousness? Or could it be a prurient taste for whatever is embarrassing, painfully paradoxical, dubious and absurd in existence? Or is it, perhaps, a kind of stew—a little meanness, a little bitterness, a bit of anti-Christianity, a touch of prurience and desire for condiments? . . . But, again, people tell me that these men are simply dull old frogs who hop and creep in and around man as in their own element—as though man were a bog. However, I am reluctant to listen to this, in fact I refuse to believe it; and if I may express a wish where I cannot express a conviction, I do wish wholeheartedly that things may be otherwise with these men—that these microscopic examiners of the soul may be really courageous, magnanimous, and proud animals, who know how to contain their emotions and have trained themselves to subordinate all wishful thinking to the truth—any truth, even a homespun, severe, ugly, obnoxious, un-Christian, unmoral truth. For such truths do exist.

II

All honor to the beneficent spirits that may motivate these historians of ethics! One thing is certain, however, they have been quite deserted by the true spirit of history. They all, to a man, think unhistorically, as is the age-old custom among philosophers. The amateurishness of their procedure is made plain from the very beginning, when it is a question of explaining the provenance of the concept and judgment *good*. "Originally," they decree, "altruistic actions were praised and approved by their recipients, that is, by those to whom they were useful. Later on, the origin of that praise having been forgotten, such actions were felt to be good simply because it was the habit to commend them." We notice at once that this first derivation has all the earmarks of the English psychologists' work. Here are the key ideas of utility, forgetfulness, habit, and, finally, error, seen as lying at the root of that value system which civilized man had hitherto regarded with pride as the prerogative of all men. This pride must now be humbled, these values devalued. Have the debunkers succeeded?

Now it is obvious to me, first of all, that their theory looks for the genesis of the concept *good* in the wrong place: the judgment *good* does not originate with those to whom the good has been done. Rather it was the "good" themselves, that is to say the noble, mighty, highly placed, and high-minded who decreed themselves and their actions to be good, i.e., belonging to the highest rank, in contradistinction to all that was base, low-minded and plebeian. It was only this *pathos of distance* that authorized them to create values and name them—what was utility to them? The notion of utility seems singularly inept to account for such a quick jetting forth of supreme value judgments. Here we come face to face with the exact opposite of that lukewarmness which every scheming prudence, every utilitarian calculus presupposes—and not for a time only, for the rare, exceptional hour, but permanently. The origin of the opposites *good* and *bad* is to be found in the pathos of nobility and distance, representing the dominant temper of a higher, ruling class in relation to a lower, dependent one. (The lordly right of bestowing names is such that one would almost be justified in seeing the origin of language itself as an expression of the rulers' power. They say, "This *is* that or that"; they seal off each thing and action with a sound and thereby take symbolic possession of it.) Such an origin would suggest that there is no *a priori* necessity for associating the word *good* with altruistic deeds, as those moral psychologists are fond of claiming. In fact, it is only after aristocratic values have begun to decline that the egotism-altruism dichotomy takes possession of the human conscience; to use my own terms, it is the herd instinct that now asserts itself. Yet it takes quite a while for this instinct to assume such sway that it can reduce all moral valuations to that dichotomy—as is currently happening throughout Europe, where the prejudice equating the terms *moral, altruistic,* and *disinterested* has assumed the obsessive force of an *idée fixe.*

• • •

IV

The clue to the correct explanation was furnished me by the question "What does the etymology of the terms for good in various languages tell us?" I discovered that all these terms lead us back to the same conceptual transformation. The basic concept is always *noble* in the hierarchical, class sense, and from this has developed, by historical necessity, the concept *good* embracing nobility of mind, spiritual distinction. This development is strictly parallel to that other which eventually converted the notions *common, plebeian, base* into the notion *bad.* Here we have an important clue to the actual genealogy of morals; that it has not been hit upon earlier is due to the retarding influence which democratic prejudice has had upon all investigation of origins. This holds equally true with regard to the seemingly quite objective areas of natural science and physiology, though I cannot enlarge upon the question now. The amount of damage such prejudice is capable of doing in ethics and history, once it becomes inflamed with hatred, is clearly shown by the case of Buckle. Here we see the plebeian bias of the modern mind, which stems from England, erupt once again on its native soil with all the violence of a muddy volcano and all the vulgar and oversalted eloquence characteristic of volcanoes.

• • •

X

The slave revolt in morals begins by rancor turning creative and giving birth to values—the rancor of beings who, deprived of the direct outlet of action, compensate by an imaginary vengeance. All truly noble morality grows out of triumphant self-affirmation. Slave ethics, on the other hand, begins by saying *no* to an "outside," an "other," a non-self, and that *no* is its creative act. This reversal of direction of the evaluating look, this invariable looking outward instead of inward, is a fundamental feature of rancor. Slave ethics requires for its inception a sphere different from and hostile to its own. Physiologically speaking, it requires an outside stimulus in order to act at all; all its action is reaction. The opposite is true of aristocratic valuations: such values grow and act spontaneously, seeking out their contraries only in order to affirm themselves even more gratefully and delightedly. Here the negative concepts, *humble, base, bad,* are late, pallid counterparts of the positive, intense and passionate credo, "We noble, good, beautiful, happy ones." Aristocratic valuations may go amiss and do violence to reality, but this happens only with regard to spheres which they do not know well, or from the knowledge of which they austerely guard themselves: the aristocrat will, on occasion, misjudge a sphere which he holds in contempt, the sphere of the common man, the people. On the other hand we should remember that the emotion of contempt, of looking down, provided that it falsifies at all, is as nothing compared with the falsification which suppressed hatred, impotent vindictiveness, effects upon its opponent, though only in effigy. There is in all contempt too much casualness and nonchalance, too much blinking of facts and impatience, and too much inborn gaiety for it ever to make of its object a downright caricature and monster. Hear the almost benevolent nuances the Greek aristocracy, for example, puts into all its terms for the commoner; how emotions of compassion, consideration, indulgence, sugar-coat these words until, in the end, almost all terms referring to the common man survive as expressions for "unhappy," "pitiable" (cf. *deilos, deilaios, poneros, mochtheros,* the last two of which properly characterize the common man as a drudge and beast of burden); how, on the other hand, the words *bad, base, unhappy* have continued to strike a similar note for the Greek ear, with the timbre "unhappy" preponderating. The "wellborn" really felt that they were also the "happy." They did not have to construct their happiness factitiously by looking at their enemies, as all rancorous men are wont to do, and being fully active, energetic people they were incapable of divorcing happiness from action. They accounted activity a necessary part of happiness (which explains the origin of the phrase *eu prattein*).

All this stands in utter contrast to what is called happiness among the impotent and oppressed, who are full of bottled-up aggressions. Their happiness is purely passive and takes the form of drugged tranquillity, stretching and yawning, peace, "sabbath," emotional slackness. Whereas the noble lives before his own conscience with confidence and frankness (*gennaīos* "nobly bred" emphasizes the nuance "truthful" and perhaps also "ingenuous"), the rancorous person is neither truthful nor ingenuous nor honest and forthright with himself. His soul squints; his mind loves hide-outs, secret paths, and back doors; everything that is hidden seems to him his own world, his security, his comfort; he is expert in silence, in long memory, in waiting, in provisional self-depreciation, and in self-humiliation. A race of such men will, in the end, inevitably be cleverer than a race of aristocrats, and it will honor sharp-wittedness to a much greater degree, i.e., as an absolutely vital condition for its existence. Among the noble, mental acuteness always tends slightly to suggest luxury and overrefinement. The fact is that with them it is much less important than is the perfect functioning of the ruling, unconscious instincts or even a certain temerity to follow sudden impulses, court danger, or indulge spurts of violent rage, love, worship, gratitude, or vengeance. When a noble man feels resentment, it is absorbed in his instantaneous reaction and therefore does not poison him. Moreover, in countless cases where we might expect it, it never arises, while with weak and impotent people it occurs without fail. It is a sign of strong, rich temperaments that they cannot for long take seriously their enemies, their misfortunes, their *misdeeds;* for such characters have in them an excess of plastic curative power, and also a power of oblivion. (A good modern example of the latter is Mirabeau, who lacked all memory for insults and meannesses done him, and who was unable to forgive because he had forgotten. Such a man simply shakes off vermin which would get beneath another's skin—and only here, if anywhere on earth, is it possible to speak of "loving one's enemy." The noble person will respect his enemy, and respect is already a bridge to love. . . . Indeed he requires his enemy for himself, as his mark of distinction, nor could he tolerate any other enemy than one in whom he finds nothing to despise and much to esteem. Imagine, on the other hand, the "enemy" as conceived by the rancorous man! For this is his true creative achievement: he has conceived the "evil enemy," the Evil One, as a fundamental idea, and then as a pendant he has conceived a Good One—himself.

WILLIAM JAMES

Despite the growth of a cosmopolitan spirit, much travel, pride in the mastery of a Western European civilization as a whole, there were still strong nationalist trends in the psychology of the mid-nineteenth century. Even unifying forces like experimentalism on the one hand and evolutionism on the other produced characteristically different responses in Britain, France, and Germany. Associationism, profoundly colored by the new experimental physiology and suffering from the first impacts of the new evolutionary outlook, could still be called the central assumption of most serious psychology. This associationism, however, was pursued in a spirit colored as deeply by philosophy as by the scientific method. There was, in short, a recognizable nineteenth-century psychology, but with national variations and with different emphases depending upon the philosophical, the experimental, the evolutionary modalities of thought.

There was no independent American psychology in this era. College students, a large proportion of whom were headed for the ministry, acquired some familiarity with associationist psychology (usually in a religious perspective), and some of them encountered German philosophical ideas as these were filtering through English channels. Among the most enterprising students a few, like Ralph Waldo Emerson, responded to the new European scholarship and even to the amazing new knowledge of Asian thought. To study psychology, however, meant for the most part to take the "mental and moral philosophy" offered in the colleges, which brought students into contact with the "Scottish school" and here and there with the associationism and utilitarianism of James and John Stuart Mill, with some contact—direct or indirect—with Kant and Hegel.

There would have been no special reason to predict any very

great American response to the new possibility of scientific psychology; that is, if one took the colleges, and even if one included the medical schools and a few individual travelers who studied in Britain or on the Continent, one would have had no reason to expect a really great figure to appear. A great figure did, however, appear and it is of interest to see what characterized him.

The steady flow of immigrants from the British Isles to the United States in the first half of the nineteenth century brought a few who had, or quickly acquired, a little capital with which to play a prominent part in the economic evolution of their adopted land. The Irishman, William James, with a Scotch-Irish business orientation, settled in Albany, New York, where the great flow of traffic from the Erie Canal and the new railroads made huge prosperity a quick reward for sharp business sense. William James became a great realty figure and made enough money to set up his five children for life. One of the five, Henry James, an eager, sociable lad, suffered an accident which involved the amputation of a leg. This forced upon him some isolation from the eager social activity of his contemporaries, and added to his relative isolation from the hurly-burly of the world to which the inheritance of a fortune predisposed him. Early he became a "seeker," one who responded warmly to the new philosophical and religious trends, seeking a definition of spiritual regeneration and salvation which would be philosophically sound and not just emotionally warming. With the understanding support of his wife, he "sought" in all sorts of ways, including much thought, much reading, and much travel. Of their five children, William, born in 1842 in New York, and his younger brother Henry, two years later, developed into two of the commanding figures in American intellectual history: our William James, the psychologist, and Henry James, the novelist.* The children, as fully at home in the Boston world as the New York world, were taken back and forth for impressions and study in England, France, Switzerland, and Germany. Such European travel was a familiar custom among

* Several biographies of the James family exist, and there is an excellent biography of William James by Gay Wilson Allen entitled *William James: A Biography* (New York: Viking Press, 1967).

well-to-do Americans of the period (cf. Van Wyck Brooks, *The Dream of Arcadia,* and the satirical picture, within which there is still reality, in Mark Twain's *A Tramp Abroad* and *The Innocents Abroad*). William James acquired an intense delight from and fascination with the customs, music, art museums, the ways of speech and expression among people of cultivation. In Cambridge, in 1861, when the Civil War broke out, it became obvious that he did not have the stamina for military service. In fact, his chemistry professor tells how he would have to lie down in the midst of experiments because he did not have strength to stand up to see them through. There were some interruptions in his education, which included a period in the Lawrence Scientific School and the Harvard Medical School, from which he graduated with an M.D. in 1869. Two other colorful details of his life: a journey with the biologist, Louis Agassiz, to the Amazon to collect specimens, which led to illness and near collapse; and a long period in the painter's colony in Newport, Rhode Island, in which he decided—for a while—that he would become a painter. Medicine, however, had prevailed. After he acquired the M.D. degree, he was still uncertain. There would be money enough in the life of a doctor. Yes, money enough for WJ, but "would there be enough for Mrs. WJ?"

In the midst of uncertainty, he was offered a lowly job as an instructor and demonstrator in physiology at Harvard. This appointment, in 1872, quickly led to his organizing a little laboratory and giving demonstrations to undergraduate students as to the ways in which the body works. Here he could make immediately useful all that he had learned in various trips abroad, especially in the lecture halls of German universities; here he could marshal all that he remembered—and that was a great deal—of the British psychology he had been reading, the French impressions, the Swiss and Italian contacts. He began writing psychological articles for the journals. So notable was he, as a vivid young physician and philosopher, too, all in one package, that Henry Holt, the publisher, asked him, in 1878, to undertake the writing of a systematic "Principles of Psychology." He agreed and started in upon an adventure which he thought he could complete in two years; actually, it took twelve. He was settling down well in the Cambridge environment. Shy and withdrawn, he might well have remained a bachelor, but his father called his attention to *just* the right girl, and he vigorously agreed. It was, from every account, a happy, sound, supporting, and satisfying relationship. The picture we get of James is one of both personal and professional adequacy to life.

It is the more surprising to encounter direct evidence that he was very far from well, subject to backaches, headaches, general stress, easy fatigue, and at times a sense of futility, even to the point of terror. The medicine of the day had little to offer. He did, however, read and reread the French philosopher Renouvier, a spiritual descendant of Kant, who had laid down the thesis that the will is central in life, and that one can remake oneself through the will. "I can, then," thought James, "remake myself and become well." He went actually quite far toward succeeding, as the testimony of the family made clear.

He finally achieved completion of the two-volume *Principles of Psychology,* and with it, a tremendous international reputation which begins to show in all sorts of ways. He becomes bold; he is willing to tackle all sorts of difficult technical problems; as a matter of fact, he moves away from psychology, and in particular moves out of the laboratory altogether; he begins to write a kind of psychology which is really an indirect expression of the new and exciting frontier life and, at the same time, of a bridging from European to American intellectual preoccupations.

Perhaps most of all, we should say, he exemplified an evolutionary spirit, for James had, from the very beginning, been an ardent and likewise a disciplined evolutionist. He thought of the living system as deriving from the struggle for existence, the survival of the fittest, and adaptation to the environment. Let the reader browse in the chapters on "Instinct" and "Emotion," and that marvelous last chapter on the "Necessary Truths," and he will see that James was looking at the whole psychic constellation of man's life in essentially Darwinian terms. We shall make our selections from James partly to show the richness and range of his spiritual contacts with the psychology of the period, but more especially to show how, in root and branch, he was always an evolutionist. Emotions, for example, are the systems of activity which nature has given us to display in crisis situations, meeting the severity of a threat by a mass mobilization of bodily energies. Emotion is simply the inner core, or the impact from the physiological activity of adapting to crisis. All the "coarser emotions" are crisis-bound. The subtler and more complicated aspects of life are still rooted in the coarser, but with the development of habit systems the coarser becomes overlaid by the subtle and complex; even, indeed, to the degree that the will steps in and takes a controlling part even in an emotionally demanding situation.

But it is not just the affective and impulsive life that betrays our evolutionary origin. Our minds, too, the ways we perceive, interpret, remember, and, above all, the ways we conceptualize and give structure to what we apprehend, spell out the way in which minds have to function because of basic Darwinian principles. We have to think as we do because this is the kind of system of activities that organisms like ours are prone to exhibit when eyes, ears, muscles, brain, etc., structure our lives through the adaptive struggle to make contact with the environment. There are not only some ways of feeling which are given by inheritance from our remote ancestors; there are also ways of thinking, imagining, conceptualizing, which give us "necessary truths." We simply have to see it this way because this is a pragmatic necessity. What James wrote in this extraordinary chapter on "Necessary Truths," in 1890, reappears in new guise in his lectures on "Pragmatism" and "The Meaning of Truth," written in the last decade of his life.

Our selections begin with the renowned chapter on "Habit."

Habit *

Habit is thus the enormous fly-wheel of society, its most precious conservative agent. It alone is what keeps us all within the bounds of ordinance, and saves the children of fortune from the envious uprisings of the poor. It alone prevents the hardest and most repulsive walks of life from being deserted by those brought up to tread therein. It keeps

* From William James, *The Principles of Psychology* (New York: Henry Holt and Company, 1890), I, 121–125.

the fisherman and the deck-hand at sea through the winter; it holds the miner in his darkness, and nails the countryman to his log-cabin and his lonely farm through all the months of snow; it protects us from invasion by the natives of the desert and the frozen zone. It dooms us all to fight out the battle of life upon the lines of our nurture or our early choice, and to make the best of a pursuit that disagrees, because there is no other for which we are fitted, and it is too late to begin again. It keeps different social strata from mixing. Already at the age of twenty-five you see the professional mannerism settling down on the young commercial traveller, on the young doctor, on the young minister, on the young counsellor-at-law. You see the little lines of cleavage running through the character, the tricks of thought, the prejudices, the ways of the "shop," in a word, from which the man can by-and-by no more escape than his coat-sleeve can suddenly fall into a new set of folds. On the whole, it is best he should not escape. It is well for the world that in most of us, by the age of thirty, the character has set like plaster, and will never soften again.

If the period between twenty and thirty is the critical one in the formation of intellectual and professional habits, the period below twenty is more important still for the fixing of *personal* habits, properly so called, such as vocalization and pronunciation, gesture, motion, and address. . . .

The great thing, then, in all education, is to *make our nervous system our ally instead of our enemy.* It is to fund and capitalize our acquisitions, and live at ease upon the interest of the fund. *For this we must make automatic and habitual, as early as possible, as many useful actions as we can,* and guard against the growing into ways that are likely to be disadvantageous to us, as we should guard against the plague. The more of the details of our daily life we can hand over to the effortless custody of automatism, the more our higher powers of mind will be set free for their own proper work. There is no more miserable human being than one in whom nothing is habitual but indecision, and for whom the lighting of every cigar, the drinking of every cup, the time of rising and going to bed every day, and the beginning of every bit of work, are subjects of express volitional deliberation. . . .

In Professor Bain's chapter on "The Moral Habits" there are some admirable practical remarks laid down. Two great maxims emerge from his treatment. The first is that in the acquisition of a new habit, or the leaving off of an old one, we must take care to *launch ourselves with as strong and decided an initiative as possible.* Accumulate all the possible circumstances which shall re-enforce the right motives; put yourself assiduously in conditions that encourage the new way; make engagements incompatible with the old; take a public pledge, if the case allows; in short, envelop your resolution with every aid you know. This will give your new beginning such a momentum that the temptation to break down will not occur as soon as it otherwise might; and every day during which a breakdown is postponed adds to the chances of its not occurring at all.

The second maxim is: *Never suffer an exception to occur till the new habit is securely rooted in your life. . . .*

The question of "tapering-off," in abandoning such habits as drink and opium-indulgence, comes in here, and is a question about which experts differ within certain limits, and in regard to what may be best for an individual case. In the main, however, all expert opinion would agree that abrupt acquisition of the new habit is the best way, *if there be a real possibility of carrying it out.* We must be careful not to give the will so stiff a task as to insure its defeat at the very outset; but, *provided one can stand it,* a sharp period of suffering, and then a free time, is the best thing to aim at, whether in giving up a habit like that of opium, or in simply changing one's hours of rising or of work. It is surprising how soon a desire will die of inanition if it be *never* fed.

> One must first learn, unmoved, looking neither to the right nor left, to walk firmly on the straight and narrow path, before one can begin "to make one's self over again." He who every day makes a fresh resolve is like one who, arriving at the edge of the ditch he is to leap, forever stops and returns for a fresh run. Without *unbroken* advance there is no such thing as *accumulation* of the ethical forces possible, and to make this possible, and to exercise us and habituate us in it, is the sovereign blessing of regular *work.* (J. Bahnsen, *Beitrage zu Charakterologie* [1867], I, 209.)

A third maxim may be added to the preceding pair: *Seize the very first possible opportunity to act on every resolution you make, and on every emotional prompting you may experience in the direction of the habits you aspire to gain.* It is not in the moment of their forming, but in the moment of their producing *motor effects,* that resolves and aspirations communicate the new "set" to the brain. . . .

No matter how full a reservoir of *maxims* one may possess, and no matter how good one's *sentiments* may be, if one have not taken advantage of every concrete opportunity to *act,* one's character may remain entirely unaffected for the better. With mere good intentions, hell is proverbially paved. And this is an obvious consequence of the principles we have laid down. A "character," as J. S. Mill says, "is completely fashioned will"; and a will, in the sense in which he means it, is an aggregate of tendencies to act in a firm and prompt and definite way upon all the principal emergencies of life. A tendency to act only becomes effectively ingrained in us in proportion to the uninterrupted frequency with which the actions actually occur, and the brain "grows" to their use. Every time a resolve or a fine glow of feeling evaporates without bearing practical fruit is worse than a chance lost; it works so as positively to hinder future resolutions and emotions from taking the normal path of discharge.

James is also celebrated for his conception that "life," "mind," and "thought" are realities spread through time; rather than cross-sectional events, the character of which may be grasped in a glance, they are rivers, like the river of Heraclitus, to whom it was a first principle that "all things flow" (see page 22). Experience moves forward. It is a temporal flow rather than a "state of consciousness," a façade which can be viewed by the introspective observer. The stream of thought is full of rich and ever-changing realities. There are relatively stable portions—"substantive" portions, James calls them—and there are fleeting evanescent portions—"transitive," he calls them. There are surface events like the chips and twigs, and deeper events, which we could compare, to carry out the simile, with the stones and the mud beneath. The stream is never the same. It widens and narrows, cascades and purls. It was probably Gertrude Stein's study under William James, at Harvard, and her own cultivation of the stream of thought that highlighted the use of this conception in fiction and drama from early in the present century until the general period of World War I and thereafter; and something may be due also to James's stream of thought in the development of existentialism and its concern with the texture of the flowing thought process.

Parallel to the chapter on "The Stream of Thought," one might well select from the brilliant chapter on "Consciousness of Self," in which James undertakes to show the different ways in which we become aware of our own individuality and the role which the self, or "self-image," plays in our steering our way through life's difficulties. We have not actually selected from this chapter, partly because we believe that James's brilliant thought here has been outdone by modern empirical research on the self. But we wish to remind the reader that thought is conceived by James as capable of becoming highly expressive of the way in which the individual views himself, and that it partakes of the biological individuality of each thinker.

The Stream of Thought *

We now begin our study of the mind from within. Most books start with sensations, as the simplest mental facts, and proceed synthetically, constructing each higher stage from those below it. But this is abandoning the empirical method of investigation. No one ever had a simple sensation by itself. Consciousness, from our natal day, is of a teeming multiplicity of objects and relations, and what we call simple sensations are results of discriminative attention, pushed often to a very high degree. It is astonishing what havoc is wrought in psychology by admitting at the outset apparently innocent suppositions, that nevertheless contain a flaw. The bad consequences develop themselves later on, and are irremediable, being woven through the whole texture of the work. The notion that sensations, being the simplest things, are the first things to take up in psychology is one of these suppositions. The only thing which psychology has a right to postulate at the outset is the fact of thinking itself, and that must first be taken up and analyzed. If sensations then prove to be amongst the elements of the thinking, we shall be no worse off as respects them than if we had taken them for granted at the start.

The first fact for us, then, as psychologists, is that thinking of some sort goes on. I use the word thinking for every form of consciousness indiscriminately. If we could say in English "it thinks," as we say "it rains" or "it blows," we should be stating the fact most simply and with the minimum of assumption. As we cannot, we must simply say that *thought goes on.*

FIVE CHARACTERS IN THOUGHT

How does it go on? We notice immediately five important characters in the process, of which it shall be the duty of the present chapter to treat in a general way:

(1) Every thought tends to be part of a personal consciousness.

(2) Within each personal consciousness thought is always changing.

(3) Within each personal consciousness thought is sensibly continuous.

* From *The Principles of Psychology,* I, 224–227, 237–239, 243–244, 284–290.

(4) It always appears to deal with objects independent of itself.

(5) It is interested in some parts of these objects to the exclusion of others, and welcomes or rejects—*chooses* from among them, in a word —all the while.

In considering these five points successively, we shall have to plunge *in medias res* as regards our vocabulary, and use psychological terms which can only be adequately defined in later chapters of the book. But every one knows what the terms mean in a rough way; and it is only in a rough way that we are now to take them. This chapter is like a painter's first charcoal sketch upon his canvas, in which no niceties appear.

(1) *Thought tends to Personal Form*

When I say *every thought is part of a personal consciousness,* "personal consciousness" is one of the terms in question. Its meaning we know so long as no one asks us to define it, but to give an accurate account of it is the most difficult of philosophic tasks. This task we must confront in the next chapter; here a preliminary word will suffice.

In this room—this lecture-room, say—there are a multitude of thoughts, yours and mine, some of which cohere mutually, and some not. They are as little each-for-itself and reciprocally independent as they are all-belonging-together. They are neither: no one of them is separate, but each belongs with certain others and with none beside. My thought belongs with my other thoughts, and your thought with your other thoughts. Whether anywhere in the room there be a mere thought, which is nobody's thought, we have no means of ascertaining, for we have no experience of its like. The only states of consciousness that we naturally deal with are found in personal consciousnesses, minds, selves, concrete particular I's and you's.

Each of these minds keeps its own thoughts to itself. There is no giving or bartering between them. No thought even comes into direct *sight* of a thought in another personal consciousness than its own. Absolute insulation, irreducible pluralism, is the law. It seems as if the elementary psychic fact were not *thought* or *this thought* or *that thought,* but *my thought,* every thought being *owned.* Neither contemporaneity, nor proximity in space, nor similarity of quality and content are able to fuse thoughts together which are sundered by this barrier of belonging to different personal minds. The breaches between such thoughts are the most absolute breaches in nature. Everyone will recognize this to be true, so long as the existence of *something* corresponding to the term "personal mind" is all that is insisted on, without any particular view of its nature being implied. On these terms the personal self rather than the thought might be treated as the immediate datum in psychology. The universal conscious fact is not "feelings and thoughts exist," but "I think" and "I feel." No psychology, at any rate, can question the *existence* of personal selves. The worst a psychology can do is so to interpret the nature of these selves as to rob them of their worth. A French writer, speaking of our ideas, says somewhere in a fit of anti-spiritualistic excitement that, misled by certain peculiarities which they display, we "end by personifying" the procession which they make—such personification being regarded by him as a great philosophic blunder on our part. It could only be a blunder if the notion of personality meant something essentially different from anything to be found in the mental procession. But if that procession be itself the very "original" of the notion of personality, to personify it cannot possibly be wrong. It is already personified. . . .

(3) *Within each personal consciousness, thought is sensibly continuous*

I can only define "continuous" as that which is without breach, crack, or division. I have already said that the breach from one mind to another is perhaps the greatest breach in nature. The only breaches that can well be conceived to occur within the limits of a single mind would either be *interruptions, time*-gaps during which the consciousness went out altogether to come into existence again at a later moment; or they would be breaks in the *quality,* or content, of the thought, so abrupt that the segment that followed had no connection whatever with the one that went before. The proposition that within each personal consciousness thought feels continuous, means two things:

1. That even where there is a time-gap the consciousness after it feels as if it belonged together with the consciousness before it, as another part of the same self;

2. That the changes from one moment to another in the quality of the consciousness are never absolutely abrupt.

The case of the time-gaps, as the simplest, shall be taken first. And first of all, a word about time-gaps of which the consciousness may not be itself aware. . . .

(We saw that such time-gaps existed, and that they might be more numerous than is usually supposed.) If the consciousness is not aware of them, it cannot feel them as interruptions. In the unconsciousness produced by nitrous oxide and other anaesthetics, in that of epilepsy and fainting, the broken edges of the sentient life may meet and merge over the gap, much as the feelings of space of the opposite margins of the "blind spot" meet and merge over that objective interruption to the sensitiveness of the eye. Such consciousness as this, whatever it be for the onlooking psychologist, is for itself unbroken. It *feels* unbroken; a waking day of it is sensibly a unit as long as that day lasts, in the sense in which the hours themselves are units, as having all their parts next each other, with no intrusive alien substance between. To expect the consciousness to feel the interruption of its objective continuity as gaps, would be like expecting the eye to feel a gap of silence because it does not hear, or the ear to feel a gap of darkness because it does not see. So much for the gaps that are unfelt.

With the felt gaps the case is different. On waking from sleep, we usually know that we have been unconscious, and we often have an accurate judgment of how long. The judgment here is certainly an inference from sensible signs, and its ease is due to long practice in the particular field. The result of it, however, is that the consciousness is, *for itself,* not what it was in the former case, but interrupted and continuous, in the mere time-sense of the words. But in the other sense of continuity, the sense of the parts being inwardly connected and belonging together because they are parts of a common whole, the consciousness remains sensibly continuous and one. What now is the common whole? The natural name for it is *myself, I,* or *me.*

When Paul and Peter wake up in the same bed, and recognize that they have been asleep, each one of them mentally reaches back and makes connection with but *one* of the two streams of thought which were broken by the sleeping hours. As the current of an electrode buried in the ground unerringly finds its way to its own similarly buried mate, across no matter how much intervening earth; so Peter's present instantly finds out Peter's past, and never by mistake knits itself on to that of Paul. Paul's thought in turn is as little liable to go astray. The past thought of Peter is appropriated by the present Peter alone. He may have a *knowledge,* and a correct one too, of what Paul's last drowsy states of mind were as he sank into sleep, but it is an entirely different sort of knowledge from that which he has of his own last states. He *remembers* his own states, whilst he only *conceives* Paul's. Remembrance is like direct feeling; its object is suffused with a warmth and intimacy to which no object of mere conception ever attains. This quality of warmth and intimacy and immediacy is what Peter's *present* thought also possesses for itself. So sure as this present is me, is mine, it says, so sure is anything else that comes with the same warmth and intimacy and immediacy, me and mine. What the qualities called warmth and intimacy may in themselves be will have to be matter for future consideration. But whatever past feelings appear with those qualities must be admitted to receive the greeting of the present mental state, to be owned by it, and accepted as belonging together with it in a common self. This community of self is what the time-gap cannot break in twain, and is why a present thought, although not ignorant of the time-gap, can still regard itself as continuous with certain chosen portions of the past.

Consciousness, then, does not appear to itself chopped up in bits. Such words as "chain" or "train" do not describe it fitly as it presents itself in the first instance. It is nothing jointed; it flows. A "river" or a "stream" are the metaphors by which it is most naturally described. *In talking of it hereafter, let us call it the stream of thought, of consciousness, or of subjective life. . . .*

This difference in the rate of change lies at the basis of a difference of subjective states of which we ought immediately to speak. When the rate is slow we are aware of the object of our thought in a comparatively restful and stable way. When rapid, we are aware of a passage, a relation, a transition *from* it, or *between* it and something else. As we take, in fact, a general view of the wonderful stream of our consciousness, what strikes us first is this different pace of its parts. Like a bird's life, it seems to be made of an alternation of flights and perchings. The rhythm of language expresses this, where every thought is expressed in a sentence, and every sentence closed by a period. The resting-places are usually occupied by sensorial imaginations of some sort, whose peculiarity is that they can be held before the mind for an indefinite time, and contemplated without changing; the places of flight are filled with thoughts of relations, static or dynamic, that for the most part obtain between the matters contemplated in the periods of comparative rest.

Let us call the resting-places the "substantive parts," and the places of flight the "transitive parts," of the stream of thought. It then appears that the main end of our thinking is at all times the attainment of some other substantive part than the one from which we have just been dislodged. And we may say that the main use of the transitive parts is to lead us from one substantive conclusion to another.

Now it is very difficult, introspectively, to see the transitive parts for what they really are. If they are but flights to a conclusion, stopping them to look at them before the conclusion is reached is really annihilating them. Whilst if we wait till the conclusion *be* reached, it so exceeds them in vigor and stability that it quite eclipses and swallows them up in its glare. Let anyone try to cut a thought across in the middle and get a look at its section, and he will see how difficult the introspective observation of the transitive tracts is. The rush of the thought is so headlong that it almost always brings us up at the conclusion before we can arrest it. Or if our purpose is nimble enough and we do arrest it, it ceases forthwith to be itself. As a snowflake crystal caught in the warm hand is no longer a crystal but a drop, so, instead of catching the feeling of relation moving to its term, we find we have caught some substantive thing, usually the last word we were pronouncing, statically taken, and with its function, tendency, and particular meaning in the sentence quite evaporated. The attempt at introspective analysis in these cases is in fact like seizing a spinning top to catch its motion, or trying to turn up the gas quickly enough to see how the darkness looks. . . .

(5) *It is always interested more in one part of its object than in another, and welcomes and rejects, or chooses, all the while it thinks.*

The phenomena of selective attention and of deliberative will are of course patent examples of this choosing activity. But few of us are aware how incessantly it is at work in operations not ordinarily called by these names. Accentuation and Emphasis are present in every perception we have. We find it quite impossible to disperse our attention impartially over a number of impressions. A monotonous succession of sonorous strokes is broken up into rhythms, now of one sort, now of another, by the different accent which we place on different strokes. The simplest of these rhythms is the double one, tick-tóck, tick-tóck, tick-tóck. Dots dispersed on a surface are perceived in rows and groups. Lines separate into diverse figures. The ubiquity of the distinctions, *this* and *that, here* and *there, now* and *then,* in our minds is the result of our laying the same selective emphasis on parts of place and time.

But we do far more than emphasize things, and unite some, and keep others apart. We actually *ignore* most of the things before us. Let me briefly show how this goes on.

To begin at the bottom, what are our very senses themselves but organs of selection? Out of the infinite chaos of movements, of which physics teaches us that the outer world consists, each sense-organ picks out those which fall within certain limits of velocity. To these it responds, but ignores the rest as completely as if they did not exist. It thus accentuates particular movements in a manner for which objectively there seems no valid ground; for, as Lange says, there is no reason whatever to think that the gap in Nature between the highest sound-waves and the lowest heat-waves is an abrupt break like that of our sensations; or that the difference between violet and ultra-violet rays has anything like the objective importance subjectively represented by that between light and darkness. Out of what is in itself an undistinguishable, swarming *continuum,* devoid of distinction or emphasis, our senses make for us, by attending to this motion and ignoring that, a world full of contrasts, of sharp accents, of abrupt changes, of picturesque light and shade.

If the sensations we receive from a given organ have their causes thus picked out for us by the conformation of the organ's termination, Attention, on the other hand, out of all the sensations yielded, picks out certain ones as worthy of its notice and suppresses all the rest. Helmholtz's work on Optics is little more than a study of those visual sensations of which common men never become aware—blind spots, *muscæ volitantes,* after-images, irradiation, chromatic fringes, marginal changes of color, double images, astigmatism, movements of accommodation and convergence, retinal rivalry, and more besides. We do not even know without special training on which of our eyes an image falls. So habitually ignorant are most men of this that one may be blind for years of a single eye and never know the fact.

Helmholtz says that we notice only those sensations which are signs to us of *things*. But what are things? Nothing, as we shall abundantly see, but special groups of sensible qualities, which happen practically or aesthetically to interest us, to which we therefore give substantive names, and which we exalt to this exclusive status of independence and dignity. But in itself, apart from my interest, a particular dust-wreath on a windy day is just as much of an individual thing, and just as much or as little deserves an individual name, as my own body does.

And then, among the sensations we get from each separate thing, what happens? The mind selects again. It chooses certain of the sensations to represent the thing most *truly,* and considers the rest as its appearances, modified by the conditions of the moment. Thus my table-top is named *square,* after but one of an infinite number of retinal sensations which it yields, the rest of them being sensations of two acute and two obtuse angles; but I call the latter *perspective* views, and the four right angles the *true* form of the table, and erect the attribute squareness into the table's essence, for aesthetic reasons of my own. In like manner, the real form of the circle is deemed to be the sensation it gives when the line of vision is perpendicular to its centre—all its other sensations are signs of this sensation. The real sound of the cannon is the sensation it makes when the ear is close by. The real color of the brick is the sensation it gives when the eye looks squarely at it from a near point, out of the sunshine and yet not in the gloom; under other circumstances it gives us other color-sensations which are but signs of this—we then see it looks pinker or blacker than it really is. The reader knows no object which he does not represent to himself by preference as in some typical attitude, of some normal size, at some characteristic distance, of some standard tint, etc., etc. But all these essential characteristics, which together form for us the genuine objectivity of the thing and are contrasted with what we call the subjective sensations it may yield us at a given moment, are mere sensations like the latter. The mind chooses to suit itself, and decides what particular sensation shall be held more real and valid than all the rest.

Thus perception involves a twofold choice. Out of all present sensations, we notice mainly such as are significant of absent ones; and out of all the absent associates which these suggest, we again pick out a very few to stand for the objective reality *par excellence*. We could have no more exquisite example of selective industry.

That industry goes on to deal with the things thus given in perception. A man's empirical thought depends on the things he has experienced, but what these shall be is to a large extent determined by his habits of attention. A thing may be present to him a thousand times, but if he persistently fails to notice it, it cannot be said to enter into his experience. We are all seeing flies, moths, and beetles by the thousand, but to whom, save an entomologist, do they say anything distinct? On the other hand, a thing met only once in a lifetime may leave an indelible experience in the memory. Let four men make a tour in Europe. One will bring home only picturesque impressions—costumes and colors, parks and views and works of architecture, pictures and statues. To another all this will be non-existent; and distances and prices, populations and drainage-arrangements, door- and window-fastenings, and other useful statistics will take their place. A third will give a rich account of the theatres, restaurants, and public balls, and naught beside; whilst the fourth will perhaps have been so wrapped in his own subjective broodings as to tell little more than a few names of places through which he passed. Each has selected, out of the same mass of presented objects, those which suited his private interest and has made his experience thereby. . . .

Looking back, then, over this review, we see that the mind is at every stage a theatre of simultaneous possibilities. Consciousness consists in the comparison of these with each other, the selection of some, and the suppression of the rest by the reinforcing and inhibiting agency of attention. The highest and most elaborated mental products are filtered from the data chosen by the faculty next beneath, out of the mass offered by the faculty below that, which mass in turn was sifted from a still larger amount of yet simpler material, and so on. The mind, in short, works on the data it receives very much as a sculptor works on his block of stone. In a sense the statue stood there from eternity. But there were a thousand different ones beside it, and the sculptor alone is to thank for having extricated this one from the rest. Just so the world of each of us, howsoever different our several views of it may be, all lay embedded in the primordial chaos of sensations, which gave the mere *matter* to the thought of all of us indifferently. We may, if we like, by our reasonings unwind things back to that black and jointless continuity of space and moving clouds of swarming atoms which science calls the only real world. But all the while the world *we* feel and live in will be that which our ancestors and we, by slowly cumulative strokes of choice, have extricated out of this, like sculptors, by simply rejecting certain portions of the given stuff. Other sculptors, other statues from the same stone! Other minds, other worlds from the same monotonous and inexpressive chaos! My world is but one in a million alike embedded, alike real to those who may abstract them. How different must be the worlds in the consciousness of ant, cuttle-fish, or crab!

But in my mind and your mind the rejected portions and the selected portions of the original world-stuff are to a great extent the same. The human race as a whole largely agrees as to what it shall notice and name, and what not. And among the noticed parts we select in much the same way for accentuation and preference or subordination and dislike. There is, however, one entirely extraordinary case in which no two men ever are known to choose alike. One great splitting of the whole universe into two halves is made by each of us; and for each of us almost all of the interest attaches to one of the halves; but we all draw the line of division between them in a different place. When I say that we all call the two halves by the same names, and that those names are "*me*" and "*not-me*" respectively, it will at once be seen what I mean. The altogether unique kind of interest which each human mind feels in those parts of creation which it can call *me* or *mine* may be a moral riddle, but it is a fundamental psychological fact. No mind can take the same interest in his neighbor's *me* as in his own. The neighbor's me falls together with all the rest of things in one foreign mass, against which his own *me* stands out in startling relief. Even the trodden worm, as Lotze somewhere says, contrasts his own suffering self with the whole remaining universe, though he have no clear conception either of himself or of what the universe may be. He is for me a mere part of the world; for him it is I who am the mere part. Each of us dichotomizes the Kosmos in a different place.

The evolutionary and the medical approach to human experience both appear clearly in James's celebrated discussion of the problem of emotion. It was the custom, in James's time, to make much of the *psychological* basis of such massive emotional states as rage and fear, but no systematic *theory* of the emotions had commanded general assent. The emotions, James concludes, are simply those states of experience which follow directly from the massive physiological response to exciting or threatening situations. During a state of upheaval there is "input," as we should say today, from the vital organs, the muscles, the mucous membranes, the whole internal apparatus. Aristotle, in the *Rhetoric,* had stressed the bodily upheaval in emotion, and Malebranche, a follower of Descartes, had given physiological upheaval its place. It remained, however, for James to *define* the emotion in terms of the back-flow, the flow from the interior of the body to the brain, which gives both the characteristic experience of shock and upheaval, and also the specific qualities of the emotions, depending upon their own areas of bodily excitation.

The Emotions *

As emotions are described in novels, they interest us, for we are made to share them. We have grown acquainted with the concrete objects and emergencies which call them forth, and any knowing touch of introspection which may grace the page meets with a quick and feeling response. Confessedly literary works of aphoristic philosophy also flash lights into our emotional life, and give us a fitful delight. But as far as "scientific psychology" of the emotions goes, I may have been surfeited by too much reading of classic works on the subject, but I should as lief read verbal descriptions of the shapes of the rocks on a New Hampshire farm as toil through them again. They give one nowhere a central point of view, or a deductive or generative principle. They distinguish and refine and specify *in infinitum* without ever getting on to another logical level. Whereas the beauty of all truly scientific work is to get to ever deeper levels. Is there no way out from this level of individual description in the case of the emotions? I believe there is a way out, but I fear that few will take it.

The trouble with the emotions in psychology is that they are regarded too much as absolutely individual things. So long as they are set down as so many eternal and sacred psychic entities, like the old immutable

* From *The Principles of Psychology,* II, 448–452.

species in natural history, so long all that *can* be done with them is reverently to catalogue their separate characters, points, and effects. But if we regard them as products of more general causes (as "species" are now regarded as products of heredity and variation), the mere distinguishing and cataloguing becomes of subsidiary importance. Having the goose which lays the golden eggs, the description of each egg already laid is a minor matter. Now the general causes of the emotions are indubitably physiological. Prof. C. Lange, of Copenhagen, published in 1885 a physiological theory of their constitution and conditioning, which I had already broached the previous year in an article in Mind. None of the criticisms which I have heard of it have made me doubt its essential truth. I will therefore devote the next few pages to explaining what it is. I shall limit myself in the first instance to what may be called the *coarser* emotions, grief, fear, rage, love, in which every one recognizes a strong organic reverberation, and afterwards speak of the *subtler* emotions, or of those whose organic reverberation is less obvious and strong.

EMOTION FOLLOWS UPON THE BODILY EXPRESSION IN THE COARSER EMOTIONS AT LEAST

Our natural way of thinking about these coarser emotions is that the mental perception of some fact excites the mental affection called the emotion, and that this latter state of mind gives rise to the bodily expression. My theory, on the contrary, is that *the bodily changes follow directly the perception of the exciting fact, and that our feeling of the same changes as they occur* IS *the emotion.* Common-sense says, we lose our fortune, are sorry and weep; we meet a bear, are frightened and run; we are insulted by a rival, are angry and strike. The hypothesis here to be defended says that this order of sequence is incorrect, that the one mental state is not immediately induced by the other, that the bodily manifestations must first be interposed between, and that the more rational statement is that we feel sorry because we cry, angry because we strike, afraid because we tremble, and not that we cry, strike, or tremble, because we are sorry, angry, or fearful, as the case may be. Without the bodily states following on the perception, the latter would be purely cognitive in form, pale, colorless, destitute of emotional warmth. We might then see the bear, and judge it best to run, receive the insult and deem it right to strike, but we should not actually *feel* afraid or angry. . . .

I now proceed to urge the vital point of my whole theory, which is this: *If we fancy some strong emotion, and then try to abstract from our consciousness of it all the feelings of its bodily symptoms, we find we have nothing left behind,* no "mind-stuff" out of which the emotion can be constituted, and that a cold and neutral state of intellectual perception is all that remains. . . .

What kind of an emotion of fear would be left if the feeling neither of quickened heart-beats nor of shallow breathing, neither of trembling lips nor of weakened limbs, neither of goose-flesh nor of visceral stirrings, were present, it is quite impossible for me to think. Can one fancy the state of rage and picture no ebullition in the chest, no flushing of the face, no dilatation of the nostrils, no clenching of the teeth, no impulse to vigorous action, but in their stead limp muscles, calm breathing, and a placid face? The present writer, for one, certainly cannot. The rage is as completely evaporated as the sensation of its so-called manifestations, and the only thing that can possibly be supposed to take its place is some cold-blooded and dispassionate judicial sentence, confined entirely to the intellectual realm, to the effect that a certain person or persons merit chastisement for their sins. In like manner of grief: what would it be without its tears, its sobs, its suffocation of the heart, its pang in the breastbone? A feelingless cognition that certain circumstances are deplorable, and nothing more. Every passion in turn tells the same story. A purely disembodied human emotion is a nonentity. I do not say that it is a contradiction in the nature of things, or that pure spirits are necessarily condemned to cold intellectual lives; but I say that for *us,* emotion dissociated from all bodily feeling is inconceivable.

Eager, intense, constantly struggling with an insoluble problem, James was obsessed with the problem of the will. Religious preoccupations and ethical preoccupations with the human struggle for the good struggled, and at times fused, with the evolutionary and the natural science viewpoint in which all things flow from their predecessors with never a discontinuity or a moment of capricious spontaneity. Spontaneity, however, was constantly winning in these battles of the mind.

The Will *

Turning now to the form of the decision itself, we may distinguish four chief types. The first may be called *the reasonable type.* It is that of those cases in which the arguments for and against a given course seem gradually and almost insensibly to settle themselves in the mind and to

* From *The Principles of Psychology,* II, 531–535, 549.

end by leaving a clear balance in favor of one alternative, which alternative we then adopt without effort or constraint. Until this rational balancing of the books is consummated we have a calm feeling that the evidence is not yet all in, and this keeps action in suspense. But some day we wake with the sense that we see the thing rightly, that no new light will be thrown on the subject by farther delay, and that the matter had better be settled *now*. In this easy transition from doubt to assurance we seem to ourselves almost passive; the "reasons" which decide us appearing to flow in from the nature of things, and to owe nothing to our will. We have, however, a perfect sense of being *free,* in that we are devoid of any feeling of coercion. The conclusive reason for the decision in these cases usually is the discovery that we can refer the case to a *class* upon which we are accustomed to act unhesitatingly in a certain stereotyped way. It may be said in general that a great part of every deliberation consists in the turning over of all the possible modes of *conceiving* the doing or not doing of the act in point. The moment we hit upon a conception which lets us apply some principle of action which is a fixed and stable part of our Ego, our state of doubt is at an end. Persons of authority, who have to make many decisions in the day, carry with them a set of heads of classification, each bearing its motor consequence, and under these they seek as far as possible to range each new emergency as it occurs. It is where the emergency belongs to a species without precedent, to which consequently no cut-and-dried maxim will apply, that we feel most at a loss, and are distressed at the indeterminateness of our task. As soon, however, as we see our way to a familiar classification, we are at ease again. *In action as in reasoning, then, the great thing is the quest of the right conception.* The concrete dilemmas do not come to us with labels gummed upon their backs. We may name them by many names. The wise man is he who succeeds in finding the name which suits the needs of the particular occasion best. A "reasonable" character is one who has a store of stable and worthy ends, and who does not decide about an action till he has calmly ascertained whether it be ministerial or detrimental to any one of these.

In the next two types of decision, the final fiat occurs before the evidence is all "in." It often happens that no paramount and authoritative reason for either course will come. Either seems a case of a Good, and there is no umpire as to which good should yield its place to the other. We grow tired of long hesitation and inconclusiveness, and the hour may come when we feel that even a bad decision is better than no decision at all. Under these conditions it will often happen that some accidental circumstance, supervening at a particular moment upon our mental weariness, will upset the balance in the direction of one of the alternatives, to which then we feel ourselves committed, although an opposite accident at the same time might have produced the opposite result.

In the *second type* of case our feeling is to a certain extent that of letting ourselves drift with a certain indifferent acquiescence in a direction accidentally determined *from without,* with the conviction that, after all, we might as well stand by this course as by the other, and that things are in any event sure to turn out sufficiently right.

In the third type the determination seems equally accidental, but it comes from within, and not from without. It often happens, when the absence of imperative principle is perplexing and suspense distracting, that we find ourselves acting, as it were, automatically, and as if by a spontaneous discharge of our nerves, in the direction of one of the horns of the dilemma. But so exciting is this sense of motion after our intolerable pent-up state, that we eagerly throw ourselves into it. "Forward now!" we inwardly cry, "though the heavens fall." This reckless and exultant espousal of an energy so little premeditated by us that we feel rather like passive spectators cheering on the display of some extraneous force than like voluntary agents, is a type of decision too abrupt and tumultuous to occur often in humdrum and cool-blooded natures. But it is probably frequent in persons of strong emotional endowment and unstable or vacillating character. And in men of the world-shaking type, the Napoleons, Luthers, etc., in whom tenacious passion combines with ebullient activity, when by any chance the passion's outlet has been dammed by scruples or apprehensions, the resolution is probably often of this catastrophic kind. The flood breaks quite unexpectedly through the dam. That it should so often do so is quite sufficient to account for the tendency of these characters to a fatalistic mood of mind. And the fatalistic mood itself is sure to reinforce the strength of the energy just started on its exciting path of discharge.

There is a *fourth form* of decision, which often ends deliberation as suddenly as the third form does. It comes when, in consequence of some outer experience or some inexplicable inward charge, *we suddenly pass from the easy and careless to the sober and strenuous mood,* or possibly the other way. The whole scale of values of our motives and impulses then undergoes a change like that which a change of the observer's level produces on a view. The most sobering possible agents are objects of grief and fear. When one of these affects us, all "light fantastic" notions lose their motive power, all solemn ones find theirs multiplied manyfold. The consequence is an instant abandonment of the more trivial projects with which we had been dallying, and an instant practical acceptance of the more grim and earnest alternative which till then could not extort our mind's consent. All those "changes of heart," "awakenings of conscience," etc., which make new men of so many of us, may be classed under this head. The character abruptly rises to another "level," and deliberation comes to an immediate end.

In the *fifth and final type* of decision, the feeling that the evidence is all in, and that reason has balanced the books, may be either present or absent. But in either case we feel, in deciding, as if we ourselves by our own wilful act inclined the beam; in the former case by adding our living effort to the weight of the logical reason which, taken alone, seems powerless to make the act discharge; in the latter by a kind of creative contribution of something instead of a reason which does a reason's work. The slow dead heave of the will that is felt in these instances makes of them a class altogether different subjectively from all the three preceding classes. What the heave of the will betokens metaphysically, what the effort might lead us to infer about a will-power distinct from motives, are not matters that concern us yet. Subjectively and phenomenally, the *feeling of effort,* absent from the former decisions, accompanies these. Whether it be the dreary resignation for the sake of austere and naked duty of all sorts of rich mundane delights, or whether it be the heavy resolve that of two mutually exclusive trains of future fact, both sweet and good, and with no strictly objective or imperative principle of choice between them, one shall forevermore become impossible, while the other shall become reality, it is a desolate and acrid sort of act, an excursion into a lonesome moral wilderness. If examined closely, its chief difference from the three former cases appears to be that in those cases the mind at the moment of deciding on the triumphant alternative dropped the other one wholly or nearly out of sight, whereas here both alternatives are steadily held in view, and in the very act of murdering the vanquished possibility the chooser realizes how much in that instant he is making himself lose. It is deliberately driving a thorn into one's flesh; and the sense of *inward effort* with which the act is accompanied is an element which sets the fourth type of decision in strong contrast with the previous three varieties, and makes of it an altogether peculiar sort of mental phenomenon. The immense majority of human decisions are decisions without effort. In comparatively few of them, in most people, does effort accompany the final act. We are, I think, misled into supposing that effort is more frequent than it is, by the fact that *during deliberation* we so often have a feeling of how great an effort it would take to make a decision *now*. Later, after the decision has made itself with ease, we recollect this and erroneously suppose the effort also to have been made then.

The existence of the effort as a phenomenal fact in our consciousness cannot of course be doubted or denied. Its significance, on the other hand, is a matter about which the gravest difference of opinion prevails. . . .

But what determines the amount of the effort when, by its aid, an ideal motive becomes victorious over a great sensual resistance? The very greatness of the resistance itself. If the sensual propensity is small, the effort is small. The latter is *made great* by the presence of a great antagonist to overcome. And if a brief definition of ideal or moral action were required, none could be given which would better fit the appearances than this: *It is action in the line of the greatest resistance.*

The facts may be most briefly symbolized thus, P standing for the propensity, I for the ideal impulse, and E for the effort:

$$I \; \textit{per se} < P.$$
$$I + E > P.$$

In other words, if E adds itself to I, P immediately offers the least resistance, and motion occurs in spite of it.

But the E does not seem to form an integral part of the I. It appears adventitious and indeterminate in advance. We can make more or less as we please, and *if* we make enough we can convert the greatest mental resistance into the least. Such, at least, is the impression which the facts spontaneously produce upon us.

❀

The mind, for James, is an evolutionary expression; it is an adaptation to reality. From one point of view we can see this doctrine pointing to James's later development of pragmatism, the philosophy which defines truth as that which combines concreteness with practicality. From another point James moved toward pluralism, the conception that the "universe" is really not tightly structured, but a collection of more or less independent phases: a "pluriverse." All the time he was expressing one or another phase of "radical empiricism," the trust in the raw root reality and vitality of that which we experience, the use of experience rather than abstract principle as a guide to what is *out there* and what is *in here* within us. And what is within us is often creative; and when one fails, it can be *re*-creative. Just as Bergson was developing a theory of "creative evolution," James was developing a conception of reality *as defined* by us, as an expression of the outer world as we ourselves give it meaning.

After the completion of the *Principles,* and the transfer to the Department of Philosophy, James appears as a reflective spirit mainly preoccupied with reading, discussing, lecturing, both at Harvard and elsewhere, and with no narrowly defined place for himself. He was a superb intellectual jack-of-all-trades, master of all, we might well say. In the last year of the century he was invited to give the Gifford Lectures on "natural religion" at Edinburgh, and he and Mrs. James sailed for Europe with the thought that there would be some months of study and preparation. Actually, his health collapsed as the ship made its way outward from the harbor of New York. (He had overtaxed his heart in the Adirondacks, and there are many signs that angina pectoris was coming on.) For months he lay in a darkened room until slowly his mind reconstituted itself. Then he plunged into the structuring of the extraordinary series of lectures: *The Varieties of Religious Experience,* a systematic study of the naturalistic view of the form and meaning of experience of ultimate things, with a place for individual difference, the religion of the healthy-minded versus the "sick soul," a trenchant analysis of the experience of conversion, and a long, tentative, sympathetic, question-asking analysis of mystic experience. It was William James who founded the modern psychology of religion.

But James founded a great deal more than new branches of psychology. He became a man for all seasons, a man of very great power and range, a first-rate evolutionist who married the evolutionary principle to the "radical empiricism" of the seeker who looks for the meaning of life wherever unexplained new areas of experience burst upon us.

RETROSPECT

Before drawing the curtain on our play, extinguishing the overhead lights, and bidding our audience a happy voyage through these older psychologies or the newer ones which now beckon to them, we should like to reflect about the meaning of the whole series of acts and scenes, the evaluation of where we stand now.

In a gross sense, the psychology of the Western world shows, as does *Asian Psychology,* a few main epochs which limit (or even to some degree predetermine) what psychology in those epochs can undertake and can carry through. The leisure, the comfort, the familiarity with other states and other peoples gave the privileged and reflective men of the Greek city-state a chance to look closely and to think deeply. It was partly the Athenian Empire and its olive-oil economics; it was partly the embattled unity of their struggle against Persia; it was partly their familiarity, through their travelers, with a variety of seminal ideas, that made the Greek philosophers capable of the first great psychological thrust in the Western world.

The collapse of the Greek city-state ushered in a series of changes and philosophies of comfort and solace supervened, within which radical ideas about a simple orderly restrained kind of comfort, and indeed about religion and ways of getting rid of the fears instilled by religion, claimed the hearts of Stoics and Epicureans alike. Then came the tidal wave of the religious revival, ushered in by Greek mystery religions, and finally, the insistent push of Christian theology and ethics, under which the Roman system began to reel, already hard-pressed by the Barbarian invasions from the north.

There came then, however, a reconstruction of the ancient

world in the form which we know as the Renaissance. Greek ideas were exhumed and, to an extraordinary degree, revitalized, while a brave new world of travel, commerce, sea power, new roads, and finally new industrial-technical inventions gave a period of "enlightenment" and of science, engineering, rationality. The psychology of all these periods is clearly built within the architecture of the main intellectual evolution. "Evolution now," in a more literal sense, as a term describing Darwin's thesis, becomes the key to the psychology of the later nineteenth century, especially in the writings of Nietzsche and William James, whose profound evolutionism gives an air of progress, confidence, and receding horizons to the psychology of the closing nineteenth century. The beginnings of experimental psychology, and of psychoanalysis, brought forth, for the twentieth century to absorb, a series of heroic ideas which can only be described and assimilated in later volumes.

This attempt to set the philosophy of an era in a broad context of its culture has, of course, some points in common with the approach traditionally associated with Karl Marx. Marx keenly recognized stages in the evolution of an economic system, with new economic enterprises such as agriculture, trade, industrial production, as exemplified in the Western world, calling into play a dominant class associated with the center of the productive enterprise. Thus at the end of the medieval period the development of the arts of transportation, trade, and banking led to developments within the towns and the rise of a prosperous merchant class, which could vie successfully with a declining landed nobility. We would expect from this point of view that literature, education, and philosophy would respond to these new cues, as, in fact, we earlier saw to be the case when we were discussing Hobbes and Locke (pages 137–165). The Marxist point of view could be pushed very much further by anyone inclined to note the influence of a particular role in society upon the way in which the individual thinks; the way he regards himself; the values—mundane and religious—which are compatible with this stance in life. Marxists have not, however, pushed very far in this direction in the explanation of the rise of philosophical schools, and hardly at all in reference to psychology. Surprising as this may be, there is really no systematic Marxist psychology. If the reader will attentively consider the very comprehensive and fertile system of modern Soviet psychology, he will see that there are indeed numerous references to Marx and to dialectical materialism, but that the class system, the relation of man to the productive process, and the relation of the various classes to one another in political, military, and international terms are not very richly developed.

One can, in fact, go somewhat further, we believe, with an eclectic, multi-faceted conception of the interdependence of the various aspects of culture—now the military, now the economic, now the political, even at times the philosophical playing a key role in the evolution of society. We should, for example, find a considerable illumination in our understanding of the psychology of India if we could see the place of each philosopher in the system. But we should soon find it difficult to predict whether a new movement, like Yoga, would begin with a priest, a warrior, or a prince, as indeed Buddhism began neither with a priest nor with a warrior, but with a prince—a prince disaffected by the sufferings of the common people. (So, too, the great Buddhist king and conqueror Asoka, after conquering much of the Indian peninsula, repented himself for the blood which his armies had shed and attempted to institute a realm of peace and good will, rather than moving forward toward the increase of his power.) In short, there are great varieties of complicating *personal* circumstances that make us very reluctant indeed to apply rigorously a systematic conception of social determination whether of a Marxist sort or of any others now available. In general, the socio-economic "determination" seems to apply a little better to the vast Asian civilizations than to the more complex, fragmented, and rapidly changing psychological systems of the West. The role of the individual thinker appears to be greater in the West, and, on the whole, psychological issues seem often to arise directly from the idiosyncrasies, the wishes, the frustrations, the modalities of integration and compromise, the devices for escaping conflict, which are available to the men of the Western world (see pages 157 ff.).

Indeed, very far from giving us a world psychology agreeing with some basic and easily observable "human nature" or "historical process," the psychologies we have come up with speak eloquently not only of time, place, and circumstance, of geography, social organization, family structure, community, city, and state, but they speak, especially in the West, about variabilities, blind spots, moments of sudden vision, deep-seated personal idiosyncrasies, and the conscious or unconscious control of thought by the way in which the individual feels it "must" be. There is indeed a "universal psychology," but it is a potentiality to be realized in the remote future, as all the methods of observation described here, and many more, are relentlessly pursued to their goals and come to terms with one another, so that a reality larger and richer than can be grasped at any one time, or by any one person, can be discovered.

The ultimate test of reality offered by many psychologists in all periods is the agreement of different observers. After watching human nature in his own case, Thomas Hobbes asked the reader to consider "if he find not the same thing in himself." So the adherents of Patanjali believe that they find reality, because, when you once know it, you can have no doubt. But what they find is rather different from what Thomas Hobbes found. In the same way, the modern existentialist is likely to report to us that he has a direct view of things as they really are in his experience and is unwilling to be put off by those who would speak to him in psychoanalytic or behavioristic terms. The trouble is that there is no one vantage point, no one "criterion of credibility" to which all must defer. This is certainly partly because we have our own deeply unconscious needs and fears, and reject and coat the truth in our own way. Partly it is because structurally, in terms of eye, ear, brain, and muscle, we necessarily perceive and act differently. Partly it is because we derive our intellectual as well as our physical sustenance from a cultural world to which we are so close that we cannot make allowances for it, "lean over backwards" to correct for its biasing role. One of the joys and despairs of psychology is that it has within it the same "uncertainty principle" which appears in modern physics, by which the very process of observation changes the thing to be observed. In psychology, as new ways of observing bring to light new worlds of experience, the very fact of observing in a new way shakes out the hidden creases, unfurls new aspects of the thinking mind.

So while the approach which we have just sketched might be called a psychology of successive epochs within a cultural whole, there is another way to cast a reflective backward glance over the path we have trodden. This is to think of the role of individual thinkers: the contingent, the local and personal, even, if you like, the "accidental" contributions which eke out, abet, and give broader meaning to the psychology of succeeding epochs. Plainly, the kind of integration sought by Aristotle could not have been successfully achieved or even imagined by the philosophers of the pre-Socratic period. The enormous personal stamp of Socrates' own personality upon Greek philosophy is paralleled by the incredible systematic organizing skill of Aristotle, which, when rediscovered in the later medieval period, very naturally overwhelmed and to some degree standardized all the efforts of the life sciences as the dawning of the Renaissance became apparent, and Greek life came to be the basis for the rebirth of European civilization.

Even in the dualistic Descartes and the mechanistic Hobbes the background of Aristotle stands massively clear. When, then, the principle of association sanctified by Aristotle, utilized by Stoics and Epicureans, revitalized by Hobbes, became a systematic psychology in the writings of David Hartley, the role of each of these giants becomes clear; and when Hartley's medical psychology, based on Newton's Law of the Pendulum and the vibratory action of the "white medullary substance of the brain," provided the basis for a new systematic psychology, Aristotle still needed to be invoked as a patron.

Evolutionism, again, would surely have had its day whether there was a Darwin or not. But the colossal figure of Charles Darwin, as these pages have undertaken to show, dominates the latter half of the nineteenth century, and all the sciences that deal with man, and the contingent and the personal can legitimately stand out as figure, while the epoch be named only as background. In the same way the twentieth century would show that the figures of Freud and Pavlov are great organizing centers around which the psychology of the twentieth century is being shaped. This is by way of saying that there is a personal as well as a socio-cultural way of viewing even the great historical changes in the thoughts held regarding the mind.

Not only the great insights, but the personal foibles and idiosyncrasies of each psychologist have plainly determined to some degree the general character of the psychology that he has constructed. "Myself and fear were born twins," said Thomas Hobbes; and later philosophers have rejoiced in finding evidence that each *psychological system* bespeaks the *character* of the man who contrived it. We believe that this is a sound note upon which an epilogue can be constructed: A note emphasizing the personal, the idiosyncratic in a few of the contributions which one may wish to understand in a deeper human sense. A psychological system may be viewed as through a reduction screen or color filter, enabling us to see more plainly just because certain phases of each man's personality are defined more sharply. The history of psychology in the West is just as fully rooted in biography as it is in Western culture.

Index